STUDIES IN IMPERIALISM

general editor John M. MacKenzie

Established in the belief that imperialism as a cultural phenomenon had as significant an effect on the dominant as on the subordinate societies, Studies in Imperialism seeks to develop the new socio-cultural approach which has emerged through cross-disciplinary work on popular culture, media studies, art history, the study of education and religion, sports history and children's literature. The cultural emphasis embraces studies of migration and race, while the older political and constitutional, economic and military concerns will never be far away. It incorporates comparative work on European and American empire-building, with the chronological focus primarily, though not exclusively, on the nineteenth and twentieth centuries, when these cultural exchanges were most powerfully at work.

Female imperialism and national identity

MANCHESTER
UNIVERSITY PRESS

Female imperialism and national identity

IMPERIAL ORDER DAUGHTERS OF THE EMPIRE

Katie Pickles

MANCHESTER
UNIVERSITY PRESS
Manchester and New York

distributed exclusively in the USA by
PALGRAVE

Published by **MANCHESTER UNIVERSITY PRESS**
OXFORD ROAD, MANCHESTER M13 9NR, UK
and ROOM 400, 175 FIFTH AVENUE, NEW YORK, NY 10010, USA
www.manchesteruniversitypress.co.uk

Distributed exclusively in the USA by
PALGRAVE, 75 FIFTH AVENUE, NEW YORK, NY 10010, USA

Distributed exclusively in Canada by
UBC PRESS, UNIVERSITY OF BRITISH COLUMBIA,
2029 WEST MALL, VANCOUVER, BC, CANADA V6T 1Z2

British Library Cataloguing-in-Publication Data
A catalogue record for this book is available from the British Library

Library of Congress Cataloging-in-Publication Data applied for

ISBN 0 7190 6390 6 hardback

First published 2002

10 09 08 07 06 05 04 03 02   10 9 8 7 6 5 4 3 2 1

Typeset in Trump Medieval
by Northern Phototypesetting Co Ltd, Bolton
Printed in Great Britain
by Bookcraft (Bath) Ltd, Midsomer Norton

CONTENTS

[v]

LIST OF FIGURES AND TABLES

Figures

Tables

LIST OF ABBREVIATIONS

BC	British Columbia
BCARS	British Columbia Archives and Records Service
CBC	Canadian Broadcasting Corporation
CCF	Canadian Communist Federation
CCIW	Canadian Council for the Immigration of Women
CFUW	Canadian Federation of University Women
CPR	Canadian Pacific Railway
CVA	City of Vancouver Archives
DEW	Distant Early Warning
GBOW	Glenbow Archives
GLWSA	Guild of Loyal Women of South Africa
IWGC	Imperial War Graves Commission
IWM	Imperial War Museum, London
LPSC	Lorne Pierce Special Collections
MULNS	Memorial University Library's Centre for Newfoundland Studies
NAC	National Archives of Canada
NB	New Brunswick
NLC	National Library of Canada
NS	Nova Scotia
NWT	Northwest Territories
PAA	Provincial Archives of Alberta
PANB	Provincial Archives of New Brunswick
PARO, PEI	Public Archives and Records Office Prince Edward Island
QUA	Queen's University Archives, Ontario
RCAF	Royal Canadian Air Force
RCMP	Royal Canadian Mounted Police
RCSL	Royal Commonwealth Society Library
SAB	Saskatchewan Archives Board
SOSBW	Society for the Oversea Settlement of British Women
UBCSC	University of British Columbia Special Collections
VPL	Vancouver Public Library
WCTU	Women's Christian Temperance Union
YWCA	Young Women's Christian Association

GENERAL EDITOR'S INTRODUCTION

What's in a name? A historian might answer 'a very great deal'. Names of organisations can be extraordinary signifiers of period, place, performance and personalities. The 'Imperial Order of the Daughters of the Empire' speaks volumes in its four principal words. It is redolent of an era, symbolising as it does not just a complete ideology but also a notable iconography. Cartoonists in the nineteenth century rejoiced in depicting Britannia as the imperial mother surrounded by her colonial daughters. The founders of the IODE (as it later became in an apparent acknowledgement of significant changes in resonance) must have been well aware of this as they chose to flag their patriotism through a title which has a formidable ring of defiance about it.

Patriotism and defiance were both characteristics of the age in which the IODE was founded, namely the era of the Anglo-Boer War, 1899–1902. It was also a time when women became more self-conscious and active politically. The suffragist movement was in full swing, though it divided women's movements and societies as much as it united them. Although in the past women had been deeply involved in pressure groups like the Anti-Slavery Society, in philanthropic activities, and in some scholarly/political organisations like the provincial geographical societies of the 1880s, they were now placing themselves in a much more central position in relation to the war. Many, like Mary Kingsley, became nurses and died of fevers along with the men. Others provided comforts and indulged in fundraising. But figures like Flora Shaw, Emily Hobhouse and Millicent Fawcett, in their very different ways, played key instrumental roles. It was in this atmosphere that the IODE was founded in Canada just as, shortly afterwards, the Victoria League appeared in London.

Although the IODE was primarily a Canadian organisation, it offers insights far beyond the confines of that dominion. Its history reflects important issues of national identity in respect of the all-too-adjacent United States, of Britain, and other dominions and imperial territories. It also illustrates the efforts of middle-class British women to dominate dominion developments and the manner in which Canadian women (as well as their counterparts in Australia, New Zealand and elsewhere) resisted the somewhat patronising and snobbish approaches that they encountered. But above all, the history of the IODE carries important messages not just for women's history at the so-called imperial periphery, but also for wider gender relations. Its

importance in illuminating a whole range of diplomatic, social, cultural and political issues is clear.

This is the first full-length study of the IODE. It covers a broad
period in the twentieth century. It illuminates the manifold web of
significance that was spun by this women's organisation. It demonstrates the many issues and methods that the IODE adopted to achieve
its goals and promote aspects of the imperial relationship. And above
all it sets its findings into the context of the rich modern historiography of gender, identities, patriotism and imperial organisations.
What emerges is that the members of the IODE were, in the end,
wholly unsatisfied with the notion of Britannia's daughters. They
sought to escape from the familial patterns and establish an autonomy
that would ultimately transcend that slightly glib nineteenth-century
iconography. Although many of its members saw the shift towards
initials as anodyne, that move was actually initiated by many new
and complex emotions. Katie Pickles succeeds in exploring all these
multiple layers and inter-relationships in considerable depth. She also
brings both a sympathetic understanding and a highly developed
critical awareness to bear upon a women's society which has a significance far beyond the very considerable boundaries of Canada.

John M. MacKenzie

ACKNOWLEDGEMENTS

At McGill University, it was my PhD supervisor Audrey Kobayashi, a past IODE War Memorial Scholar herself, who wrote 'What about the IODE?' in the margin of an early thesis proposal. Thus began the study that has eventually led to this book. Together with my thanks to Audrey, I wish to express my gratitude to the rest of my PhD committee, the late Theo Hills, Andrée Lévesque and Sherry Olson, and to Barbara Welch who put me in touch with two of the party of girls who formed the 1928 English Schoolgirl Tour of Canada.

More recently, valuable guidance and encouragement have been offered by my colleagues in New Zealand: at the University of Canterbury, Garth Cant, Graeme Dunstall, Miles Fairburn, David McIntyre, Philippa Mein Smith, Ann Parsonson and Luke Trainor; at the University of Otago, Barbara Brookes, Melissa Kerdemelidis and Dot Page; at the University of Auckland, Don Kerr and Wendy Larner; and from afar and during visits to Vancouver, Myra Rutherdale of the University of British Columbia.

I owe an enormous thanks to my family and friends, and to everyone who has supported and helped me along the way. For their assistance with records, I am grateful to numerous archivists across Canada, and at the Royal Commonwealth Society Library and the Imperial War Museum, London, UK. Tim Nolan and Pauline Wedlake at the University of Canterbury, New Zealand, provided technical assistance. The contributions of the series' editor John MacKenzie, the anonymous readers and the staff at Manchester University Press are greatly appreciated.

A version of part of chapter eight originally appeared as 'Forgotten colonizers: the Imperial Order Daughters of the Empire (IODE) and the Canadian north', *The Canadian Geographer*, 42: 2 (1998), 193–204, as also has a version of part of chapter four, which appeared as 'Exhibiting Canada: Empire, migration and the 1928 English Schoolgirl Tour of Canada', *Gender, Place and Culture*, 7:1 (2000), 81–96.

Without the support and assistance of members of the IODE across Canada, and of the two women from the 1928 English Schoolgirl Tour, this would be a very different book. I have appreciated their sharing of memories and opinions with such wisdom, honesty, warmth and hospitality. Meeting with them has been an experience that I shall treasure always.

For my parents, Geraldine and Jim Pickles

Introduction

In 1978 the Imperial Order Daughters of the Empire, an organization of Canadian women founded in 1900 and still in existence, changed its name to 'just IODE', an often used informal abbreviation. As one member put it: 'IODE really doesn't stand for anything.'[1] That was the hope of publicity officers at national headquarters in Toronto, who initiated the name change keen to overcome what they perceived to be the unwelcome connotations of 'empire'. The now peculiar and elusive name conjures up faint memories and suspected intrigue, with little actually known of the IODE and its vital place in twentieth-century imperial history. In this book I redress the neglect and place the IODE in the spotlight, resurrecting it from a contemporary shadow of a presence. I position the IODE in historical context, revealing its substantial contribution in the making of an Anglo-Canadian identity in the image of Britain.

At a first glance the IODE appears as one of the many women's philanthropic organizations that emerged from the second part of the nineteenth century onwards. With an increase in the status given to what was deemed women's 'natural' work of nurturing and domestic matters, women of the upper classes throughout the Western world busied themselves with philanthropic activities. Sometimes benevolent activities were organized in women-only clubs, that were in the main infused with first-wave feminist concerns of health and welfare for women and children. Other women's groups were branches of empire-wide organizations that were underpinned by Christianity and devoted to providing aid with war relief, immigration and colonization. The IODE's working relationship with a variety of organizations, such as the National Council of Women, the Federation of University Women, the Salvation Army, the Young Women's Christian Association (YWCA), the Girls' Friendly Society, the Society for the Oversea Settlement of British Women (SOSBW) and the Red Cross, appears throughout this book.

[1]

More specifically, the IODE was first and foremost a patriotic organization, advancing its own particular brand of female imperialism.
Although unusual, as women's patriotism was an awkward fit with
the gendered masculine domain of politics, nation and empire, here
the IODE was not alone, as there were other groups of solely patriotic
women – most notably, the Victoria League, the South African Guild
of Loyal Women and the American Daughters of the Revolution. What
is so interesting about the IODE is that, from the Dominion of Canada,
it confidently positioned itself at the centre of the British Empire,
declaring itself to be the Empire's 'premier' women's patriotic organization. It was certainly the largest in membership, and, for many
years, went about its work proudly advancing its patriotic intentions.
But how successful was it? Although its 'good works' in education,
health and welfare were extensive and were arguably ahead of government initiatives, the growing embarrassment and the attempt to
forget the past suggest that the beliefs of the IODE express once-dom-
inant ideas now in decline, rather than a concern with shaping the
future.

The move to erase all historical reference from the IODE's name has
met with considerable debate and dissension among individual members: 'There are some of us who are still saying "Order" in the prayer.
We stumble over it, it's stupid, but I call it "The Order". It's distinctive.'[2] A past member from Quebec City considers the move silly: 'In
this province all you need is an acute and you're *iodé*, and we're not
iodine!' Her personal name for the Order was the Irresistible Daughters of the Evening.[3] Unable to completely change from the old name
due to the sentiments of members, the IODE is stuck with a name that
represents its identity crisis: transformed from its past, yet still
strongly attached to it. What sort of a past had it been?

There are matters dealt with in this book that the IODE would
rather were forgotten. By the late 1970s the IODE had developed a
sense of uneasiness about its history, a sense which has continued into
the present. These feelings concern ideas on and attitudes towards
race, immigration and citizenship now eclipsed and found generally
unacceptable. Specifically, the embarrassment involves the IODE's
past as an organization of female imperialists, and its part in the construction of an Anglo-Canadian identity that celebrated all things
British and advanced Canada's destiny as a part of the British Empire.
It is the uncovering of such identity that forms the core of this book.
In a country as diverse as Canada, there were obviously dissenting
opinions and regional differences throughout the IODE's history, and I
reveal some of these in the course of the book. Yet, in order to explore
the IODE's overall construction of a pro-British Anglo-Canadian iden-

tity, I privilege general statements, and am most preoccupied with and fascinated by the official opinions that emerged from individual members to *speak for* the Order. This is a book about a *group* of women and the collective identity and vision they forged, rather than a study of women as individuals.

Gender and hegemony

Taking my lead from a variety of scholars concerned with themes of nation, empire and colonization, I excavate the IODE's history to reveal the characteristics of an Anglo-Canadian identity. I argue that this was a hegemonic identity that appealed to an enlightenment sensibility of unquestioned conquest and colonization of native peoples. Economic and cultural 'progress' were supported, and the assimilation of all difference was demanded. Throughout, it had an unfailing belief and confidence in knowing best. Canada was to become a nation through conformity to a grand narrative, the contents of which were to be based upon British democracy and constitutional monarchy, the Christian myths and saintly symbols of the British Isles, and economic and cultural 'progress' through new innovations and technologies. Thus, along with the other 'pink' parts of the map, colonial Canada was situated as British territory. Canada was a 'child', one which through copying the 'mother country' would grow up to be a nation whose identity was situated in its own space. Due to my geographical training, a preoccupation with *space* underpins this book. Influenced by work on geographers' oft-times support of empire builders, I approach the history of the IODE from a post-colonial critique of the construction of colonialism.[4] The shifting *location* of Anglo-Canadian identity is a continual theme. I follow Homi Bhabha when he writes of the need to 'think beyond narratives of originary and initial subjectivities and to focus on those moments or processes that are produced in the articulation of cultural differences', of 'in-between' spaces and interstices of difference where 'the intersubjective and collective experiences of nationness, community interest, or cultural value are negotiated'.[5] In centring Canada, rather than Britain, an examination of the IODE's history holds insights for the study of British imperialism.

Over the twentieth century the British Empire itself became history, and Canada as a nation dramatically changed. From mimicking a British imperial centre in population, economics, politics and culture, Canada has moved beyond dominion status to become a globally powerful multicultural nation state, whose identity is centred in its geographical location. French Canadian identity is now partially recognized, with on-going tension and controversy over the right to self-determination. If the future relationship between Quebec and Anglo-Canada is unknown, it is clear that the IODE's narrative and vision are now history. Absolutist truth-claims are now under question, and 'diversity' is the order of the day. We have experienced a sense of the 'loss of European history and culture as History and Culture, the loss of their unquestioned place at the centre of the World'.[6] Nations themselves are narrations (Said[7]), they are contestable, imagined (Anderson[8]), invented traditions (Hobsbawn and Ranger[9]), and steeped in ever-changing memory (Samuel[10]).

With the shift from colonial to post-colonial understandings of imperial history, new genealogies of the previously taken-for-granted are appearing. Work is now turning to 'the sense in which Europeans' constitution of reality had its own exotic and hegemonic quality'.[11] Influenced by Gramsci and the legitimation of domination, Kay Anderson's work on Vancouver's Chinatown focuses on the construction of Chinatown according to European ideologies of race and the hegemonic policies those ideas have shaped.[12] In *The Mountie from Dime Novel to Disney*, Michael Dawson deconstructs the meaning of the mountie to represent changing Anglo-Canadian nationalism.[13] Also concerned with icons, Daniel Francis takes a critical look at national identity through an examination of 'myths' in Canadian history such as the Royal Canadian Mounted Police (RCMP) and the Canadian Pacific Railway (CPR), and the myth of unity with Quebec.[14] The shaping of Canadian culture, history, politics and health care is investigated in *Painting the Maple*, a book of interdisciplinary essays on race, gender and the construction of Canada. The editors state that 'one purpose of this work-in-progress is to problematize the construction of Canada by *discovering* assumptions, biases, and hegemonic practices'.[15] Likewise, Karen Dubinsky's work on honeymooning and tourism at Niagara Falls deconstructs hegemonic heterosexual citizenship.[16]

This book focuses on the IODE's invention of 'Britishness' as a part of its vision for Anglo-Canada. That focus makes necessary the complicating of notions of imperialism as beginning in a European metropole and expanding outwards. Instead colonialism becomes 'a moment when new encounters with the world facilitated the formation of categories of metropole and colony in the first place'.[17] For such purposes, I look at the imposition of hegemony, not by the direct force of a colonizing power, but by the mimicry of descendants from the constructed British imperial centre. Hence, Canada as a 'white settler society' shapes my research. The process of European settlement in past empires is now problematized and un-settled.[18] Conquest, domination, colonization and assimilation, the tools of imperialism and nation building in societies, such as that of Canada, to which Anglo-Celtic settlers migrated and there became dominant, are now questioned. But, as Phillip Buckner has suggested, Canadian historiography has down-played the significance of the imperial experience in shaping the identity of British Canadians.[19] This book takes up Buckner's challenge, and examines the development of a British Canada through the work of a group of female imperialists. It sheds new light on the complex relationship between Britishness and national identity. It is time for Canadian historians to re-acknowledge the British influence on the Canadian nation, albeit in a way that draws upon recent post-colonial work in other settler societies, and that does not do so at the expense of the histories of indigenous peoples, French Canadians, or migrants from outside of Britain and France.

For Canada, claiming colonial status as part of the British Empire has not necessarily meant subjugation, but rather, the advancement of nationalism. In his influential 1970 study of Canadian imperial ideology, Carl Berger proposed that, for Canada, imperial ties to Britain could be a way of increasing the power of the nation.[20] Indeed, colonial nationalism was premissed on Canada proving itself within an imperial context. Such ideas were always embedded in the beliefs of the IODE. Berger's study focused on male intellectuals, and stopped at 1914. The IODE was destined to outlive Berger's men, and to outweigh their significance. To contribute to an understanding of Canada's 'sense of power' I focus on a group of women, and shift from the space of 'public' men to that of women's voluntary work. Vital to its longevity was the IODE's ability to change with the times.

Tracing, through the IODE's history, the shifts in Anglo-Canadian identity and Canada's place in the British Empire, I argue that hegemonic identity was constructed in relation to the very difference that it dominated. As Raymond Williams informed us (in his now much-used phrase), hegemony 'does not just passively exist as a form of dominance. It has continually to be renewed, recreated, defended and modified. It is also continually resisted, limited, altered, challenged by pressures not all of its own.'[21] Such a dynamic process is witnessed to in the IODE's behaviour of attack and defence: either silencing perceived 'threats' that challenged its vision for Canada, or assimilating – *canadianizing* – otherness. Beyond merely mimicking an imagined Britain, the IODE invented Anglo-Canada in response to what it perceived to be threats and resistance to its narrative. This recursive relationship between marginal and dominant groups in producing hegemonic identity was explained by Raymond Williams twenty years ago when he stated that 'the reality of cultural process must then always include the efforts and contributions of those who are in one way or another outside or at the edge of the terms of the specific hege-mony'.[22] Since the making of that statement, the place of 'the other' has received such attention that our understanding of domination has been dramatically altered.

So what of *gender*? This book wrestles with a current tension in feminism. On the one hand, I retain a group of women subjects as the standpoint of my research. I possess a great respect for and a sense of awe towards the IODE, an influential, efficient, clever, sometimes ruthless, and proud organization. Through its work this group of women, albeit affluent and Anglo-Celtic women, has struggled to make an impact in a sexist society, playing no small part in improving the lot of women. It has done so with sharp and organized efficiency. To have survived for so long is evidence enough of a powerful organization. There are reasons to be proud of this unique and feisty group of women.

As an organization the IODE has displayed great zeal and commitment in its efforts to produce a strong Canada and strong Canadian citizens in the image of an imagined Britain. This has involved hard work and careful thought. The IODE has been an innovator in education, health and welfare throughout its existence. It has laboured away in fighting tuberculosis, improving health care, and members have exerted an impressive presence both inside and outside the classroom. Women's voluntary work, such as placing pictures of monarchs in classrooms, offering school prizes for 'imperial' essays, providing school libraries and scholarships, as teachers themselves, providing care at ports, and catering at citizenship courts, allowed the IODE access to immigrants and children. Privileged social position allowed access to education boards, government and commerce. All of these activities were united by an overarching patriotic mission, and deemed suitably 'female' because of underlying maternal motivations.

Yet, although I want to boast about how much of an impact the IODE has had on Canada and the Empire, this book is not an uncritical celebration of the IODE. While I want to show the IODE as an integral and important part of the British imperial past, it is my task to place the IODE in the context of the making of Anglo-Canada. That involves an engagement with work on gender, race and colonialism. I build upon insights into the relationship between white women and imperialism to examine the IODE, and in turn contribute its Canadian context in order to enrich the international literature. Thanks to works by women's historians, it is now clear that women are not uniformly marginalized, and the work of the IODE that I choose to display provides the evidence to form my arguments about the IODE's complicity in racism and oppression; its representation of Anglo-Canadian hegemonic identity. It is my intention to grapple with this group of women as representative of hegemonic discourse; to show them, as Iris Marion Young has described cultural imperialism, universalizing a dominant nation's experience and culture, and establishing them as the norm.[23] This involves moving beyond the uniform celebration of women's work and examining the contradictory and complex position of, on the one hand, extending help to those perceived to be in need, while, on the other, supporting the patriarchal and imperial practices which had led to that need in the first place.

Feminist history and the loss of confidence

By 1971 the IODE had become insecure about the extent to which it was perceived to be influential, and when it sent a brief to the Special Joint Committee on the Constitution of Canada it sought the support of 'other' groups, 'those with Canadian backgrounds of several generations but of other than British heritage, for example Italian, Ukrainian, Chinese, thus widening the base of operations and avoiding the inevitable WASP label'.[24] Here there was evidence of a limited acceptance of multiculturalism, although the IODE still believed that all Canadians should accept the British monarch as their head of state. It is not surprising that the IODE saw no need for the Canadian flag to be changed in 1965 or for the Canadian Constitution to be repatriated in 1981. Yet, increasingly aware of its complicity in an outmoded past, the IODE expressed itself with decreasing confidence. Along with involving 'others', the cure was to attempt a clean-up and a face lift. First, the name was 'changed', and then the badge abandoned its Union Jack with outward radiating stars for each corner of the Empire, in favour of a logo of four maple leaves. Symbolically, the IODE became more Canadian-centred than ever before.

Of great significance was that in 1979 the IODE cleaned out its closets and donated the most of its documented history to the Public Archives of Canada, physically moving its written memory away from its national offices in Toronto and its everyday activities, rendering its past 'history'. At approximately the same time, chapters across Canada began to make local deposits to provincial archives (see Note on sources). Physically out of sight, it would perhaps be possible for the IODE's history to be out of mind, locked in the past. The result was that a meticulous collection of minute books, scrapbooks, memorabilia, a full run of the IODE's quarterly magazine *Echoes*, and other publications, was handed over to a safe resting place. Ironically, the IODE's collection was professionally preserved and made available for historians so that they could consult the details of what was often considered a secret and mysterious organization.

Why did the IODE not follow the example of other organizations scared of future exposure and light a bonfire, letting its history go up in smoke? Such an action would have contradicted the very essence of the Order. The IODE has always taken itself seriously as a maker of history. In the post-Second World War years the IODE even purchased the services of a press agency so that its activities would be comprehensively recorded. It has constantly worked to perpetuate the memory of selected Canadian citizens and has invented 'Canadiana'. It was simply not possible for the IODE to make a clean break from its past because, as this book shows, the history of the IODE is about representation: the past as process.

The story related here is told from the perspective of a feminist historian, informed by the post-1970s debates over and developments in the writing of women into history . Thus far, women's historians have paid little attention to the IODE. There are the publications that the IODE has itself produced (see Note on sources), but, to date, critical work on the IODE is limited to five MA dissertations, my own PhD thesis and some articles by Nancy Sheehan. Sheehan's useful work focuses on the IODE's early years, and its endeavours with children and education.[25] That it has taken so long for a history of the IODE to be written can be explained by a number of factors. First, as subsequent chapters will discuss in detail, the IODE is a conservative organization. Hence, its patriotism and politics have not fitted the agenda of a women's and gender history intent on recovering past women's organizations as role-models for a leftist second-wave feminism. Second, as an organization of female imperialists, and with citizenship and democracy at its centre, the IODE has not fitted neatly with the widely influential *public* and *private* spheres framework which has held so much sway with women's historians. Overall, both inside and outside of the academy, there has been a lack of recognition given to women's everyday influence in matters of citizenship and democracy.

Historians are only just beginning to grasp the past realms of a 'separate spheres' framework that has considered nation, empire and government to be located in a 'public' sphere of commerce and economy, separate from women's 'natural' place in a 'private' realm of care and nurture.[26] Despite acknowledgements of the limits to the separate spheres framework, as Carol Pateman indicated a while ago now, 'the dichotomy between the private and the public is central to almost two centuries of feminist writing and political struggle'.[27] The task of refining and nuancing our understandings of such complex, diverse and ever-changing spheres has for long captured the attention of women's historians. Work during the past ten years has challenged the assumption of two discrete realms, and has shown how closely linked and intertwined family, sexuality, gender, imperialism, nation and citizenship were. I build upon this literature and contribute new insights about a female imperialist organization's relationship to the British Empire and the Canadian nation state. My perspective elaborates on the work of women's historians. That there is now a vibrant field of gender and history is testament to the efforts of such historians from the 1970s onwards.[28] In this book I continue many of the themes of Canadian women's history, such as the significance of women's voluntary work, immigration, welfare and children, and education. I also develop newer themes of colonization, gender and hegemony, along lines similar to those of Karen Dubinsky regarding Niagara Falls as a 'contact zone' between travel and race/ethnicity, of Cecilia Morgan on Laura Secord and narratives of Canadian loyalist history, of Myra Rutherdale on Anglican women missionaries as agents of colonization in the Pacific northwest and the Arctic, and Adele Perry on gender, race and sexuality in nineteenth-century British Columbia.[29] In centring Canada and examining Anglo-Celtic women as empire builders, nation builders and colonizers, this book makes a distinctively Canadian contribution to the international literature on women and imperialism.

In rendering the IODE essential to the construction of Anglo-Canadian identity, I continue to grapple with the historical construction of the public and private spheres, and how women were placed, and how they placed themselves, at once in the spaces of domesticity and citizenship. I follow Anne McClintock in accusing male theorists – of imperialism and post-colonialism – of failing to explore the gendered dynamics of the subject. It is time to gender national, imperial and colonial spaces. The cult of domesticity was 'a crucial, if concealed, dimension of male, as well as female identities, shifting and unstable as these were, and an indispensable element both of the industrial market and imperial enterprise'.[30]

Along with gender, race and class must be taken into consideration, and the admission made that not all women are the same: that identities are multiple and complex. Writing about the female subject in history, Denise Riley states that 'most commonly, you will skate across the several identities which will take your weight, relying on the most useful for your purposes of the moment'. She is quick to caution, however, that while 'it is impossible to thoroughly be a woman, it's also impossible never to be one'.[31] Such re-thinking does, however, allow the admission that, because of race and class identities, women sometimes oppress other women. Vron Ware has suggested that 'gender played a crucial role in organizing ideas of "race" and "civilization", and women were involved in many different ways in the expansion and maintenance of the Empire'.[32]

There is now a vast historical literature on gender, race and colonialism. The 1990s saw prominent feminist journals devoting special issues to research and discussion.[33] Conferences were devoted to the importance of gender and race in the history of nation, empire and colony,[34] while edited collections brought together an array of diverse work.[35] Anna Davin's 1978 article 'Imperialism and motherhood' set the trajectory for an examination of the importance of gender to imperialism.[36] Subsequent work set out to recover and celebrate a unified white woman subject and her presence in imperial projects.[37] Such an approach was quickly problematized by those who linked gender and race, grappling with the complicity of women in imperial projects. It was startlingly clear that it was not enough merely to recover and chronicle women's presence in the imperial project, and that race would have to be taken seriously.[38] This led to admissions that white women have 'benefited from the economic and political subjugation of indigenous people and shared many of the accompanying attitudes of racism, paternalism, ethnocentrism, and national chauvinism'.[39] White women were not 'the hapless onlookers of empire, but were ambiguously complicit both as colonizers and colonized, privileged and restricted, acted upon and acting'.[40] There was a deconstruction of 'white' women, to 'get away from the assumption that to be white is to be normal, while to be not-white is to occupy a racial category with all its attendant meanings'.[41] The awkward question of the white feminist response to racism added another dimension to the history of the women's club movement and first-wave feminism.[42] Such concerns provide a context for my history of the IODE. An examination of the IODE's work and beliefs reveals the organization as a forgotten colonizer.

Another concern in the proliferation of work on gender, race and colonialism is the reconfiguration of 'home' and 'away'. Here, work on travel literature, notably that of Mary Louise Pratt, collapses 'cores' and 'peripheries'.[43] Antoinette Burton suggests that 'the United Kingdom could be as much of a "contact zone" as the colonies themselves'.[44] This book centres Canada as its contact zone, and continues the complication of national and imperial borders. Yet, it is important to retain a strong sense of uneven power, and of the irony in the IODE's attempt to mimic a revered British core that was considered, and considered itself to be, superior.

We should also be wary of limiting definitions of 'travel' to adventure and exploration. Sara Mills has made a call to 'resist the projection of imperial expansion as adventure, and concentrate more on the lived experience of all those involved in colonial life, to analyse domestic and women's spaces and see beyond the "heroic" adventures of male travellers'.[45] Travel should not be viewed as separate from the 'everyday'. Indeed, historically, immigration accounts for the greatest volume of travellers. The IODE and other patriotic organizations were well aware of the essentially pragmatic need for immigration in order to realize their goals.[46] The renewed focus on domesticity and 'the everyday', however, means asserting, in a modified way, that colonialism is about motherhood and domesticity beyond élite women travellers or the viewing of women as symbols of home and purity, marginal to the process of colonialism.[47] It is between the spaces of imperialism and nationalism, of 'public', 'private' and 'the everyday', that I tell the story of the IODE. The terrain I explore is replete with tensions, contradictions and ironies.

The first chapter offers a genealogy of the IODE, detailing the structure of the organization and placing it in imperial context. I show how the IODE's set-up has itself represented its vision for Anglo-Canadian identity, and Canada's place within the Empire. The second chapter covers the beginning years of the IODE, through to the end of the First World War. It introduces the 'racial hierarchy' of the IODE, and its preference for British immigration, that was to prove so important during the twentieth century. It covers the IODE's work with immigrants, and then its maternal war-time labour. The third chapter looks at the 1920s and the growing importance of 'canadianization': the assimilation of all 'others' into Canadian identity. In the fourth chapter the focus is on the lengths to which the IODE would go to produce a Canada that emulated Britain, with a case study of the 1928 English Schoolgirl Tour of Canada. The tour also provided a statement of what an Anglo-Canada in the late 1920s should be. The persistence of and the changes in Anglo-Canadian identity through the 1930s are examined in the fifth chapter, which also documents the effects of the Second World War in re-defining and shifting this identity towards centring Canada. The sixth chapter examines the innovative work of the IODE in memorialization and considers war memorials as producers of identity, again tracing the shifts from colonial British space to national Canadian space. Chapter seven looks at Cold War Canada, including the often ignored gendering of democracy, and considers the effects of the perceived Communist threat on Canadian identity. It argues that the IODE's representation of democracy changed during the Cold War and that this change involved an ideological as well as a spatial shift away from Britain toward North America. The eighth chapter continues consideration of the influence of the USA and looks to the IODE's most recent projects in the Canadian north. It covers the demise of the 'racial hierarchy' and the IODE's corresponding shift of focus away from immigrants to the canadianizing of 'new' Canadians.

This chapter shows the IODE negotiating a position increasingly away from that of government, moving towards children and individuals as the focus of its 'charity'. The Conclusion examines the contemporary fragmented construction of an Anglo-Canadian identity based upon mimicking Britain, while also revealing the considerable continuity with and re-presentation of the past that exists.

Notes

1 Interview, 8 November 1993: Kingston, Ontario.
2 Interview, 18 April 1994: Regina, Saskatchewan.
3 Interview, 12 February 1994: Sillery, Quebec.
4 See Felix Driver, *Geography Militant: Cultures of Exploration in the Age of Empire* (Oxford: Blackwell, 1999); Morag Bell, Robin Butlin and Michael Heffernan (eds), *Geography and Imperialism 1820–1940* (Manchester: Manchester University Press, 1995); Derek Gregory, *Geographical Imaginations* (Oxford, and Cambridge, MA: Blackwell, 1994); Anne Godlewska and Neil Smith (eds), *Geography and Empire* (Oxford, and Cambridge, MA: Blackwell, 1994); David N. Livingstone, *The Geographical Tradition: Episodes in the History of a Contested Enterprise* (Oxford, and Cambridge, MA: Blackwell, 1993); and David R. Stoddart, *On Geography and its History* (New York: Blackwell, 1986).
5 Homi Bhabha, *The Location of Culture* (London and New York: Routledge, 1994), 2.
6 Robert Young, *White Mythologies: Writing History and the West* (London and New York: Routledge, 1990), 20.
7 Edward Said, *Culture and Imperialism* (London: Vintage, 1993).
8 Benedict Anderson, *Imagined Communities: Reflections on the Origin and Spread of Nationalism*, 2nd edn (London and New York: Verso, 1991 [1983]).
9 Eric Hobsbawn and Terence Ranger (eds), *The Invention of Tradition* (Cambridge: Cambridge University Press, 1983).
10 Raphael Samuel, *Theatres of Memory*, vol. 1: *The Past and Present in Contemporary Culture* (London and New York: Verso, 1994); Raphael Samuel and Paul Thompson (eds), *The Myths We Live By* (London and New York: Routledge, 1990).
11 Kay Anderson and Fay Gale (eds), *Inventing Places: Studies in Cultural Geography* (Melbourne: Longman, 1992), 33.
12 Kay J. Anderson, *Vancouver's Chinatown: Racial Discourse in Canada, 1875–1980* (Montreal: McGill–Queen's University Press, 1991).
13 Michael Dawson, *The Mountie from Dime Novel to Disney* (Toronto: Between the Lines, 1998).
14 Daniel Francis, *National Dreams: Myth, Memory, and Canadian History* (Vancouver: Arsenal Pulp Press, 1997).
15 Veronica Strong-Boag, Sherrill Grace, Abigail Eisenberg and Joan Anderson, *Painting the Maple: Essays on Race, Gender, and the Construction of Canada* (Vancouver: University of British Columbia Press, 1998), 11.
16 Karen Dubinsky, *The Second Greatest Disappointment: Honeymooning and Tourism at Niagara Falls* (Toronto: Between the Lines, 1999).
17 Nicholas Dirks (ed.), *Colonialism and Culture* (Ann Arbor: University of Michigan Press, 1992), 6.
18 Daiva Stasiulis and Nira Yuval-Davis (eds) *Unsettling Settler Societies: Articulations of Gender, Race, Ethnicity and Class* (London: Sage, 1995).
19 Phillip Buckner, 'Whatever happened to the British Empire?' *Journal of the Canadian Historical Association*, 4 (1994), 3–32.
20 Carl Berger, *The Sense of Power: Studies in the Ideas of Canadian Imperialism, 1867–1914* (Toronto: University of Toronto Press, 1970).
21 Raymond Williams, 'Selections from Marxism and literature', in Nicholas B. Dirks

and Sherry B Ortner (eds), *Culture/Power/History: A Reader in Contemporary Social Theory* (Princeton, NJ: Princeton University Press, 1994), 585–608, at 598.

22 *Ibid.*, 599.

23 Iris Marion Young, *Justice and the Politics of Difference* (Princeton, NJ: Princeton University Press, 1990), 59.

24 National Archives of Canada (hereafter NAC) MG28 I 17, 10.

25 Nancy Sheehan, 'Philosophy, pedagogy and practice: the IODE and the schools in Canada 1900–1945', *History of Education Review*, 2: 2 (1990), 307–21; Nancy Sheehan, 'Women's organisations and educational issues, 1900–1930', *Canadian Women's Studies/Les Cahiers de la femme*, 7: 3 (1986), 90–4; Nancy Sheehan, 'The IODE, the schools and World War I', *History of Education Review*, 13: 1 (1984), 29–44.

26 For a critique of the spheres, see: Linda J. Kerber, 'Separate spheres, female worlds, woman's place: the rhetoric of women's history', *Journal of American History*, 75: 1 (1988), 9–39; Linda J. Kerber, Nancy F. Cott, Robert Gross, Lynn Hunt, Carol Smith-Rosenberg and Christine M. Stansell, 'Beyond roles, beyond spheres: thinking about gender in the early republic', *William and Mary Quarterly*, 46: 3 (1989), 565–85, at 566; Jean Bethke Elshtain, *Public Man, Private Woman: Women in Social and Political Thought* (Princeton, NJ: Princeton University Press, 1981); and Dorothy Kelly and Susan M. Reverby (eds), *Gendered Domains: Rethinking Public and Private in Women's History* (Ithaca, NY: Cornell University Press, 1992).

27 Carole Pateman, *The Disorder of Women: Democracy, Feminism and Political Theory* (Cambridge: Polity Press, 1989), 118.

28 For examples of works on Canadian women's history, see Kathryn McPherson, Cecilia Morgan and Nancy M. Forestell (eds) *Gendered Pasts: Historical Essays in Femininity and Masculinity in Canada* (Don Mills: Oxford University Press Canada, 1999); Franca Iacovetta and Wendy Mitchinson (eds), *On the Case: Explorations in Social History* (Toronto: University of Toronto Press, 1998); Alison Prentice, Paula Bourne, Gail Cuthbert Brandt, Beth Light, Wendy Mitchinson and Naomi Black, *Canadian Women: A History*, 2nd edn (Toronto: Harcourt Brace Canada, 1996); Joy Parr and Mark Rosenfeld (eds), *Gender and History in Canada* (Mississauga: Copp Clark Ltd, 1996); Franca Iacovetta and Mariana Valverde (eds), *Gender Conflicts: New Essays in Women's History* (Toronto: University of Toronto Press, 1992); The Clio Collective, *Quebec Women: A History* (Toronto: Women's Press, 1987); Alison Prentice and Susan Mann Trofimenkoff (eds), *The Neglected Majority: Essays in Canadian Women's History*, vol. 2 (Toronto: McClelland and Stewart, 1985); Linda Kealey (ed.), *A Not Unreasonable Claim: Women and Reform in Canada 1880s–1920s* (Toronto: Women's Press, 1979).

29 Karen Dubinsky, 'Vacations in the "contact zone": race, gender, and the traveler at Niagara Falls', in Ruth Roach Pierson and Nupur Chaudhuri with Beth McAuley (eds), *Nation, Empire, Colony: Historicizing Gender and Race* (Indiana: Indiana University Press, 1998), 251–69; Cecilia Morgan, '"Of slender frame and delicate appearance": the placing of Laura Secord in the narratives of Canadian loyalist history', in Parr and Rosenfeld, *Gender and History in Canada*, 103–19; Myra Rutherdale, *Women and the White Man's God: Gender and Race in the Canadian Mission Field* (Vancouver: University of British Columbia Press, forthcoming); Myra Rutherdale, 'Revisiting colonization through gender: Anglican missionary women in the Pacific northwest and the Arctic, 1860–1945', *BC Studies*, 104: winter (1994), 3–23; Adele Perry, *On the Edge of Empire: Gender, Race, and the Making of British Columbia, 1849–1871* (Toronto: University of Toronto Press, 2000); and Adele Perry, '"Oh I'm just sick of the faces of men": gender imbalance, race, sexuality, and sociability in nineteenth-century British Columbia', *BC Studies*, 105–6: spring–summer (1995), 27–43.

30 Anne McClintock, *Imperial Leather: Race, Gender and Sexuality in the Colonial Contest* (London and New York: Routledge, 1995), 5.

31 Denise Riley, *'Am I that Name?': Feminism and the Category of 'Women' in History* (Basingstoke: Macmillan, 1988), 114.

32 Vron Ware, *Beyond the Pale: White Women, Racism and History* (London and New York: Verso, 1992), 37.

33 For example, see the following journals' special issues: *Women's Studies International Forum*, 21: 3 (1998): 'Women, imperialism and identity'; *Gender and History*, 10: 3 (1998): 'Feminisms and internationalism'; and *Feminist Review*, 65: summer (2000): 'Reconstructing femininities: colonial intersections of gender, race, religion and class'.

34 See Roach, Pierson and Chaudhuri, *Nation, Empire, Colony*.

35 Antoinette Burton (ed.), *Gender, Sexuality and Colonial Modernities* (London: Routledge, 1999); Clare Midgley (ed.), *Gender and Imperialism* (Manchester: Manchester University Press, 1998); Julia Clancy-Smith and Frances Gouda (eds), *Domesticating the Empire: Race, Gender and Family Life in French and Dutch Colonialism* (Charlottesville and London: University of Virginia Press, 1998); and Nupur Chaudhuri and Margaret Strobel (eds), *Western Women and Imperialism: Complicity and Resistance* (Bloomington: Indiana University Press, 1992).

36 Anna Davin, 'Imperialism and motherhood', *History Workshop*, 5 (1978), 9–65.

37 See Joanna Troloppe, *Britannia's Daughters: Women of the British Empire* (London, Melbourne, Auckland and Johannesburg: Cresset, 1983). Troloppe is a writer of historical novels who celebrates women's contribution in building and sustaining the British Empire. Claudia Knapman, *White Women in Fiji, 1835–1930: The Ruin of Empire?* (Sydney: Allen & Unwin, 1986), Helen Callaway, *Gender, Culture and Empire: European Women in Colonial Nigeria* (Basingstoke: Macmillan, 1987).

38 Jane Haggis, *Women and Colonialism: Untold Stories and Conceptual Absences. A Critical Survey* (Manchester: University of Manchester, Sociology Department, Special Series, 1988).

39 Margaret Strobel, *European Women and the Second British Empire* (Bloomington: Indiana University Press, 1991), xi.

40 McClintock, *Imperial Leather*, 6.

41 Ware, *Beyond the Pale*, 18. See also Ruth Frankenberg, *White Women, Race Matters: The Social Construction of Whiteness* (Minneapolis: University of Minnesota Press, 1995).

42 Antoinette Burton, *Burdens of History: British Feminists, Indian Women, and Imperial Culture, 1865–1915* (Chapel Hill and London: University of North Carolina Press, 1994), 1.

43 Mary Louise Pratt, *Imperial Eyes: Travel Writing and Transculturation* (London and New York: Routledge, 1992).

44 Antoinette Burton, *At the Heart of Empire: Indians and the Colonial Encounter in Late-Victorian Britain* (Berkeley, Los Angeles and London: University of California Press, 1998).

45 Sara Mills, 'Knowledge, gender and empire', in Alison Blunt and Gillian Rose (eds), *Writing, Women and Space: Colonial and Postcolonial Geographies* (New York and London: Guilford Press, 1994), 29–50, at 47.

46 Julia Bush, *Edwardian Ladies and Imperial Power* (Leicester: Leicester University Press, 2000).

47 Margaret Jolly, 'Colonizing women: the maternal body and empire', in Sneja Gunew and Anna Yeatman (eds), *Feminism and the Politics of Difference* (New South Wales: Allen & Unwin, 1993), 103–27; and Kalpana Ram and Margaret Jolly, *Maternities and Modernities: Colonial and Postcolonial Experiences in Asia and the Pacific* (Cambridge: Cambridge University Press, 1998).

CHAPTER ONE

Genealogy of an imperial and nationalistic Order

The IODE began as it would continue: on a footing of attack and defence, amid a climate of patriotism fuelled by the South Africa War (1899–1901). Margaret Clark Murray, a sometime journalist, philanthropist and wife of an influential McGill professor, returned to Montreal from London, where she had experienced much pro-war jingoism, and decided to act on the public outpourings of Anglo-Canadian patriotism that she sensed around her. Her intentions were to seek an opportunity to strengthen Canadian national ties as well as imperial connections, her imperialist outlook stemming, in part, from her upbringing in Scotland. Murray had ambitious plans to form an empire-wide Federation of Daughters of the British Empire and Children of the Empire. She would start the organization in Canada, where she resided, and fan outwards to the other parts of the Empire, including Britain.

After a period of fervent writing of national histories, scholars are now exploring the connections, tensions and ironies between national and imperial identities. Benedict Anderson's work has been instrumental in destabilizing the absolute power ascribed to empires by suggesting that they were 'imagined'. Anderson has drawn attention to cases of colonized peoples 'who have every reason to feel hatred for their imperialist rulers' instead being inspired by the power of patriotism and racism to 'love and often profoundly self-sacrificing love'.[1] In the case of the formation of the IODE, it was Anglo-Celtic 'colonials' who did not feel hatred for their rulers, as they were 'white settlers', attempting to create a 'British' Canada. In this vein Clark Murray's gutsy enthusiasm was simultaneously nationalistic and imperial. She began her task by methodically sending out telegrams to the mayor of the capital city of each province, asking them to call together women to form regional chapters of her proposed organization. She asserted that it was time to 'stand by our Queen at all costs, to shake our fists if necessary, in the face of the whole of Europe, and show them what we are made of'.[2] A contemporary member explains the IODE's patriotism: 'It all made perfect sense in 1900. We *are* a patriotic organization who love Canada and are patriotic to Canada. We have been accused for years of being patriotic to Britain, which is not true. It's always been a Canadian organization'.[3] In recalling 1900, she evokes the co-dependence of national and imperial identities, and the need for Canadian nationalism to grow out of an imperial attachment. This, indeed, is the essence of Carl Berger's work on how Anglo-Canada gained a 'sense of power'.[4] Along with Berger's blindness to the IODE in his work on Canada and the South Africa War, Carman Miller similarly finds little place for the IODE's initial work or sentiments.[5] Yet, as Julia Bush's work on Edwardian ladies and imperial power argues, a 'spiritual creed of Empire was as attractive to many British women as it was to their male counterparts'.[6] I argue that, along with patriotic women in other countries, such as the members of the Victoria League and of the South African Guild of Loyal Women, the women of the IODE displayed their own enthusiastic patriotism. As Clark Murray declared: 'do not forget that the destiny of our Empire lies in the hands of our women and our children, more than in politics and in parliaments'.[7] Thus, Clark Murray and other patriotic women around the British Empire expressed a *female* imperialism, that placed great importance in, and was justified by, an appeal to women's perceived maternal capabilities.

Patriotic clubs and imperialism

In its activities, initial class composition and political affiliations, the IODE fitted very closely with the imperial propaganda clubs, a number of which were founded at the end of the nineteenth century in Canada and other parts of the Empire.[8] These were conservative movements that sought to foster imperial patriotism. Utilizing textbooks, exhibitions and entertainments to promote their ideas, their varied constitutions and their defensive and cultural concerns all came together in the theme of imperial unity.[9] The Navy League, the Victoria League, and the Girl and Boy Scout Movements epitomised such organizations. The IODE was clearly a part of this historical moment, enjoying strong links to imperial defence and collaboration with the Navy League.[10] The symbols of the IODE's organization also reflected empire unity. The motto was 'one flag (the Union Jack), one throne (the British Monarchy), one Empire (the British Empire)'. Likewise, the badge cast imperial foundations in metal, with the crown symbolizing the British monarchy, the Union Jack for Britain and the Empire, surrounded by a seven-pointed outward-radiating star, one point for each of the major territories of the Empire.

Clark Murray's way of going about organizing her Order involved tapping into an élite network of individuals representative of the Canadian establishment, her connections spanning outwards from affluent Anglo-Celtic Montreal society. Fredericton was the first place to assemble a group of women at a meeting, on 15 January 1900, where the mayor read Clark Murray's telegram: 'Will the women of Fredericton unite with the women of Montreal in federating as "Daughters of the Empire" and inviting the women of Australia and New Zealand to unite with them in sending to the Queen an expression of our devotion to the Empire and an emergency war fund to be expended as Her Majesty shall deem fit?'[11] As well as involving Britain's antipodean Empire in unity, Clark Murray's empire-wide ambitions included plans to set up an imperial chapter in London as soon as possible.[12] That ambition, however, tested the limits of 'Empire unity' for a Britain that still considered itself the superior core of that Empire. Clark Murray's ambitions of empire-wide membership were soon crushed, blocked by the rival British women's patriotic organization, formed in 1901 and taking its name from the matriarch of imperialism herself, the Victoria League.

With an aim similar to the IODE's, of promoting closer union between British subjects living in different parts of the Empire, the Victoria League took strong objection to Clark Murray's plans for an imperial chapter of her organization in London, seeing the Canadian counterpart as competition. In a letter to Canada, the Victoria League demanded that Clark Murray hand over to them the contacts that she had made in London. Much to Clark Murray's dismay, self-interested and perhaps meek Toronto members sided with the Victoria League, took 'Federation' out of the name, and made Toronto the national centre of a re-named Imperial Order Daughters of the Empire.[13] Clark Murray's health suffered, and it was a long time before the deeply upsetting events of formation were smoothed over and she came to be celebrated as the IODE's foundress.

Out of such beginnings, the IODE has itself often treated other women's organizations as the competition. While there has been considerable cooperation between the IODE and other organizaions, especially during wartime, the Order has attempted to maintain control over the activities that it has chosen to participate in. But being considered inferior by the Victoria League and the SOSBW is a theme that recurs through this book. The clashes over control and respect highlight the unique position of the IODE, as a Canadian organization that promoted imperial ideals. While it was staunch in voicing its opposition to other Canadian women's organizations, when it came to groups based in Britain the IODE always deferred – indeed such were the hierarchies of the Empire that it had no choice but to fall in with the intentions of the Victoria League and the SOSBW. Here the IODE was trapped by the reverence in which it held all things British.

Clark Murray envisioned a large international membership eventually, to be run along fairly egalitarian lines. In a written retrospective she held that she had founded her 'Daughters on a new principle, namely, to prove what could be done without asking for high patronage', but capitulated when those working with her demanded a patroness.[14] Known for her own patriotic and charitable work, Lady Minto became the first *honorary* president. The first president of the IODE, from 1901 to 1910, was Edith Nordheimer. A well-connected member of the Canadian upper-classes, Nordheimer set the standard for presidents to come. As Margaret Gillett's work on Edith Nordheimer reveals, her grandfather, D'Arcy Boulton, was attorney-general of Upper Canada, an uncle was governor-general of Nova Scotia and later governor of Ceylon, while her father, James Boulton, was a well-established barrister. At the age of 24, she married the extremely wealthy 42-year-old businessman Samuel Nordheimer. Moving in élite Toronto circles, Edith Nordheimer was a member of a variety of charitable organizations, from the Working Boys' Home, and the Children's Aid Society, to the Victorian Order of Nurses and the Red Cross Society.[15] With Edith Nordheimer's presidency came an assurance to the Victoria League that the IODE would not compete for members in Britain or in other places where the Victoria League existed.

Over the course of the twentieth century, the possibility of expansion outside of Canada sporadically re-emerged for the IODE, each time to be met with cold defensive opposition from the Victoria League. With the exception of small and tenuous satellite chapters in pre-confederation Newfoundland, the USA, Bermuda, the Bahamas and India, the IODE was restricted to Canada. In the USA the Daughters of the British Empire consisted of a small number of loyal chapters on the eastern seaboard. In common with women involved in Bermuda and the Bahamas, they were largely British ex-patriates.[16] Alternatively, in India in 1905 Miss Susie Sorabji, a Parsee Christian teacher, organized the Kaiser-I-Hind Chapter in the Bombay district of Poona. She and her group of 'Empire-thinking Indian women' worked mainly in education.[17] The IODE in Canada raised funds for St Helena's School, of which Sorabji was the principal. In 1930 money was pledged to complete the building of the science block, named 'Canada Wing'.[18] Such work, however, was very small in scale. The frosty reception that Clark Murray's and subsequent Canadian initiative to enact 'Empire unity' met with in Britain served to highlight hierarchies of the Empire that were not supposed to be breached. And, despite being shunned, the IODE continued to celebrate an imagined Britain. Such admiration of Britain was possible because, as Carl Berger argues, imperial ties to Britain were believed to be the way forward for Canadian nationalism. That Anglo-Celtic settlers were in control of the Dominion of Canada meant that Canada's 'colonial' positioning was very different from the positioning of those deemed 'third world' parts of the Empire. Indeed, the IODE considered itself in a position to extend aid to India.

Patriotic expression was the initial primary objective of the IODE. Formed during wartime, the IODE set out to bolster and support nation and Empire, and all work took place in such a patriotic context that was concerned with citizenship. In this way, the IODE differed from other charitable organizations which did not have patriotism as their primary concern. The IODE's brand of patriotism was often gendered. Engaging with the maternal ideology of care and nurture, patriotism was to be non-partisan and non-sectarian.[19] Vron Ware writes of the manipulation of women's sexuality to serve imperial ends: 'Whether as Mothers of the Empire or Britannia's Daughters, women were able to symbolize the idea of moral strength that bound the great imperial family together.'[20] In accordance, the IODE's objectives were to stimulate patriotic sentiment, to foster a mind of union among women and children throughout the British Empire, to care for the dependants of military personnel, and to preserve the memory of brave and historic deeds.[21]

Reinforcing its primary patriotic objectives, strong distinctions between patriotism and charity were made clear. In 1905 a national executive meeting was strongly of the opinion that specifically charitable work should not 'direct the energy and funds of the chapters from purely patriotic ends which the Order stood for', and it was recommended that a 'liberal and varied list' of suggestions for active work be published in *Echoes*, for the benefit of the chapters.[22] There were guidelines on how work that verged on charity could be made more patriotic. For example, aid given to prevent the spread of tuberculosis should be approached from the patriotic perspective that it was of national concern to maintain a healthy population.[23] It was suggested that members combine working in hospital wards with reading to patients on imperial topics.

In the formative years fundraising, wherever it was possible, also served patriotic ends. As elsewhere in the Empire, this meant lectures by guest speakers and the production of pageants and plays. John MacKenzie has demonstrated the importance of entertainment in fostering imperial attachments in Britain, and in Canada that medium was also used by patriotic organizations such as the IODE.[24] A member in Regina recalls performances given from 'year one' in people's homes and church basements, as well as bazaars and crafts' sales.[25] Prince Edward Island held a number of notable entertainment fundraisers. In 1913 there was a Kirmess at the Opera House, Charlottetown. The programme included 'A Fate in Fairyland and Pyramid Ballet', chaperoned by Mrs James Warburton, 'The Wood Nymphs', chaperoned by Mrs Bulman, 'A Night in Koko's Garden' from the Mikado, and it ended with the singing of *God Save the King*.[26] In keeping with the past, from 1963 to 1971 the Prince Edward Island Chapter staged five popular variety performances called 'Red Glove Reviews'.[27]

The IODE's society connections allowed for some élite entertainment. At the beginning of the twentieth century there were grand balls, which were often held to celebrate imperial holidays. In 1925 the birthday of British Columbia was celebrated at a 'brilliant ball', one of many held in that province.[28] The ball was hosted by the Lady Douglas Chapter, whose regent for the years 1912–33, Mrs McMiking, had dressed as Queen Victoria at the Victoria Day parade in May 1923, as she did also in 1931.[29] A member in British Columbia recalls that the IODE was a society 'leader'. Receptions were held for influential Canadians, and when the Hotel Vancouver opened it was the IODE which put on the reception. In 1939, at an empire fête held at the Hotel Georgia in Vancouver, thirty chapters participated under the auspices of the Municipal Chapter of Vancouver. The event was opened by IODE member Mary Bollert, first dean of women at the University of British Columbia.[30] Bollert was also involved in the Canadian Federation of University Women. Before her appointment at UBC she had administered Sherbourne House Club, Toronto's largest residence for single 'business women and girls', a popular modern hostel that operated according to 'democratic principles of self-management'.[31]

As an organization of female imperialists, the IODE was situated between the mostly male patriotic clubs and the women's organizations. While, in common with the patriotic clubs, the IODE offered imperial lectures and provided opinions on imperial matters, it was also expected to perform maternal work. Unlike male patriotic organizations, which held lectures and offered prizes, from the outset the IODE undertook *work*. Yet with patriotism came a sense of seriousness, and separation from other women's organizations considered charitable. This view was to persist for many years. Later on in the century, Charlotte Whitton, a prominent and influential long-time IODE member, and Canada's first woman mayor, considered women's auxiliaries to be 'the butterers of bread, the cutters of cake, the brewers of tea, folders of letters, lickers of stamps – generally the hand-maidens of the social trivialities'.[32] Whitton was among the policy makers of the IODE, rather than of the membership offering maternal care at ports and courts. She aligned herself with affairs that she con-sidered to be of importance, and believed that women belonged in political leadership. Branded by her biographers a 'feminist on the right', Whitton considered women's progress into the political arena to be motivated by an intent not to alter the system but to improve it.[33] Her forthright and pragmatic approach found an outlet in the IODE, and generated considerable admiration among the membership. But just as she was an exception and pioneer in her work at the Canadian Council on Child Welfare, and later as the mayor of Ottawa, Whitton was not a 'typical' member of the IODE. The vast majority of members *were* active in voluntary work in their local communities, serving cake and tea. Meanwhile, Whitton's presence in Ottawa gave the more typical members a voice in the national arena.

To what extent Whitton and other women of strong political opin-ions used the IODE as a vehicle for their missions is hard to determine. Whitton was the driving force behind the IODE's 1947 study of welfare in Alberta. The IODE's report alleged inadequate and unprofessional child welfare procedures, in particular 'babies for export', the cross-border adoptions of Alberta children. The IODE's allegations led to the 1948–49 Alberta Royal Commission on Child Welfare, which found that the IODE was right in its expression of concern. In this case, the members of the IODE in Alberta had sought the professional advice of Whitton, and collaborated with her in the study. The result was the impressive Royal Commission and a series of recommendations for improvement.[34]

With a clear patriotic mission and an emphasis on citizenship that extended beyond a focus on women and children, the IODE in its ini-tial years fitted only partially with other Canadian women's organiza-tions. Canadian women's historians have written much about the women's club movement of the late nineteenth and early twentieth centuries, the organization of women in different Western countries into collectives dealing with education, culture, philanthropy, reform, politics, professions and religion.[35] The members of women's clubs have been described by Veronica Strong-Boag as 'largely middle class women who were moved by humanitarian, class and egalitarian con-cerns to attempt the redemption of society'.[36] These organizations were a product of a time that saw an ideological distinction between *public* and *private* spheres. Thanks to the work of women's historians, we know much about women's maternal role and their place in a con-structed 'private' sphere, and of the influence of a 'cult of domesticity'.

We know about feminist-friendly clubs whose activities were cast as expressions of benevolence or as working towards legislative reform for women's rights. Research on women's Christian societies, such as the YWCA and the Women's Christian Temperance Union (WCTU), has shown the importance to women of moral regulation. Although the impact of class, race and politics was not the primary focus of the study of Canadian women's organizations, their importance has not gone unnoticed.[37]

Because women have for so long been considered marginal to imperialism, it is only now that women's patriotic organizations are receiving in-depth consideration. The IODE is sometimes confused with its southern neighbour, the Daughters of the American Revolution, founded in 1890, which also had patriotism as its central concern. Their similar names, dates of foundation and emphases on patriotism and 'heritage' help to explain the confusion. A key difference, however, keenly felt among the IODE membership, was that the Order's sense of loyalty stemmed from support for Britain; its members' sympathies – and in some cases even their blood-lines – derived from the Loyalists who headed for British North America at the time of the American Revolution. The IODE's promotion of connections with Britain has meant that its pragmatic similarities to the Daughters of the Revolution have been downplayed. As I argue in this book, however, the IODE's identity was increasingly situated in North America, and its élite politics, family membership and displays of patriotism were North American. It makes sense, however, to seek similar organizations within the British Commonwealth.

Women's organizations in the British Commonwealth are being read for their contributions to citizenship.[38] Historians are now turning to women's patriotic organizations' imperialism and its outreach to the white settler colonies, examples of which are the work of Julia Bush on the Girls' Friendly Society, the Primrose League, the British Women's Emigration Association, and Bush and Reidi on the Victoria League.[39] Bush's latest work, on Edwardian ladies and imperial power, considers how 'the leading ladies of female imperialism sought to impose their gendered, class-bound values upon the national and imperial scene'.[40] As already noted, the Victoria League had intentions of promoting Empire unity that overlapped, as well as clashed with, those of the IODE. The IODE, however, was more 'hands-on' than the Victoria League, working beyond the tea-party and lecture series, seeking to directly influence Canadian citizenship through immigration and canadianization. Here the IODE had much in common with immigration organizations such as the Oversea League, the Girls' Friendly Society, the Salvation Army and the YWCA. These were empire-wide voluntary organizations doing much work in the settlement of migrants. As a part of what is sometimes termed 'the women's club movement', the IODE did collaborate with these organizations, but it was also keen to retain its own identity. Where the Victoria League situated itself at the centre of the Empire, the IODE existed to make Canada within the Empire, and attempted to enact its rhetoric through maternal voluntary work.

The IODE also had much in common with other Canadian branches of imperial organizations. Within Canada the IODE was a supporter of the 'evangelical muscular Christianity movements', especially the Girl Guides, that also aimed to create appropriate colonial citizens.[41] In 1923 the IODE entered into cooperation with the Girl Guides. It did so in the belief that the aims and ideals of both organizations were similar 'as regards a clean, healthy, practical citizenship, based on love of God, King and country'.[42] With similar objectives and activities to the Girl Guides', junior chapters of the IODE existed sporadically, experiencing strong and weak phases. During the 1950s and 1960s there were teenage chapters for the daughters of members, which held fashion evenings and beauty contests.

It was typical for IODE members to be 'clubswomen', being themselves involved also in several other women's groups at any given time. Indeed, it would have been unusual for a member of the IODE to belong solely to the IODE. IODE members were particularly active in the Canadian Club, various church groups, the Women's Press Club, local and national Councils of Women, various 'heritage' committees, and the Royal Commonwealth Society. The sense emerges, however, that members considered the IODE a unique organization, one that appealed directly to their affiliation as Canadians within the British Empire.

Inventing traditions

Officially, membership in the IODE was open to 'all women and children in the British Empire or foreign land who hold true allegiance to the British Crown'.[43] The unofficial reality of membership was more restricted, and varied in different provinces and at different times during the century. The social status of patriotic clubs was highest in the pre-First World War years, and the activities and attitudes of the IODE reflected such status. John MacKenzie has written of the turn-of-the-century patriotic organizations in Britain that 'all of these organizations were middle class and elitist; only one or two enjoyed a wider, more populist membership'.[44] The initial membership of the IODE fits such categorizing. Despite her more general intentions mentioned above, it was, after all a Canadian élite which Clark Murray targeted in order to set up initial meetings. It followed that it was the wives of élite males who became the first members.

Out of its élite beginnings, the IODE cultivated its own segregated social hierarchy. Membership was by and large by invitation. There is evidence that potential members, once invited along, were voted in or out through ballot.[45] In turn, the administrative structure of the IODE developed a hierarchy, best reflected in the structure of the 'Order' itself, which was referred to as a business, a militia, or a parliament where the first members assembled together as first ministers.[46] In 1916 an IODE publication from Manitoba claimed: 'We like best the definition which calls it [the IODE] a great SISTERHOOD OF SERVICE on which the Empire can rely in war and peace to further all that stands for the betterment of the Race.'[47] The structure of the IODE was the idea of Clark Murray, and has remained largely the same throughout the Order's history. Considered 'simple, but none the less effective' in a 1925 IODE publication, the simplicity came through a series of federated 'levels'.[48] At the bottom level were the primary chapters, hopefully to be 'in every city and town of the Dominion, and also other parts of the Empire'.[49] From the outset, an urban geography was a part of the IODE. Primary chapters sent representatives to municipal chapters, which in turn sent representatives to provincial chapters, which in turn fed the national chapter in Toronto. Hence, primary, municipal, provincial and national chapters were the ascending levels of the Order. While individual chapters worked on their own selected projects, there were also projects at the municipal, provincial and national levels. Annual meetings were held at the provincial and national levels. The provincial meetings were usually held in March, in order to give time for proposals to be put before the national meeting held during May. Provincial chapters took turns in hosting the national annual meetings.

The annual national meetings provided the most visible mechanism by which members, spread out over a vast geographic distance, were able to remain united. In an attempt to secure the membership and to make each region feel included, the locus shifted back and forth across Canada. These meetings were held in Canada's grand hotels, such as the York in Toronto, the Beaverbrook in Fredericton, and the Hotel Vancouver. Attending such meetings from afar required considerable funds, and the appropriate attire, including hat and gloves, to meet the formality and the pomp and circumstance of these occasions. The programmes for the meetings displayed much continuity in the format of proceedings. Remembering the war-dead with a march through the streets of the hosting town to lay a wreath at the war memorial was an enduring feature of the annual meetings. There was also a service in a Protestant church of one or other denomination. Formal reports were made by the various committees of the Order, at the provincial and national levels, and the president always made a substantial address.

Because the national headquarters was in Toronto, at 182 Lowther Street, in a home donated by the Eaton family, the department-store magnates, the IODE's national presidents have come largely from Toronto, or nearby parts of Ontario. Prior to the Second World War it was not unusual for national presidents to serve for many years. In the postwar period, however, two-year terms became standard. Provincial presidents became vice-presidents of the national chapter of the IODE, also enjoying a two-year term. Like the national presidents, committee secretaries at the national level tended to be from Ontario or the relatively near-by Quebec. The heads of primary and municipal chapters were majestically named 'regents'.

All levels of the IODE were divided into the same committees, each with a secretary. The committees covered services, education, organization, citizenship and Empire study. Each level of the Order also chose a standard bearer for official ceremonies. Before the Second World War the services committee was split into child and family welfare, war and postwar services, and ex-services' personnel. In the post-Second World War years the services committee dealing with war was re-named 'service at home and abroad'. The range of work covered under services included family welfare, cancer clinics, drugs and x-rays, and clothing supplies for Europe and Asia, distributed through the British Save the Children Fund. A percentage of the IODE's service work in the postwar years went outside of Canada. As Chapter eight reveals, the Canadian north became another postwar focus.[50] After the Second World War, the Empire study committee evolved into the Commonwealth relations committee,[51] an indicator of the changing times; and the combating Communism and democratic action committees were specifically Cold War innovations. As chapter seven details, these committees were responsible for selecting and sending out articles which were intended for use as study material by the chapters.[52] Meanwhile, the film committee encouraged the showing of 'suitable' films and British pictures, and urged that matrons be appointed for all children's showings.[53]

Without fail, from its beginnings, the IODE published its own quarterly magazine, *Echoes*, which was edited by a series of long-serving women journalists, in particular May Kertland and Agnes Mary Pease. As well as reports of the Order's work at all levels, its lavish and professional format included general interest articles, particularly on topics of national and imperial concern. For example, during the interwar years there was a series of articles on different parts of the Empire. On the eve of Elizabeth II's coronation in 1953 there was an article by Hamilton IODE member Marjorie Freeman Campbell titled 'Six queens have ruled England'.[54] Current affairs often featured, such as a 1952 article on the Malayan emergency by the national convener of the Empire and world affairs committee, Mrs H. S. Angas.[55] Such reports of world politics were printed alongside film, fashion, 'kitchen alchemy' and book reviews, written, from the early 1920s into the 1960s, most notably by Wilhelmina Gordon. The sense of community built by *Echoes* was vital in uniting chapters across Canada.

From the outset, the IODE grew more rapidly in Ontario than else-where. Chapters outside of central Canada were boosted by two grand recruitment train trips, one in 1909 to the western provinces, the other in 1910 to the eastern. There was continuity in the membership remaining relatively urban; with membership highest in medium-sized cities such as Regina, Saskatoon or Fredericton, Saint John, Sarnia and London. Anglophone areas such as the eastern townships of Quebec were strongholds, as were former Empire loyalist settlements such as Fredericton, St John, and the region along the Saint Lawrence River in Ontario and Quebec. Overall, membership grew steadily until the First World War, when it peaked at 50,000. That war saw the reten-tion of dominance by the chapters of central Canada as well as the thickening of chapters in the east and west. The huge increase in num-bers brought much diversity into the Order, and threatened to swamp the initial membership. This prompted calls by the established élite to change as little as possible. Membership during the interwar years dropped down to 20,000, before receiving a boost to 35,000 during the Second World War. In the postwar years membership has steadily declined, with provincial proportions remaining uniform.

Over the years, Ontario has retained by far the largest membership. British Columbia, Alberta, Nova Scotia and New Brunswick have had memberships of a similar size, with Nova Scotia and New Brunswick declining less in numbers since the Second World War than British Columbia and Alberta. Once on a par with these four provinces, Quebec's membership has declined the most rapidly, with only the chapter in Stanstead remaining. Given the rise of Quebec nationalism, this is perhaps not surprising. Manitoba and Saskatchewan have been next in size, followed by the smaller, but loyal, Prince Edward Island and Newfoundland. The Yukon and the Northwest Territories have had the smallest memberships, but it is significant that the IODE reached, and maintained chapters in, all provinces of Canada. Table 1.1 charts IODE membership, giving provincial proportions for the years for which data exist. Membership is currently at approximately

7,000. (I consider the reasons for membership decline in the Conclusion.)

Although officially non-denominational, in reality the IODE was overwhelmingly Protestant, and this Protestant identity was an important component of the IODE's power. One member explains her belief that it was, in equal measure, by choice and chance that at the IODE's beginning it was women from 'rich Protestant Anglo-Saxon families' who had the time to join and that it 'just happened that those were the people who arrived' when the mayors called meetings after receiving Clark Murray's telegram.[56] All forms of Protestantism were represented, from Anglican to Presbyterian to the United Church of Canada. Although members and written documents insist that denomination was not important, with closed membership there are recollections of excluding and blackballing Catholics.[57] Judging from the other groups to which members belonged, the leadership in the early years was decidedly Protestant. The IODE's second president, from 1911 to 1919, Mrs A. E. Gooderham, was also the first president of the 1922 Protestant Federation of Patriotic Women.[58] The divisive potential of such exclusion of other denominations was not missed by the *Globe*, which declared on March 6 that '[t]olerance, and patriotism, and study of the Empire should be Catholic as well as Protestant qualifications', and that 'a society whose aims are mainly patriotic ought not to start out by excluding more than one-third of the people of Canada'.[59]

What of the diversity of women represented among the IODE membership? Among the IODE's membership were many prominent Canadian women. Their achievements include Canadian 'firsts' for women in many political positions, from Mayor Charlotte Whitton, to Lieutenant-Governor Pauline McGibbon to Federal Government Minister Ellen Fairclough.[60] As already noted, of particular importance was Charlotte Whitton, professional welfare worker, social commentator and first woman mayor of Ottawa, who kept the IODE up to date on welfare and educational issues, formed IODE policy and used the IODE as a platform for her beliefs. Among the membership were many respected educators, including Wilhelmina Gordon, first woman lecturer at Queen's University, and Mary Bollert, first dean of women at the University of British Columbia, both of whom used their expertise to execute the IODE War Memorial Scholarships.[61] Indeed, if there were prominent Canadian women who were not themselves members of the IODE, then there were strong connections to them among the membership. This was also the case with élite Canadian families, such as the Eatons and Gooderhams. Although the Order became increasingly non-élitist as the century progressed, class distinctions remained.

Table 1.1 Summary of IODE membership by province, 1940–93

Year	Alberta	BC	Manitoba	NB	NS	Ontario	PEI	Quebec	Sask	Yukon	Nfld	NWT	Total
1940	2626	2500	1100	1689	2064	12000		2685	1545				26473
1941	2650	3100	1350	1793	2582	14600		3093	1949				31293
1942	2814	3222	1385	1950	2987	15500		3199	2080				32676
1943	2583	3153	1660	1991	2969	15580		3702	2170				33808
1944	2588	3100	1632	2044	2931	15858	204	3769	2086				34309
1945	2782	3222	1677	2084	2852	15970	204	3740	2053	92			34676
1946	2808	3122	1531	2136	2690	15723	188	3375	1960	101			33634
1947	2575	3083	1315	2103	2629	15172	182	287	1804	107			31807
1948	2458	3020	1266	2165	2512	15210	185	2673	1662	122			31273
1949	2184	2936	1180	2219	2509	15566	181	2530	1665	98			31068
1950	2245	2914	1148	2209	2507	15745	181	2413	1667	101			31144
1951	2267	2809	1008	2262	2604	16024	178	2458	1658	132	11		31411
1952	2167	2685	1045	2299	2672	16465	166	2346	1682	142	15		31695
1953	2061	2636	1036	2336	2723	16476	168	2371	1642	132	75		31656
1954	2114	2595	1103	2307	2720	16956	170	2302	1669	149	80		32165
1955	2053	2545	1089	2355	2746	17048	167	2219	1653	146	77		32098
1956	2076	2476	1044	2348	2817	17137	169	2204	1632	141	96		32140
1957	2083	2506	1035	2348	2876	16467	161	2092	1595	121	119		31403
1958	2044	2453	996	2310	2828	16733	163	2142	1585	113	122		31489
1959	2048	2339	983	2350	2905	16424	166	2059	1596	96	160		31126
1960	2168	2252	962	2348	2909	16015	173	1976	1571	114	177		30665
1961	2076	2117	911	2284	2841	15918	204	1978	1460	79	214		30286
1962	2113	2101	944	2281	2785	15270	227	1935	1441	83	221		29401

1963	2062	2099	920	2269	2749	14795	212	1849	1426	70	225		28676
1964	2012	2053	902	2226	2707	14460	200	1714	1407	65	192		27938
1965	1963	2034	841	2239	2663	14883	204	1577	1415	65	200		28084
1966	1925	1975	853	2242	2641	14650	181	1441	1378	74	195		27555
1967	1883	1913	830	2148	2612	14141	182	1366	1268	59	188		26590
1968	1748	1885	817	2068	2540	13664	175	1261	1104	40	195		25497
1969	1637	1844	778	1961	2281	12668	187	1149	1071	31	198		23707
1970	1557	1731	840	1881	2114	12125	198	1049	953	35	199		22682
1971	1446	1623	77	1866	2090	11189	165	912	891	28	203		21196
1972	198	1501	740	1818	1979	11167	174	787	862	34	201	32	20693
1973	1357	1424	711	1838	1905	10311	163	752	800	30	190	26	19507
1974	1328	1254	637	1854	1849	9985	170	654	764	34	185	36	18750
1975	1297	1300	623	1903	1917	10010	177	613	784	42	186	30	18882
1976	1246	1265	569	1891	177	9207	202	588	741	36	172	23	17677
1977	1246	1205	537	1811	1755	9033	204	538	695	30	170	21	17173
1978	1178	1225	548	1778	1768	8906	198	519	680	23	165	23	17011
1979	1123	1137	559	1758	1683	8459	187	44	666	28	174	25	16242
1993	623	828	277	1131	1311	5503	184	148	348	15	110	13	10551

Notes: BC = British Columbia; NB = New Brunswick; Nfld = Newfoundland; NWT Northwest Territories; NS = Nova Scotia; PEI = Prince Edward Island; Sask = Saskatchewan.
Source: NAC MG28 I 17, 11–13

A leading post-Second World War example of a revered long-time member was Pauline McGibbon, IODE national president from 1963 to 1965. McGibbon was the British Commonwealth's first woman lieutenant-governor (1974–81) serving as the queen's representative in Ontario. McGibbon was, among her other achievements, the first woman chancellor of the University of Toronto (1971–74). In some ways her life started out like many other Canadian women's. Born in Sarnia, Ontario, McGibbon did well at school, where she met her future husband Don McGibbon. In 1932 Don took a job with Imperial Oil Ltd, a company within which he would rise to become vice-president and treasurer. Soon after her marriage to Don in 1935, Pauline McGibbon joined the IODE and helped to found a new chapter.[62] She then embarked on a life of community service. Pauline McGibbon was a member of many clubs, including the Canadian Club, the Empire Club, the Ladies' Club of Toronto, the volunteers' committee of the Art Gallery of Ontario, as well as being involved in supporting the performing arts.[63] With no children, and with no need to be in paid employment due to the support of her husband, Pauline McGibbon was able to devote time to her voluntary work. While in many ways her lifestyle had much in common with earlier, Edwardian, IODE members, at a time of second-wave feminism she was able to reach positions of leadership previously reserved for men.

Despite the changing class composition that accompanied the growth in numbers, there was an overall continuity in IODE membership formed from family and social networks. The Anglo-Celtic Canadian membership, defined in terms of the Anglo-Canadian identity that the IODE has promoted, still dominates. A member in Regina defends her background, against the snobbish treatment she received from the Victoria League in London:

> And I have quite the background. I think that I can stand up with the best of them. I'm very proud of the fact that my grandfather came out to this area at 16 years old in 1882, and his mother followed the next year as a widow with eight children – and homesteaded and got her land claim in her name. Grandpa was mayor of Regina twice. There are several buildings named after him in Regina. He was a very prominent person, a lawyer. The other side of my family, my mother's side, have been here from 1912 on. Grandpa was an entrepreneur, very active in the church and Masons and things like that, very involved, but a farmer, that too. We're all very basic people. And I myself have been honoured to have received several awards, volunteer awards and what have you, and I've been very involved in heritage.[64]

As Cecilia Morgan has shown in the placing of Laura Secord within the narratives of Canadian loyalist history, this telling of family history evokes memory and tradition when calling for inclusion in the 'imagined community' of Canada.[65] It is a pioneering narrative of ordinary people succeeding in an egalitarian society.

'Daughters of the Empire' was intended by Clark Murray to capture the symbolic connection of women through the Empire, but over the years the name also took on literal meaning and has contributed to the longevity of the Order. There is much evidence of inter-generational family membership of the IODE, with family networks particularly evident among members in national positions. Members are often well-aware of their family's history in the IODE. A Toronto member recalls: 'My mother was in it, a life member of Toronto, Ontario and national. I grew up with it and then joined in 1976.'[66] Another member says that she was 'born into IODE'. Her grandmother was a member in Regina, her mother was national president and her daughter is a fourth-generation IODE member.[67]

Joining the IODE after marriage, invited by her new mother-in-law, was a frequent practice that has made many a member literally a 'daughter'. A Toronto member joined in the late 1950s when her mother-in-law's chapter, which had been together since before the First World War, was looking for new members. They took in a group of younger members and became a two-level chapter, 'which was not entirely successful, because we were all so polite and nice, and didn't say "Sit down, mother, and be quiet, we're going to do it this way"'.[68] In eastern Ontario a member was invited by her mother-in-law to join the IODE soon after she was married: 'It had closed membership at that time. We had seventy people in the chapter, and you had to wait your turn.'[69] Another member, in British Columbia, joined just before her marriage. Her sister-in-law to be, who lived in west Vancouver, called her to see if she was interested in joining a new chapter that was forming.[70] A Regina member's great-aunt had been a provincial president and was happy to hear that her relative had joined: 'She was so pleased when I went up and told her that I had joined IODE, and she didn't have any family of her own, so I had made her day.'[71]

Local chapter names are a fascinating testament to the IODE's quest to assimilate difference into the dominant narrative of Anglo-Canada. The chapters illustrate Edward Said's assertion that 'the power to narrate or block other narratives from forming and emerging … is very important to culture and imperialism and constitutes one of the main connections between them'.[72] In the chapters' names there is an employment of diverse traditions, drawing upon people, places and achievements that all come together in support of Anglo-Canadian identity.[73] Some names celebrate famous men, often war heroes, usually from Britain. Other names were taken from the geographical area in which the chapter met, or from the regiment with which the chapter was associated. Among the chapter names in British Columbia in 1953 were Captain Cook, the British explorer and hero; Ruskin, the British philosopher of aesthetic anti-modernism; Canadian Scottish; Unknown Warrior; Memorial Silver Cross, for wartime self-sacrifice; and Kitsilano and Kerrisdale, after two Vancouver suburbs.[74] Chapters were sometimes named after women. There was the Emily Carr Chapter in British Columbia, named for the painter, and the Pauline Johnson Chapter named for the native Canadian poet. In an annual ceremony members placed daffodils, her favourite flower, on her monument in Stanley Park, and then took tea.[75] In their promotion of Anglo-Canadian identity, chapter names evoked a sense of idealism, of a romantic chivalry that extended to the dramatic idea of being a Daughter of the Empire whose badge was a seven-pointed star. Such anti-modernism is not surprising given the salience of such sentiments within Canadian imperialism of the turn of the century period. Naming chapters after literary figures and glorious imperial and Canadian figures endorsed the promotion of a strongly British Canada.

The IODE's way of dealing with diversified and marginal groups as its members was containment within distinct chapters. Local chapters acted as local containers of identity, especially where non-Protestant and non-Anglo-Celtic members were concerned. Such chapters at once served to emphasize the possibilities of assimilation into the Canadian mainstream, yet were containers of religion, such as the Catholic chapters in Quebec; containers of ethnicity, such as the Jon Sigurdsson Chapter of Winnipeg, made up of Icelandic immigrants, the Saint Margaret of Scotland Chapter of Alberta, made up of Hungarian immigrants[76] and the Native Chapter in British Columbia; or containers of class, such as the First World War blue-collar Ross Rifles Chapter, chapters of nurses,[77] the professional women's Elizabeth Tudor Chapter in Ottawa during the 1930s;[78] and military chapters, in which members were through their husbands attached to specific regiments, such as the Argyle IVth in Belleville, Ontario, or the RCMP Scarlets in Regina. Chapters also segregated along occupational, ethnic, religious and age lines for pragmatic reasons. Particular meeting times, as well as areas of expertise, suited chapters of teachers, and chapters of Catholics and Jews found camaraderie from meeting with women of the same religion amid a predominantly Protestant Order.

The structure of the IODE provides an insight into the workings of an organization that has by a long stretch outlived the Empire that it was formed to defend. Much of the IODE's strength was found within its structure, its stable organizational hierarchy and its ability to swing into action. Family networks played a big part in keeping membership alive from generation to generation, and also contributed to continuity in the social composition of membership. Although the women who belonged to the IODE were the very women likely to belong to other women's organizations, there was a sense of joining the IODE for life, and that members saw the Order as an outlet for their sense of imperial and national identity. The IODE's structure also reflected its vision for Anglo-Canada. Early chapter names displayed the formation of an Anglo-Canadian identity constructed from British influences. As the century progressed, more local heroes and heroines appeared in chapter names. The dominant narrative was ever-changing, and appeared more encompassing, yet the assumption of assimilation was not abandoned. Rather, the organizing principles of the early years of the century were re-presented.

Notes

1 Benedict Anderson, *Imagined Communities: Reflections on the Origin and Spread of Nationalism*, 2nd edn (London and New York: Verso, 1991), 142.
2 NAC MG28 I 17, 18, 3, 11a, 13 Feb 1900, At Windsor Hotel parlours, Montreal.
3 Interview, 25 February 1994: Toronto, Ontario.
4 Carl Berger, *The Sense of Power: Studies in the Ideas of Canadian Imperialism, 1867–1914* (Toronto: University of Toronto Press, 1970).
5 Carman Miller, *Painting the Map Red: Canada and the South African War 1899–1902* (Montreal and Kingston: McGill–Queen's University Press, 1993). Miller is a past IODE War Memorial Scholar.
6 Julia Bush, *Edwardian Ladies and Imperial Power* (Leicester: Leicester University Press, 2000). This is an argument also made by Elizabeth L. Riedi in her PhD thesis, 'Imperialist women in Edwardian Britain: the Victoria League 1899–1914', PhD thesis, St Andrew's University, 1998.
7 Margaret Polson Murray, 'The Order: its past and its future. By the founder', NAC MG28 I 17, Misc. files, document 4; Clark Murray was also known as Polson Murray.
8 W. David McIntyre, *The Significance of Commonwealth, 1965–90* (Basingstoke and London: Macmillan, 1991).
9 John M. MacKenzie, *Propaganda and Empire: The Manipulation of British Public Opinion, 1880–1960* (Manchester: Manchester University Press, 1984), 148.
10 *Ibid.*, 150.
11 Provincial Archives of New Brunswick (hereafter PANB), MC 200 MS 1/A/1.
12 NAC MG28 I 17, 18, 3, 3 and 12.
13 NAC MG28 I 17, 11, 1902–4.
14 Polson [Clark] Murray, 'The Order: its past and its future', 2.
15 Margaret Gillett, 'Growing pains: Mrs Murray, Lady Minto, Mrs Nordheimer and the early years of the IODE', Address to the James McGill Society, Montreal, 24 January 2000, 2–3.
16 IODE, 'A brief history 1900–1958', 1. Document housed at IODE national headquarters in Toronto.
17 *Ibid.*, 2.
18 *Ibid.*
19 NAC MG28 I 17, 2, 2 Feb. 1911.
20 Vron Ware, *Beyond the Pale: White Women, Racism and History* (London and New York: Verso, 1992), 162.
21 Pamphlet (IODE, 1982).

22 NAC MG28 I 17, 16 March 1905.
23 NAC MG28 I 17, 4 October 1905.
24 MacKenzie, *Propaganda and Empire*.
25 Interview, 18 April 1994: Regina, Saskatchewan.
26 Public Archives and Records Office, Prince Edward Island (hereafter PARO, PEI), Acc. 3995, 7, Souvenir programme for 18–20 December 1913.
27 Interview, 27 October 1993: Charlottetown, Prince Edward Island.
28 Vancouver City Archives (hereafter VCA), NI/IM/ 7L, 1, Scrapbook of Lady Douglas Chapter 1919–39: 'Lady Douglas Chapter IODE hosts annual function'.
29 VCA, reel #0286 IODE, 24.
30 VCA, Publications, 99, 25 November 1939, Empire fête, ballroom and lounge, Hotel Georgia, Vancouver Municipal Chapter.
31 Carolyn Strange, *Toronto's Girl Problem: The Perils and Pleasures of the City 1880–1930* (Toronto: University of Toronto Press, 1995), 178–85.
32 P. T. Rooke and R. L. Schnell, *No Bleeding Heart: Charlotte Whitton, a Feminist on the Right* (Vancouver: University of British Columbia Press, 1987), 211.
33 *Ibid.*
34 NAC MG20 E 256, vol. 34, IODE Province of Alberta, 'Report on a report', 1949; *Echoes* (summer 1947), 'Welfare study in Alberta', 7.
35 Veronica Strong-Boag, *The Parliament of Women: The National Council of Women in Canada 1893–1929* (Ottawa: National Museums of Canada, 1976), 2. See also Prentice *et al.*, *Canadian Women*.
36 Strong-Boag, *Parliament of Women*, vii.
37 See Barbara Roberts, '"A work of Empire": Canadian reformers and British female immigration', in Linda Kealey (ed.), *A Not Unreasonable Claim* (Toronto: Women's Press, 1979), 185–202.
38 See Fiona Paisley, *Loving Protection? Australian Feminism and Aboriginal Women's Rights, 1919–39* (Carlton South: Melbourne University Press, 2000); Fiona Paisley, 'Citizens of their world: Australian feminism and indigenous rights in the international context, 1920s and 1930s', *Feminist Review*, 58: spring (1998), 66–84; and Angela Woollacott, 'Inventing Commonwealth and Pan-Pacific feminism: Australian women's internationalist activism in the 1920s–30s', *Gender and History*, 10: 3 (1998), 425–48.
39 Julia Bush, 'Edwardian ladies and the "race" dimensions of British imperialism', *Women's Studies International Forum*, 21: 3 (1998), 277–89; and see Bush, *Edwardian Ladies and Imperial Power*; and Reidi, 'Imperialist women in Edwardian Britain'.
40 Bush, *Edwardian Ladies and Imperial Power*, 13.
41 MacKenzie, *Propaganda and Empire*, 243.
42 National Library of Canada (hereafter NLC), *The Imperial Order Daughters of the Empire 1900–1925* (IODE, 1925), 30.
43 NAC MG28 I 17, 2, 6 November 1912.
44 MacKenzie, *Propaganda and Empire*, 148.
45 British Columbia Archives and Records Service (hereafter BCARS), Add. MS 255, 3, Emily Carr Chapter Minutebook 1960–70. Membership was by ballot, and majority vote.
46 Interview, 24 April 1994: Calgary, Alberta.
47 Royal Commonwealth Society Library, London (hereafter RCSL), IODE, *Manitoba Souvenir*, 1916.
48 *IODE 1900–1925*, 5.
49 *Ibid.*
50 IODE, 'A brief history 1900–58', 4.
51 *Ibid.*, 3.
52 *Ibid.*, 4.
53 *Ibid.*
54 Marjorie Freeman Campbell, 'Six queens have ruled England', *Echoes* (summer 1953), 3 and 19.

55 Mrs H. S. Angus, 'The war in Malaya', *Echoes* (Christmas 1952), 7.
56 Interview, 25 October 1993: Saint John, New Brunswick.
57 Interview, 26 October 1993: Charlottetown, Prince Edward Island; interview, 27 August 1995. Stanstead, Quebec.
58 Hopkins, J. Castell, *The Canadian Annual Review of Public Affairs* (Toronto: Annual Review Publishing Co., 1922), 392.
59 *Ibid.*
60 For the life of Pauline McGibbon, see Norma West Linder and Hope Morritt, *Pauline: A Warm Look at Ontario Lieutenant-Governor Pauline McGibbon* (Sarnia: River City Press, 1979); for Charlotte Whitton, see Rooke and Schnell, *No Bleeding Heart*; and for Wilhelmina Gordon, see David G. Dewar, *Queen's Profiles* (Kingston, Ontario: Office of Endowment and Public Relations of Queen's University, 1951).
61 See Katie Pickles, 'Colonial counterparts: the first academic women in Anglo-Canada, New Zealand and Australia', *Women's History Review*, 10: 2 (2001), 273–97.
62 West Linder and Morritt, *Pauline*, 71.
63 *Ibid.*, 120.
64 Interview, 18 April 1994: Regina, Saskatchewan.
65 Cecilia Morgan, '"Of slender frame and delicate appearance"', 103–19, at 115.
66 Second interview, 24 February 1994: Toronto, Ontario.
67 Interview, 4 November 1993: Ottawa, Ontario.
68 Interview, 25 February 1994: Toronto, Ontario.
69 Interview, 9 October 1993: Campbellford, Ontario.
70 Interview, 29 April 1994: Vancouver, British Columbia.
71 Interview, 18 April 1994: Regina, Saskatchewan.
72 Edward Said, *Culture and Imperialism* (London: Virago, 1993), xiii.
73 See Eric Hobsbawn and Terence Ranger (eds), *The Invention of Tradition* (Cambridge, Melbourne and London: Cambridge University Press, 1983).
74 VCA, Vancouver and Municipal Chapter Records, Chapter highlights, 1952–53.
75 VCA, Matthews Collection, 'IODE honors Indian poetess', 18 March 1946. See Veronica Strong-Boag and Carole Gerson, *Paddling Her Own Canoe: The Times and Texts of E. Pauline Johnson (Tekahionwake)* (Toronto: University of Toronto Press, 2000).
76 Interview, 29 April 1994: Vancouver, British Columbia; and second interview, 24 February 1994: Toronto, Ontario.
77 *Echoes*, 68 (June 1917), 89.
78 Lorne Pierce Special Collections, Queen's University (hereafter LPSC), IODE, *Ottawa Souvenir*, 1935.

CHAPTER TWO

Female imperialism at the periphery: organizing principles, 1900–19

From the beginning of the twentieth century, it was a common sight to see members of the IODE frequenting Canada's major ports. Proudly pinned to their smartest clothes were their badges with Union Jack, crown and stars radiating outwards to the corners of the Empire. In a close working relationship with government, taking advantage of élite contacts and putting forward its maternal role, the IODE negotiated a position to welcome immigrants from many countries at ports of arrival. A 1904 article by Mabel Clint commented that at the Port of Quebec '[t]he wearers of the badge have been the only outsiders allowed in the Immigration Buildings after the arrival of an ocean liner, and have met with every courtesy from the officials'.[1] The 'wearers of the badge' thus began their work commanding a respect that they would sustain and extend in future years.

The IODE was greatly excited by, as well as concerned about, the arrival of immigrants. As part of its mission to produce a Canada that mimicked Britain, the IODE sought British immigrants to populate Canadian space. A framework of powerful racial preferences was constructed as the norm to which all others must assimilate. Examining the preference for British immigrants, this chapter shows how, as was the case with other ethnic labels, 'Britishness' was very much an invented tradition.

During the early years of the twentieth century women's place was often ideally located as a wife, mother or daughter in private domestic space. The IODE was involved in utilizing such maternal identity in the production of its own brand of female imperialism. As Dominic Alessio suggests in his examination of female personifications in the 'white' British 'colonies' from 1886 to 1940, women were constructed as 'agents of civilization', their role moving beyond the symbolic to that of active racial and moral agents.[2] As Anna Davin articulated in 1978, such maternal civilizing work was deeply infused with race ideology and population dynamics.[3] More recently, Mariana Valverde has documented the commonplace discussion of 'race degeneration', eugenics and salvation through social purity among a broad spectrum of Canadian women's organizations.[4] In this vein, the IODE was very outspoken, and made extremely strong connections between race and populating Canada, that it then sought to enact. The First World War provided the opportunity for the IODE, backed by such ideology, to exert its energies in defence of the Empire.

Constructing Anglo-Celts and racial hierarchies

The IODE forthrighly articulated belief in a 'British' race, and it is important to survey the implications of Britishness in the Canadian context. Kay Anderson's work on Canadian racial discourse in Vancouver's Chinatown makes visible the components of such racism, reading Chinatown as a representation of Anglo-Celtic Canadians' hegemonic constructions of race.[5] Studies attempting to show 'the British' or 'the English' as an ethnic group in Canada are very recent and are testimony to the extent of the hang-over of hegemonic constructions of Britishness.[6] The lack of attention is also to do with the tension in treating the English the same as other ethnic groups. As Greenhill cautions, 'there is a danger that a valorized English ethnicity will be linked with power in such a way as to make it even more hegemonic, a culture to which all others must aspire. But invisibility is also problematic; subversive parodies and travesties of power are impossible when its workings are unrecognised.'[7] Rather than become entangled in whether Englishness or Britishness was or was not ethnic, it is more helpful to look to the localized invention of Britishness. Catherine Hall's anti-essentialist conceptualization of identity is useful. She considers the make-up of mid-nineteenth-century Englishness to 'unpick the stories which gave meaning to the national and imperial project, and to understand the ways in which English identity was constructed through the active silencing of the disruptive relations of ethnicity, gender and of class'. Rather than reconstituting she attempts to destabilize Englishness, uncovering contingency in its historic specificity, and looking at the dependences, inequalities and oppressions which were hidden in its celebration of national identity.[8]

In considering 'contingency', 'historic specificity' and the silencing of difference, Hall's approach has much in common with that of Robert Young, who argues that 'Englishness' was 'fissured with difference and a desire for otherness'.[9] This was clearly the case in Canada, where the construction of Britishness was unique. The identity of 'the English' or 'the Anglo-Canadian' has often uncritically blended the

English, Irish, Scottish and Welsh into a single group. Greenhill suggests that this confusion was deliberate and served to disempower other groups: 'English ethnicity's most salient characteristics are submerged by a variety of forces that make its hegemonic status obscure.'[10] As Howard Palmer suggests, 'Anglo-Celts', Canadians of English, Scots, Welsh or Irish descent, did not always think of themselves as an undifferentiated group: 'They could and did have differences of opinion among themselves when it came to their own ethnic identity. But when it came to the other ethnic groups, the Anglo-Celts closed ranks.'[11] It is this closing of ranks, what it was composed of, and how it retained and fostered its dominance, that interests me. Tangled up with the policies and thought of the time, here, the IODE's history provides much insight.

Theories of race had a great influence on the IODE; members attended lectures and read books and articles to keep well-versed on contemporary developments. One book that contained ideology which influenced the IODE was J. S. Woodsworth's *The Stranger at Our Gates*. In 1909, the Canadian reformer and founder of the Co-operative Commonwealth Federation, in a book sponsored by the Methodist Church, captured the prevailing Canadian 'racial hierarchy'.[12] Immigrants were ordered according to proximity to a British core, and the 'unusual' races were to be welcomed in the degree to which they approached the ideal of 'Anglo-Saxons', the British and the Americans first, followed by the Northwestern, then the Central and Eastern Europeans, then the Jews, the Asians and the blacks. This hierarchy of races was reflected in Canadian immigration law, where British immigrants were legislated as the 'first choice'. An Act in 1906 consolidated and revised all immigration legislation since 1869.[13] A 1910 Act excluded persons deemed undesirable because of 'climatic, industrial, social, educational, labour or other conditions or requirements of Canada or deemed undesirable because of their customs, habits, modes of life and methods of holding property and their probable inability to become readily assimilated'.[14] Such subjective categorizing left the way open to favour preferences for British origins.

It was during the early years of the twentieth century that the IODE formed and solidified its own racial ideology. Its beliefs were steeped in powerful ideas of the time, such as the superiority of an Anglo-Celtic race that was interpreted as being biological, and which was demonstrable from imperial conquests such as the South Africa War. It drew upon a diversity of racial theories, and Darwin was invoked to give scientific credibility to the theory of Anglo-Celtic superiority,[15] while it was widely believed that 'the breeding of humans followed the same mendelian laws and was as predictive in nature as that of other sexually reproducing organisms'.[16] In 1883 Galton coined the term 'eugenics' to describe 'the study of the agencies under social control that may improve or impair the racial qualities of future generations, either physically or mentally'.[17] As Angus MacLaren has suggested, eugenic arguments also claimed scientific justifications for deep-seated gendered, racial and class assumptions.[18] The belief that race could be scientifically controlled and manipulated led to calls for 'race regeneration' and 'purity'. There was new faith in the efficacy of regu-lation, management, administration and science in remaking society.[19] As Carol Bacchi and Mariana Valverde have argued, women, as moth-ers, had an important part to contribute to the cleaning-up of the 'lesser races'.[20] Furthermore, it was believed that racial improvement could be brought about by improved environmental immersion.[21]

Geographers such as Ellsworth Huntington and Griffith Taylor pro-moted the idea that the character of a race was influenced by physical environment, natural selection and historical development.[22] As Liv-ingstone notes, 'the idioms of political and moralistic evaluation were simply part and parcel of the grammar of climatology'.[23] Environmen-tal suitability was used to justify the racial hierarchies such that the Northern European races were suited to Canada. As Marilyn Barber has written:

> [T]o the northern races were assigned the virtues of self-reliance, initia-
> tive, individualism, and strength, whereas the southern races were seen
> as degenerate and lacking in energy and initiative. Canada was a north-
> ern country, and the myth of the northern race, a hardy race created by
> a stern and demanding climate, had been used to express Canadian
> nationalism and pride in country since Confederation.[24]

Such theories, however, could also be applied to South Africa, empha-sizing the benefits of warm weather for health. If biological theories of race meant that a distinct hierarchy was created, other theories of environment introduced the possibility for assimilation. As Morag Bell notes for South Africa at this time, in acclimatization, sexual dif-ference took on moral as well as ecological meaning, being tied to social and environmental change.[25] Ironically, environmental deter-minist arguments added weight to the arguments of those who wanted to settle Canada with people other than the British occupying the posi-tions that needed to be filled. This led to the contradiction that while assimilation may appear all-encompassing, on the one hand, on the other, biology determined that such assimilation was impossible for those of 'inferior stock'. Nevertheless, the belief in assimilation was strong and programmes to achieve it were carried out by the IODE with on-going determination.

In practice, there was an on-going tension between race and immigration in Canada at this time, just as later on in the century there was between race and labour. There was a pragmatic need to expand the economy through an influx of immigrants who were prepared to perform heavy labour and farm work. The practical and economic concerns of federal government and the railways in settling the Canadian west ran counter to the ideological preoccupations of many Anglo-Canadian intellectuals; as Angus MacLaren argues: 'most realized that Canada needed immigrants to do the hard, dirty work of building a country, but they worried about the sort of country that would result'.[26] Influential in the settlement of the Prairies, Clifford Sifton, minister of the interior in the Laurier Government from 1896 to 1905,[27] saw the importance of the skills, as well as the origin, of the settler.[27] While Sifton wanted farmers from the American mid-west and Britain, he perceived finding them to be a difficult task, and saw that the need might be met by peasant farmers from Europe, 'people who had been born on the land who were accustomed to a pioneering life'.[28]

The IODE, still in its organizing stages, was not yet well enough established on the Prairies to offer comprehensive services for new immigrants during the first ten years of the century, but it had definite ideas as to how Canada's immigrants should be recruited and assimilated, and, not surprisingly, exhibited a clear preference for immigrants from Britain. In 1907, the women of the IODE's St George Chapter of Toronto listened to an address by a Dr Kilpatrick in which he said:

> Population, accordingly, is the need of the day. Multitudes are wanted to subdue physical nature to the uses of man and to afford the material basis for national greatness. But as long as immigration flows toward Canada a very large proportion will always consist of aliens. No sooner do these people touch our shores than the problem of assimilation and integration emerges for us in its profound difficulty.[29]

While the IODE did not want aliens, if they were to be admitted to Canada they would have to be quickly and effectively 'canadianized'. And so 'canadianization' emerged as the term for the assimilation of newcomers into Anglo-conformity.[30]

In the pre-First World War years, women's clubs, as 'surrogate mothers' for young women immigrants from diverse countries, were responsible for setting up a variety of Canadian welcome hostels. At a time of rigid patriarchal structures, the IODE saw a need for hostels to protect women upon arrival and was active in supporting such hostels, working with other women's organizations to supply board and training. The scope of the IODE's work was not as extensive as that of the

YWCA or the Salvation Army, but none the less the IODE was very involved in these ventures, with the expressed purpose of keeping women, as Agnes Fitzgibbon said in a 1913 address on women's welcome hostels, 'safe from the temptations which assail them on every side in the new and strange surroundings far from home and their home influence' and to 'keep the purity of their womanhood and the future of new generation of which they are the potential mothers, for no one can count, no one can ever estimate the harm done by women who have lost their sense of womanhood'.[31] Agnes Fitzgibbon was regent of the IODE Fitzgibbon Chapter of Toronto and superintendent of the Women's Welcome Hostel at 52 St Alban's Street, Toronto. Agnes Fitzgibbon and others of like mind considered that women's sexuality was clearly linked to nation building, and virtue would ensure respectable mothers for the next generation of Canadian citizens.[32] In such an endeavour, although always keen to claim the glory for their own efforts, often at the expense of down-playing the work of others, there was a sense of collaboration between the various women's organizations.

The IODE differentiated immigrants, not only along racial and gender lines, but by class and age. Holding preferences for the 'right kind' of British migrant was, of course, neither new nor unique to the IODE. As the work of Marilyn Barber – and of Adele Perry for nineteenth-century British Columbia – has shown, class preferences were idealistically commonplace.[33] The IODE was pragmatic as well as idealistic about its class preferences, and was active in encouraging educated women of high social standing to emigrate to Canada. Again, it was hoped that hostels could 'isolate and educate' British women before they went out into the small towns where they were perceived to be at risk.[34] Work by Marilyn Barber has shown that at the Queen Mary's Coronation Hostel in Vancouver, guests had to be 'gentlewomen',[35] and, of course, of the preferred race as well.[36] It was important that women immigrants be young, flexible and fertile. At a national meeting, a member contributed: 'I would say if they would send to us women of the right age they would be all right ... We had an example sent to us, by the Settlers' Welcome only last year; a lady of fifty, a trained nurse. Poor thing, what opportunity has she here?'[37] This member was opposed to old women, 'whose ideas are set and formed', and who lacked the ability to adapt to Canada. Mrs Hannington, a British Columbia member reported to the national executive:

We see it out there; the English woman, they come out to our land, expensively educated, they can paint miniatures and play on the piano beautifully, but she does not know which end of her baby to hold uppermost ... You give a Canadian or American woman a few yards of cheesecloth and a keg of nails and she will make you a drawing room while you wait.[38]

This statement suggests that living in Canada led to greater pragmatism and innovation, to 'the simplification of Europe overseas'.[39] Ironically, adaptability to the Canadian environment did not entail any change in British racial characteristics. The same member declared: 'and I think the children of the coast are the most beautiful in the world. They haven't lost their red English cheeks and the gold in their hair.'[40] There is a quandary here of whether acclimatization led to improvements in those already considered at the top of the constructed racial hierarchy. In this case it did not, although eugenic arguments would have suggested otherwise.

Constructing the maternal during the First World War

The patriotic sentiments responsible for the founding of the IODE during the South Africa War were quick to surface again at the outbreak of the First World War. In 1915, the president of the IODE proudly stated:

> Every British woman is a daughter of the Empire, but when she joins our organization she then becomes a subject militant in the service of our king and country – in times of peace we drill and otherwise prepare ourselves, so that when the call to arms comes, we may be ready. Since the war began, we have considered ourselves on active service ... and we have responded nobly to the call.[41]

As British subjects, members of the IODE were simultaneously 'daughters' of the Empire. The power of the maternal was clearly important, as it was through such prevailing ideology that the IODE was able to contribute to fighting the war. Not only did the IODE work defensively during the First World War, but it concurrently produced articulate imperial, national and colonial ideologies that clarified Canada's place in the war – and, ultimately, in the Empire.

War is the time when identities become polarized into good or bad, for or against, friend or foe, enemy or compatriot. Despite the unification of a nation around one cause, providing new opportunities for women, war is also a time when gender identities are accentuated. The maternal identity was of particular significance to the IODE's place during the First World War. Genevieve Lloyd draws attention to how 'nurturant motherhood has been so readily enlisted in the cause of patriotism, which seems on the surface to be so much at odds with it'.[42] Lloyd shows how motherhood was constructed to support war and how, in giving up their sons, 'women are supposed to allow them to become real men and immortal selves. Surrendering sons to significant deaths becomes a higher mode of giving birth. Socially constructed motherhood, no less than socially constructed masculinity, is at the service of an ideal of citizenship that finds its fullest expression in war.'[43] To follow Lloyd, maternal identity was very important to the IODE, which valued a women's culture of activities and beliefs centred around mothering, and wanted to infuse a male-dominated public sphere with those values in order to 'keep the home fires burning'. The IODE's war effort involved the kind of voluntary work which was considered 'natural' and associated with mothering: providing food, clothing and bedding; setting up clubs and entertainment for soldiers; counselling the wounded; and giving emotional support to soldiers' families. The scale of IODE contributions during the First World War was spectacular. It included provision of 19 ambulances, 3 motor trucks, 2 automobiles, 22 sterilizing units, 12 operating tables, 3 huts for convalescent soldiers, 22 field kitchens, 942 cots, and equipment for 36 wards, plus thousands of knitted items.[44]

Strongly gendered distinctions were drawn between paid and voluntary work. When supplies and weapons were donated by the IODE, they were justified with an appeal to domesticity. Such was the case with the IODE's first project for the First World War, which was to provide a fully equipped hospital ship for the British Admiralty. The ship was feminized, and placed in a 'private' realm of care. Referring to the ship, the national executive noted: 'It is felt that this will be an opportunity [for] every Canadian woman to show her loyalty and devotion to the Empire and most fitting as it is the woman's part to minister to the sick and wounded.'[45]

The privileged social position of IODE members was important in its war work. As noted in the previous chapter, membership was at its most elitist at the beginning of the First World War. More generally at the time, as Wayne Roberts's work on maternal feminism in Toronto from 1877 to 1914 indicates, élite women had considerable influence, despite being split in their positions on suffrage.[46] For the IODE, the presence of wealthy members influenced the scope of IODE projects since those members could afford to donate their homes, money and resources. There were some impressive examples. On 4 August 1914, just before war was declared, National President Gooderham called an emergency meeting at which it was decided to place the fully equipped hospital ship at the service of the British Admiralty. Collections were started, with a considerable boost being made by Lady Gibson of Hamilton who promised $1,000, as did Mrs Gooderham herself. Mrs Herbert Molson of Montreal contributed $2,500, and Lady Van Horne and Lady Drummond each sent $1,000. HRH the Duchess of Connaught, at a meeting in Ottawa the same day, subscribed $1,000.[47] Soon afterwards, Mrs C. D. Crerar donated her home 'Dunedin', in Hamilton, as a hospital for convalescent soldiers.[48] The names Gooderham, Molson and Van Horne signal extremely wealthy Canadian business interests in alcohol and the railways. These prominent IODE figures were the wives of élite businessmen, and as members of family dynasties were able to channel money into patriotic and philanthropic causes.

Consistent with the IODE's maternal identity, the meaning of 'home' was extended to encompass any place where the war took Canadians. In such locations the IODE provided safe havens, homes away from home. The IODE was quick to realize that the forces had leisure time and that hostels and clubs offered a way of regulating the behaviour of potentially wayward men. The IODE therefore set up the Royal King George and Queen Mary Maple Leaf Club in London, England, to serve as a safe house for Canadian soldiers, with preference given to officers on war leave.[49] There meals and beds were provided; at the height of activity 1,200 beds were available every night. Contributing to this considerable undertaking, during the club's operation over a million meals were served.[50] A home for nurses, less impressive, and a hospital on Hyde Park Road were also provided in London. The home for Canadian nurses at 95 Lancaster Gate was formerly the town house of Lady Minto, the IODE's first patroness. HRH the Princess Patricia opened the home and appreciation was expressed for 'the value and comfort of this haven of rest to the nurses after their trying, tedious and often most sorrowful duties'.[51] The IODE's contribution can be read as a group of imperial daughters providing the comforts associated with their place in the domestic sphere of the family and as mothers of the nation, from the homefront of Canada to the frontlines of the war.

Defending Britain and democracy

Fighting to defend Britain was all-important to the IODE. During the South Africa War and the First World War, Canada was a junior partner, seizing a chance to prove its value to the imperial centre. Evidence of the shift to a stronger Canadian identity can be seen in IODE National President Gooderham's annual speech, in 1917: 'Is it not fitting that we, as Daughters of the Empire, should ask ourselves at this time if we are worthy of the sacrifices that so many noble spirits have made for our Empire? It is a never-to-be-forgotten demonstration of what a nation will do for a national ideal.'[52] To defend the Empire loyally, the IODE's First World War projects were imperial in scope, with the home for nurses a 'concrete expression of the spirit of humanity that is binding the different portions and peoples of the Empire together in bonds that do not perish'.[53] Again the rhetoric indicates a sense of Canadian national identity amid the Empire's unity, the joining of 'the great members of the Anglo-Saxon family' who must come together to 'win and guarantee enduring peace for the World'.[54]

To defend Britain, the IODE drew upon its maternal skills. Knitting had significant racial as well as gendered meanings. In *Echoes* in 1918 a caption under a picture of a young film star read: 'Two weapons of the Anglo-Saxon race are doing tremendous work to win the war for freedom – the bayonet of our soldiers and the needle of our loyal women. The knitting, the sewing, and the unparalleled helpfulness of women in all lines of activity have doubled the effectiveness of our men in the field.'[55] Knitting was also therapeutic and solitary, as expressed in a 1917 poem:

A peaceful valley in the West,
The evening shadows flitting;
A trembling heart, a glist'ning tear,
A lonely mother knitting.

Knit, Mother, Knit. The cross is thine;
The cross that mothers borrow;
For all must knit and some must mourn,
While war brings need and sorrow.

Dream, Mother, Dream. The night is here;
Dream that its shadows borrow;
A radiance from the great beyond,
To light a blest to-morrow.[56]

The benefits of work to the overcoming of grief were often expressed during the First World War years, with grief a domain for maternal help. An IODE postwar publication recalled: 'In the dark days of the world conflict the Order was a means of salvation to mind and body of many women (who had given their all) from a settled sorrow and despair, its activities provided a stimulus for alleviating their own grief in working for others, which alone constitutes true happiness.'[57] IODE members visited soldiers' wives and families. In 1915 Toronto's municipal chapter alone reported having made 5,029 visits.[58] At the end of the war the IODE printed the words of the British prime minister, praising women for their bearing of 'their burden of sorrow and separation with unflinching fortitude and patience', as well as for their assuming of 'an enormous share of the burdens necessary to the practical conduct of the war'.[58] Likewise, in a letter to IODE National President Gooderham, the commander of the Canadian armed forces, Sir

Arthur Currie, endorsed the IODE's gendered work, writing that 'the men in the field will never forget the noble work of the mothers, wives and sisters during the war, now so happily past'.[60]

The IODE was certainly not a pacifist organization. During the First World War the goal was victory for Canada and the Empire. Its military involvement refutes the arguments of some contemporary theorists, such as Jean Bethke Elshtain, who consider war and peace as opposites, with women as 'beautiful souls' and life-givers, and men as 'just warriors' and life-takers.[61] For example, Sara Ruddick bestows upon women a 'preservative love', innate to their maternal experience.[62] The IODE's support of war, while appealing to maternal identities, demonstrates the need to complicate the experience of women in times both of war and of peace, and question whether women are by nature, socialization, ideology or experience more pacific than men.[63] Indeed, re-presentation of women and war is now a focus of research,[64] with new attention to how images of women are constructed, and what functions they serve. Through such an approach women's responses to war become much messier; and, to follow Ruth Roach Pierson, 'there has not been a consistent women's response to war and revolution any more that there has been a uniform feminist position on women's relation to organized violence'.[65]

Given its goal of victory, it is not surprising that the IODE persuaded men to enlist and was an active campaigner for compulsory military service. In Victoria the IODE held a 'silent recruiting week' for one battalion, with each member wearing a badge urging enlistment.[66] It is also not surprising that the IODE took strong objection to the peace movement. Its opposition was singular and focused:

> It is not too much to say that the continuance of the present war depends upon the support of the women of the Empire, so that any discussion which may confuse the issue must be regarded as dangerous. The women know that this generation has been called upon to make tremendous sacrifices in order to leave peace and liberty in the world for their children and their children's children. That is the reason why peace talk, no matter how sincere, cannot be tolerated.[67]

The IODE's position was justified by a call to the maternal. Women, from their moral and nurturing position, were to make sacrifices for future generations. Thus the 'private sphere' justification echoed the 'public sphere' Tory politics of conserving for future generations, demonstrating the interconnectedness of what were constructed as separate spheres.

The IODE expressed a strong disdain for Germany, and in 1916 associated itself with the Anti-German League, stating:

The purpose of the Anti-German League is not to perpetuate international hatreds. It is simply a sane measure of self-preservation aimed against a nation which has made itself an outlaw of civilization. All members who join this league pledge themselves never willingly or knowingly to buy German or Austrian goods, and to do their utmost to prevent such goods beings brought into Canada either now or after the war.[68]

Boycott was a wartime strategy, but the violence of the expression is striking. In 1915 Mrs P. D. Crerar suggested the pledge, 'From this day until the day of my death I pledge myself never willingly nor knowingly to buy an article made by the bloody hands that killed our boys.'[69] Fearing for the safety of Canadian prisoners in Germany, the IODE suggested that the pledge be made in secret.[70]

It is easy to understand, in a nation at war, a belief in the cause and a rallying of beliefs to secure victory. Specific episodes suggest a convergence in perceptions of both race and gender in the defence of the Empire. When, in 1915, the British nurse Edith Cavell was executed by the Germans in Belgium on a charge of 'escorting troops to the enemy', gender sharpened the sense of outrage expressed empirewide.[71] The IODE chapter bearing her name, and appropriately comprised of Montreal nurses, was one of the many Cavell memorials that sprung up around the Empire.[72] It was stated in *Echoes* after the close of the war:

Among all the horrible deeds perpetrated by the Germans during the great war none perhaps excited more loathing and disgust in the minds of British people than the brutal murder of this gloriously loyal Englishwoman ... Her execution can only be regarded as a brutal murder, and another illustration of the many which the Germans have given in the late war, that in spite of all their vaunted culture they are in fact still a semi-barbarous people and destitute of the very elements of any true culture.[73]

This was an attack on a white British woman, a symbol of purity and the Empire, in which she was rendered defenceless by an enemy constructed as racially inferior and barbaric.

Despite the maternal identity that it cultivated as a representative of the Empire, in maintaining a patriotic purpose supportive of the status quo the IODE did not limit its work solely to issues that concerned gender. This would lead the IODE to fall out of agreement with other women's organizations. For example, in 1919 the IODE resigned from the National Council of Women of Canada to protest the Council's affiliation with the International Council of Women, on the grounds that the latter included 'enemy' affiliates.[74] Given that the IODE was first and foremost a patriotic organization, its resignation is not surprising. It demonstrated the multiple positioning of the IODE as a patriotic group of women with the primary objective of winning the war for Britain and the Empire.

Votes for women

Despite its primarily patriotic endeavours and its general support of women's traditional place in society, highlighting the complexity of conservative women and feminism, in 1917 the IODE was at the centre of a key feminist cause when the issues of suffrage and conscription converged to achieve victorious outcomes. By the advent of the First World War, Canada had a strong women's suffrage movement that was tapped into and was a part of an international movement and a first wave of feminism. Within a decade of Canadian confederation, in 1867, though with the exception of Quebec, the push for women's suffrage had taken hold. Canada's federal system, with a House of Representatives and a Senate, as well as provincial government, meant that agitation had to take place in a variety of arenas in order to be effective. By the end of the nineteenth century, there were organizations active in Ontario, the western provinces and the Maritimes. Bills were introduced in provincial legislatures and petitions were signed. The campaign exhibited a Canadian quality in its orderliness, lawfulness and lack of confrontational tactics seen elsewhere.[75]

How was it that the IODE came to play an important part in the granting of suffrage to women? Julia Bush has identified that in Britain there were rifts between 'imperial feminists', those women who were a part of overtly feminist groups with suffrage as their primary cause, and 'female imperialists', women, such as those of the Victoria League, who had patriotism as their primary cause and who advocated conservative politics.[76] It appears that such divisions were not as strong in Canada as they were in Britain, with the differences between groups less demarcated. Some members of the IODE were supporters of suffrage, while others were not. This was not the case among women's patriotic organizations in Britain at the time. As a place with more fluid class relations, and as a 'colony', Canada was different. Carol Lee Bacchi has suggested that Anglo-Celtic, Protestant, well-educated élite women and wives of professionals were sympathetic to the objectives of the suffrage.[77] As the case of the IODE shows, it was not as simple as that all such women supported suffrage, but, certainly, among the membership there were suffragists, most notably Constance Hamilton. It is not surprising, then, that in recognizing the diversity of opinions among its membership the IODE, as an officially non-partisan organization, did not explicitly endorse the franchise for women. In fact, in 1916, the IODE national executive appeared to put issues other than winning the war 'in abeyance', urging 'all patriotic women to concentrate all their energy, strength and means upon the immediate war'.[78]

A year later, however, conscription was the hinge issue in the election facing Borden's Conservative Government. By the time the Conservatives joined forces with the pro-conscription wing of the Liberal Party, forming the Union Government Coalition on 12 October 1917, the IODE had become active in doing all that it could to bring about conscription. It couched its support for the Union Government with its old rhetoric of securing a 'decisive victory in the war'.[79] At this time, National President Gooderham, along with IODE member Constance Hamilton in her capacity in the Canadian Suffrage Association, and the presidents of the National Council of Women and the WCTU, at the request of the prime minister, tested the effect that a selective female franchise would have on the election. The result was the controversial 1917 Wartime Elections Act that boosted the support for conscription by excluding from voting all conscientious objectors and those born in foreign countries and naturalized since 1902; and muting French Canadian and other dissenting voters by extending the franchise to women who were British subjects 21 years of age or over with a close relative serving in the armed forces of Canada or Great Britain.[80]

Hence, after years of struggle, approximately 500,000 women in Canada won the vote.[81] In supporting conscription with the objective of winning the war, the IODE was directly implicated in this fundamental step towards securing the vote for all women in Canada. The IODE went so far as to make it clear that members should use their vote 'and influence as a citizen in the campaign to secure a government that will press the war aggressively to a victorious conclusion'.[82] It was Catherine Cleverdon's 1950 contention that it was the hard work of women in the war effort that convinced politicians of the worth of giving women the vote.[83] That being the case, as the largest patriotic organization in the Empire, along with other organizations such as the YWCA and the Red Cross, the IODE made a strong contribution here. Always at the forefront were the issues of motherhood and morality, and of seeking justice for the men in the forces overseas.

During the IODE's first years, immigration and war work had in common the intended construction of a strong British Canada. The IODE was able to use its élite social status and gender to achieve its objectives. It supported a 'racial hierarchy' which asserted that British people and their Anglo-Celtic Canadian descendants were superior to all other races, and discriminatory immigration laws which legislated this preference. The First World War provided the opportunity for the IODE to draw upon prevailing strong constructions of the maternal to defend the Empire. Its maternal position was vitally connected to an idealization of an Anglo-Celtic race: it was female British subjects who were given the vote in 1917. Founded to rally to the cause of the South Africa War, fighting for the 'mother country' as loyal 'daughters' during the First World War the IODE acted out its motives on a far larger scale than it had imagined in 1900. Membership peaked during the war, and was never again to climb to the 50,000 it then reached. An IODE member and author of a Masters' thesis on the IODE centred her studies on the first twenty-five years, 'because it was the corner-stone for the whole organization, because everything else has been elaborated or detracted from that twenty-five years... they covered so much in ... [those] years'.[84] Indeed, the IODE's organizing principles would shift over the century, but the formative years provided the base that, as the rest of this book will show, remained of importance in its attitudes towards gender, race and class. The war also solidified the IODE's sense of national identity, albeit within the British Empire, and strengthened its resolve to go on the offensive and 'canadianize' immigrants during the postwar years.

Notes

1 *Echoes*, 18 (October 1904), 6.
2 Dominic David Alessio, 'Domesticating "the heart of the wild": female personifications of the colonies, 1886–1940', *Women's History Review*, 6: 2 (1997), 239–69, at 249.
3 Anna Davin, 'Imperialism and motherhood', *History Workshop*, 5 (1978), 9–65.
4 See Mariana Valverde, '"When the mother of the race is free": race, reproduction, and sexuality in first-wave feminism', in Franca Iacovetta and Mariana Valverde (eds), *Gender Conflicts: New Essays in Women's History* (Toronto: University of Toronto Press, 1992), 3–26; and Mariana Valverde, *The Age of Soap, Light and Water: Moral Reform in English Canada 1885–1925* (Toronto: McClelland & Stewart, 1991).
5 Kay Anderson, *Vancouver's Chinatown: Racial Discourse in Canada, 1875–1980* (Montreal and Kingston: McGill–Queen's University Press, 1991).
6 John Porter, *The Vertical Mosaic* (Toronto: University of Toronto Press, 1965). Porter's study was the first to critically investigate differences in the social situation of 'English' Canadians. More recent works on Canadian 'British ethnicity' have been Pauline Greenhill, *Ethnicity in the Mainstream: Three Studies of English Canadian Culture in Ontario* (Montreal and Kingston: McGill–Queen's University Press, 1993); Ross McCormack, 'Networks among British immigrants and accommodation to Canadian society: Winnipeg, 1900–1914', *Histoire sociale/Social History*, 17: 34 (1984), 357–74; and Ross McCormack, 'Cloth caps and jobs: the ethnicity of English immigrants in Canada, 1900–1914', in Jorgen Dahlie and Tina Fernando (eds), *Ethnicity, Power and Politics in Canada* (Toronto: Methuen, 1981), 38–57.
7 Greenhill, *Ethnicity in the Mainstream*, 157.
8 Catherine Hall, *White, Male and Middle-Class: Explorations in Feminism and History* (New York: Routledge, 1992), 206. See also Catherine Hall, '"From Greenland's

icy mountains ... to Afric's golden sand": ethnicity, race and nation in mid-nineteenth-century England', *Gender and History*, 5: 2 (1993), 212–30.

9 Robert Young, *Colonial Desire: Hybridity in Theory, Culture and Race* (London and New York: Routledge, 1995).

10 Greenhill, *Ethnicity in the Mainstream*, 153.

11 Howard Palmer, 'Reluctant hosts: Anglo-Canadian views of multiculturalism in the twentieth century', in Gerald Tulchinsky (ed.), *Immigration in Canada: Historical Perspectives* (Toronto: Copp Clark Longman Ltd, 1994), 297–333, at 300.

12 James S. Woodsworth, *Strangers at Our Gates or Coming Canadians*, 2nd edn (Toronto: University of Toronto Press, 1972 [Young People's Forward Movement Department of the Methodist Church, 1909]).

13 Valerie Knowles, *Strangers at Our Gates: Canadian Immigration and Immigration Policy, 1540–1990* (Toronto: Dundurn Press, 1992), 78.

14 Freda Hawkins, *Critical Years in Immigration: Canada and Australia Compared* (Montreal and Kingston: McGill–Queen's University Press, 1989), 17. This important clause was to be active for fifty years.

15 Marilyn Barber, 'Introduction' to 2nd edn of Woodsworth, *Strangers at Our Gates*, xiv.

16 Angus MacLaren, *Our Own Master Race: Eugenics in Canada 1885–1945* (Toronto: McClelland & Stewart, 1990), 23.

17 *Ibid.*, 15.

18 *Ibid.*, 49.

19 *Ibid.*, 165.

20 Carol Lee Bacchi, *Liberation Deferred? The Ideas of the English–Canadian Suffragists, 1877–1918* (Toronto: University of Toronto Press, 1983); and 'Race regeneration and social purity: a study of the social attitudes of Canada's English-speaking suffragists', *Histoire sociale/Social History*, 11: 22 (1978), 460–74; Valverde, *The Age of Light, Soap, and Water*.

21 David N. Livingstone, *The Geographical Tradition: Episodes in the History of a Contested Enterprise* (Oxford, and Cambridge, MA: Blackwell, 1993).

22 Ellsworth Huntington, *The Character of the Races, as Influenced by Physical Environment, Natural Selection, and Historical Development* (New York: Scribner, 1924); Griffith T. Taylor, 'The evolution and distribution of race, culture, and language', *Geographical Review*, 11 (1921), 54–119.

23 Livingstone, *The Geographical Tradition*, 221.

24 Barber in Woodsworth, *Strangers at Our Gates*, xiv.

25 See Morag Bell, 'A woman's place in "a white man's country": rights, duties and citizenship for the "new" South Africa, c. 1902', *Ecumene*, 2: 2 (1995), 129–48; and '"The pestilence that walketh in darkness": imperial health, gender and images of South Africa c. 1880–1910', *Transactions of the Institute of British Geographers*, 18 (1993), 327–41.

26 Angus MacLaren, *Our Own Master Race*, 48.

27 Hawkins, *Critical Years in Immigration*, 5.

28 *Ibid.*

29 *Echoes*, 28 (June 1907), 40.

30 MacLaren, *Our Own Master Race*, 47.

31 *Echoes*, 52 (June 1913), 29–31. The first hostel was started in Winnipeg.

32 For a discussion of motherhood in Canada at the time, see Katherine Arnup, Andrée Lévesque and Ruth Roach Pierson (eds), *Delivering Motherhood: Maternal Ideologies and Practices in the Nineteenth and Twentieth Centuries* (London and New York: Routledge, 1990).

33 In particular see Marilyn Barber, 'The gentlewomen of Queen Mary's Coronation Hostel', in Barbara K. Latham and Roberta J. Pazdro (eds), *Not Just Pin Money* (Victoria: Camosun College, 1984), 141–58; and Adele Perry, '"Oh I'm just sick of the faces of men"'.

34 NAC MG28 I 17, 11, 5, 51.

35 Barber, 'The gentlewomen', 150. See also James Hammerton, *Emigrant Gentle-*

women: *Genteel Poverty and Female Emigration, 1830–1914* (London: Croom Helm, 1979).

36 Marilyn Barber, *Immigrant Domestic Servants in Canada* (Ottawa: Canadian Historical Association with Government of Canada's Multiculturalism Programme, 1991). At that time, the IODE was less concerned than were others over the numbers of domestics and other nationalities entering Canada.

37 NAC MG28 I 17, 11, 5, 51, 1913, IODE National Executive Minutes. Mrs Wilson-Smith is speaking.

38 NAC MG28 I 17, 11, 5, 49, 1913, IODE National Executive Minutes.

39 For developments of this argument see R. C. Harris, 'The simplification of Europe overseas', *Annals of the Association of American Geographers*, 67: 4 (1977), 469–83.

40 NAC MG28 I 17 11, 5, 46.

41 NAC MG28 I 17, 11, 7, 1915 National Meeting, Halifax. President's speech.

42 Genevieve Lloyd, 'Selfhood, war and masculinity', in Carol Pateman and Elizabeth Gross (eds), *Feminist Challenges: Social and Political Theory* (Boston, MA: Northeastern University Press, 1986), 63–76, at 76.

43 *Ibid.*

44 *A Brief History of the IODE* (Toronto: IODE National Headquarters, 1981).

45 NAC MG28 I 17, 2, 3, 119, 4 August 1914, National Executive Meeting.

46 See Wayne Roberts, '"Rocking the cradle for the world": the new woman and maternal feminism, Toronto, 1877–1914', in Linda Kealey (ed.) *A Not Unreasonable Claim* (Toronto: Women's Press, 1979), 15–46. Roberts provides a discussion of Toronto élites, suffrage and activism.

47 J. Castell Hopkins, *The Canadian Annual Review of Public Affairs 1914* (Toronto: Annual Review Publishing Co.), 232.

48 J. Castell Hopkins, *The Canadian Annual Review of Public Affairs 1915*, 209.

49 NAC MG28 I 19, 1, King George and Queen Mary Maple Leaf Club Minutes 1915. The first meeting of the organizers was held on 23 June 1915 in Mrs Rudyard Kipling's rooms. The largest individual donations were from Sir Thomas Shaughnessy, Lady Drummond, Lady Peiley, Lindsays, Mrs Rudyard Kipling, McLennans. The IODE's *Manitoba Souvenir* 1916 (RCSL) records that the premises was purchased by Mrs Gooderham.

50 *Echoes*, 78 (1919–20), 57. The sum of approximately $40,000 was raised by voluntary subscription, and that was supplemented by donations from the Ontario government.

51 NLC, *IODE 1900–1925*, 13.

52 *Echoes*, 69 (October 1917), 13.

53 *Echoes*, 73 (June 1918), 3.

54 *Ibid.*, 155. The article goes on to state that 'the Hand that Rocks the Cradle is the hand that keeps the Ship of State from Rocking'.

55 *Echoes*, 72 (May 1918), 29.

56 Chas J. North, 'Women of the West work to support our boys in the trenches', *Echoes*, 69 (October 1917), 31

57 NLC, 'IODE 1900–1925', 15.

58 Castell Hopkins, *Canadian Annual Review 1915*, 333.

59 *Echoes*, 75 (December 1918), 15, statement by David Lloyd George.

60 *Echoes*, 76 (March 1919), 9, letter to Gooderham from Sir Arthur Currie dated and addressed 26 December 1918, Headquarters of the Canadian Army Corps.

61 J. Elshtain, *Women and War* (New York: Basic Books Inc., 1987).

62 Sara Ruddick, *Maternal Thinking: Toward a Politics of Peace* (Boston, MA: Beacon Press, 1989).

63 H. M. Cooper *et al.* (eds), *Arms and the Woman: War, Gender, and Literary Representation* (Chapell Hill: University of North Carolina Press, 1989), xv.

64 For examples see S. MacDonald, P. Holden and S. Ardener (eds), *Images of Women in Peace and War: Cross Cultural and Historical Perspectives* (London: Macmillan, 1987); and Claire M. Tylee, *The Great War and Women's Consciousness: Images of Militarism and Womanhood in Women's Writings, 1914–64* (Basingstoke: Macmil-

lan, 1990).

65 Ruth Roach Pierson, '"Did your mother wear army boots?"'. Feminist theory and women's relation to war, peace and revolution', in MacDonald, Holden and Ardener, *Images of Women in Peace and War*, 255.

66 Castell Hopkins, *Canadian Annual Review 1915*, 783.

67 Editorial on peace movements, *Echoes*, 60 (December 1915).

68 'The Anti-German League', *Echoes*, 66 (December 1916), 8.

69 NAC MG28 I 17, 2, 3, National Executive Meeting Minutes, 8 October 1915.

70 *Ibid*.

71 See Katie Pickles, 'Edith Cavell – heroine: no hatred or bitterness for anyone?', *History Now*, 3: 2 (1997), 1–8.

72 Marcel Dirk, 'The Imperial Order Daughters of the Empire and the First World War', unpublished MA dissertation, Carleton University, Institute of Canadian Studies, 1988, 59.

73 Article on Edith Cavell, *Echoes*, 77 (June 1919), 33–5.

74 Veronica Strong-Boag, *The Parliament of Women: The National Council of Women of Canada 1893–1929* (Ottawa: National Museums of Canada, 1976), 105.

75 *A History of the Vote in Canada* (Ottawa: Minister of Public Works and Services Canada, 1997), 62–8.

76 Julia Bush, 'Edwardian ladies and the "race" dimensions of British imperialism', *Women's Studies International Forum*, 21: 3 (1998), 277–89, at 282.

77 Bacchi, *Liberation Deferred?*, 149.

78 NAC MG28 I 17, 2, National Executive Minutes, 6 December 1916.

79 NAC MG28 I 17, 2, National Executive Minutes, 17 October 1917.

80 Catherine Lyle Cleverdon, *The Woman Suffrage Movement in Canada* (Toronto: University of Toronto Press, 1950), 123.

81 *Ibid.*, 129.

82 NAC MG28 I 17, 2, National Executive Minutes, 17 October 1917.

83 Cleverdon, *The Woman Suffrage Movement*, 119.

84 Doreen Hamilton, 'Origins of the IODE: a Canadian women's movement for God, king and country, 1900–1925', unpublished MA dissertation, Department of History, University of New Brunswick, 1992. Information from interview, 25 October 1993: Saint John, New Brunswick.

CHAPTER THREE

Women, race and assimilation: the canadianizing 1920s

During the 1920s the IODE was heavily involved with immigration and the canadianization of immigrants. Ideally, canadianization involved assimilating all immigrants into the Canadian mainstream of the time. As canadianization was based upon mimicking Britain as much as possible, British people were considered the easiest to canadianize. A special interest was displayed in British single women, who the IODE hoped might migrate to Canada and there become wives and mothers. Well aware of the importance of mothers in passing on culture, the IODE performed a considerable amount of maternal work with new immigrants. It was the IODE members' place to attempt assimilation in the homes of 'foreigners', this being considered 'women's work'. As female imperialists, they used techniques familiar to those of other patriotic organizations around the Empire, promoting the English language and an imperial curriculum at every opportunity. During the interwar years the IODE's preference for British immigration was strengthened through collaboration with both Canadian and British governments, attempting to overcome the contradictions between the policies of the two nations. To assimilate people of other than British origin, the IODE devoted increasing effort to its canadianization programme. For all involved with Canadian immigration, the 1920s started as a time of great hope and potential.

Preference for 'British stock'

The IODE was a firm supporter of the 1919 Canadian Immigration Act which, amending the Act of 1910, prohibited immigrants deemed unsuitable and made even clearer the immigrants' need to assimilate. During the interwar years the IODE frequently reiterated its preference for British immigration, forthrightly stating: 'The consensus of opinion regarding that important feature of our national life, immigration, is the fact that the IODE considers a selection policy should be pursued by the Government and that there should be a predominance of British Settlers.'[1] The sacrifices of the First World War were used as a justification for preserving the predominance of Anglo-Celtic immigration, such as in a 1920 address in Manitoba in which Mrs C. C. Hearn of Brandon told the women's section of the Grain Growers' Convention: 'We sent our splendid men overseas to fight for us and for our country, and surely now ours is the great responsibility of preserving and building up from them the land for which they made such great and supreme sacrifices.'[2]

Given its preference for British immigration, it is not surprising that the IODE supported the British Government in its postwar emigration plans for British people. After the First World War, the British State renewed its tradition of the settlement of British people overseas in British territories, especially in the 'white' Dominions of Canada, Australia, New Zealand and South Africa.[3] State involvement centred around the 1922 Empire Settlement Act, which authorized assistance for passages and land settlement for fifteen years, with £3 million allocated each year.[4]

Gender was of vital concern in post-First World War British emigration to Canada, and it was here that the IODE focused its attention. The Empire Settlement Act was motivated by the perception that there was a surplus of women in Britain. Citing figures according to which women exceeded men in Britain by more than a million, Secretary of State for the Dominions Leo Amery argued that women from the 'centre of empire' were needed on the 'peripheries'. He proposed that salvation for redundant female workers in the stagnant postwar economy lay in the British colonies, where there was still an overabundance of men.[5] The idea of 'redundant women' was not a result solely of First World War battlefield losses. The mythology had been popping up in Britain since the 1850s, and was associated not just with Britain's changing social dynamics but with the populating of the Empire.[6]

In addition to ridding Britain of its 'surplus' was the benefit of potential economic, strategic and cultural development of the dominions.[7] In Canada, it was believed, there were vast expanses of land waiting to be populated with 'fresh British stock'.[8] According to Bernard Semmel, writing in 1960, a social imperialist doctrine of the 1920s saw the open resources as an opportunity for economic development and a means of renewal for a British race polluted by industrial urbanization, all of which would serve to strengthen the Empire.[9] As Stephen Constantine so neatly sums it up:

The claimed benefits of female migration were therefore essentially conservative: the confirmation of women's traditional roles and the satisfaction of masculine needs, the preservation of British cultural and
political predominance in the dominions by the breeding of new generations from fresh British stock, and the sustaining of economic production and prosperity through the stimulus of more marriage, higher birth
rates, population growth and larger markets.[10]

Despite an overall enthusiasm for British immigration to Canada,
and its legislated preference for British immigrants, the Canadian
Government was concerned that Canada was viewed in Britain as a
'dumping ground' for the unfit.[11] Those Canadians who were themselves of the lower classes, such as trades unionists and veterans, were
protective of their own interests and viewed immigration as an
attempt to flood the labour market.[12] In this tug of war, the IODE, sen-
sitive to class distinctions, admitted that there could be 'absolutely
worthless British immigrants'.[13] Thus, IODE National Education
Secretary Constance Boulton of Toronto stated in an address on immigration:

> I am convinced the foreign immigrant is as varied in quality and type as
> the British immigrant. We have magnificent British immigrants, and
> absolutely worthless British immigrants, and among those foreigners
> whom we call dirty, filthy and ignorant (I hear it on every hand), are you
> not sure among those immigrants there are magnificent types of men?
> The lower classes of foreigners in Europe have I venture to say a far
> greater appreciation of music and art.[14]

Here, class concerns dampened the IODE's usual uncritical enthusiasm for Britishness, and there was a mystique attaching to European
'otherness', a bonding with an imagined form of culture.

Canada was particularly eager to attract male agriculturalists and
female domestics.[15] Considerable efforts were made to obtain British
male agriculturalists. It was veterans of the First World War and their
families who were offered the first passages to take up land in the
British dominions under the Returned Servicemen's Scheme.[16] Under
the Empire Settlement Act, there were further special provisions for
veterans to take up work on the land.[17] Such attempts to get British settlers on to the land were not very successful. Of the 8,500 British har-
vesters who went to Canada, most returned and the scheme was called
a failure.[18] As Barbara Roberts's work on deportation at this time has
shown, what was not publicized back in Britain was that those who
did not live up to expectations would be sent back.[19] There were not as
many immigrants as were wanted by Canada, and the qualities of
British immigrants were not always found satisfactory.

[56]

Children were among those in Britain who were perceived as needing to escape from urban decay. As child migration continued under the Empire Settlement Act, between 1870 and 1930 Canada received more than 100,000 children.[20] At the end of the First World War the number of British immigrants who had gone to Canada as children and who subsequently 'flocked to the colours in Canada during the war' was used as evidence by government officials of the good citizenship promoted by the scheme.[21] In the 1920s, however, the IODE began to question the scheme, raising doubts about the conditions for children. The IODE's criticisms of child migration were influenced both by its connections to the new welfare organizations and by the fact that the children were British and hence deserving of better treatment. At the 1924 IODE convention Charlotte Whitton, IODE member and director of the Canadian Council on Child Welfare, spoke:

> Why are so many children being sought for placements in homes and on conditions which the Canadian authorities will not accept for our children? It does not redound to the credit of Canada that in an official publication of the Dominion Government we should speak of getting farm helpers from ten to thirteen years of age. Do not these facts bear out a contention of a cheap labour demand, a cheap labour that approaches perilously near a form of slavery?[22]

As a professional social worker, Whitton was critical of emigration agencies and their inspection processes, and of the guardianship of children.[23] To treat British children as cheap labour made the scheme all the more distasteful. Later in the twentieth century, the IODE's criticisms of the scheme would become widely held. Joy Parr's work on child migration to Canada has revealed tales of suffering and abuse, as well as of happiness and success.[24] Child migration to Australia extended to the 1950s and 1960s, and was the subject of a 1990s' inquiry by the British Government, as Alan Gill has documented.[25]

'Surplus' British women

The targeting of British domestics in the Empire Settlement Act appealed to both British and Canadian interests. While Britain held ambitions of lessening the surplus in its number of women, Canada hoped that an inflow of domestics would alleviate the shortage of domestic labour in Canada. Over 170,000 British women came to Canada between 1900 and 1930 declaring their intended occupation to be domestic service, about half arriving in the decade before the First World War and the rest in the 1920s.[26] Marilyn Barber has looked to the motivations of those women who chose to emigrate:

Women often have been portrayed as passive or adaptive in the emigration process, sharing the consequences of a move initiated by men. Yet
in all periods, single women came to Canada, many as domestic servants, for reasons of individual or family betterment very similar to
those motivating male immigrants. Those emigrating as domestics were
young women of prime marriageable age. While some were very aware
of improved chances for marriage in Canada, and others used domestic
service as a way to join fiancés who had emigrated, most domestics
came primarily for economic reasons.[27]

To the IODE, occupation was secondary to race and, with its preference for British immigrants, the IODE backed the British domestics.
In encouraging this British immigration, the IODE moved across a
number of spaces that transgressed constructed 'public' and 'private',
as well as national, boundaries. The imperial context was an overriding framework. In its work, the IODE was but one actor among many
interested parties who were also imperial in attitude and scope. Voluntary organizations such as the YWCA, the Salvation Army, the
Girls' Friendly Society, the Oversea League and the Navy League were
all hard at work to foster British migration.

During the 1920s immigration, especially of single women, was controlled by a complicated combination of state and voluntary interests.
Increased government bureaucracy was attempting to manipulate, and
replace, an extensive system of private philanthropic agencies and voluntary societies. While women's immigration gained importance
through the Empire Settlement Act, the bureaucracies set up were still
heavily dependent upon the voluntary work of women, and they often
involved those women in their structures. The new Women's Division
of the Department of Immigration, for example, sent staff officers to
Britain to give final approval in the selection of British domestics. In
Canada the division established a chain of women's hostels to receive
parties of domestics, who were then placed by a new government
employment service.[28] These agencies took over tasks previously controlled by women's voluntary organizations. Women's voluntary work
as the maternal care givers of a private domain was increasingly professionalized.

Increased state involvement led to multiple positionings for the
IODE. The new bureaucracy involved collaboration between voluntary and state interests, and the IODE positioned itself in both arenas.
An added benefit was that among the IODE membership were 'insid-
ers', prominent members such as Charlotte Whitton and Margaret
Grier who were part of Ottawa's new professional 'femocrats'. Femocrats were women who, thanks to the efforts of a first wave of feminism, had received higher education. By the 1920s they were employed

by governmental and private organizations, largely in welfare work. Although not often overtly feminist, and while necessarily a part of the public sector, these women were well aware of their position, and gathered together for support and networking. For example, the Elizabeth Tudor Chapter, formed in Ottawa in 1929, drew its limited membership of thirty-five from women who were occupied in public welfare work, nursing, teaching and various branches of civil service. It was characterized by highly educated, unmarried, professional women, such as Charlotte Whitton and Margaret Grier. Among its many activities was organizing parties for the entertainment of women brought to Canada by the Women's Division of the Department of Immigration.[29]

Besides its well-placed members, the IODE was represented on Canadian boards such as the Canadian Council for the Immigration of Women (CCIW) that was made up of women's voluntary organizations and had been set up in 1919 as an advisory body to government. The CCIW's main concerns were to aid British women immigrants, either out of work after the war or generally disrupted by the war, and to set up a network upon their arrival in Canada, as Mariana Valverde puts it, 'to ensure that once in Canada the prospective domestic servants did not escape their fate and seek other kinds of work or relationships with men'.[30] Extending the pre-Second World War hopes for female migrants, their protection and surveillance were increased by the provision of matrons on boats and trains, and eight hostels were set up across the country to provide single female immigrants with accommodation and supervision.

Ambitious plans were only partially fulfilled. Although it had grand professional intentions, the CCIW was dormant from 1922 until 1927. In 1927 the IODE, dismayed at the lack of coordination of the 119 organizations involved in immigration work, arranged a meeting between its president and the head of the Women's Immigration Department, Miss Mary Burnham.[31] Ever ready to promote its objectives, the IODE thought that the Government should call together the CCIW and attempt better coordination in order to attract more female British immigrants.[32] At the same time as it publicly expressed a desire to collaborate with other organizations, such as the Salvation Army, the IODE was weary of committing energy to those organizations' projects and demands, and attempted to concentrate its efforts. In 1928, caution was expressed before agreement was reached to participate in the Navy League's migration scheme. In considering whether to take on the welcoming and welfare of these families, Whitton pointed out that chapters throughout Canada were already doing such work, in particular for the YWCA in the Essex Peninsula and with the SOSBW.[33]

The IODE's connections and collaborations with state bureaucracies extended beyond Canada, encompassing imperial organizations. As part of its preference for 'British stock' the IODE was in close contact with agencies in Britain, especially the SOSBW. That organization was another example of an increasing state involvement in activities that were still gendered female and private, a tendency manifesting the State's still heavy reliance upon the voluntary work of women. The SOSBW was a part-voluntary, part-statal organization, whose goal was to increase the number of white British women throughout the Empire outside of Britain. Founded in 1919 by the amalgamation of the British Women's Emigration Association, the South African Colonization Society and the Colonial Intelligence League, in 1920 the SOSBW was recognized as the Women's Branch of the Oversea Settlement Department of the Colonial Office. Its provincial representatives, who were all voluntary workers, served on the local employment committees of the Ministry of Labour when women applicants for oversea settlement were interviewed.[34] The interwar years marked a new era for those women who, bolstered by first-wave feminism, were able to exert an influence on official imperial matters, especially where they concerned other women. As Julia Bush argues, in the area of British female emigration, it was clubwomen and women bureaucrats who were able to exert such a considerable formal influence.[35]

Class continued to be an overt concern of the IODE. While it was supportive of domestic servants, the IODE continued to encourage the immigration of educated and middle- and upper-class women. In 1926, for example, the IODE's immigration committee articulated its conception of class in this way:

> While the need for household workers in Canada is unlimited it is not desirable that Canadian stock should be replenished solely by that one class of British newcomer. Surely it is important that a certain number of women of education and training of various kinds should be encouraged to come to help populate our vast areas to be 'home-helps' in families in the more remote districts, or in whatever part such openings could be provided. The Government furnishes wonderful assistance and opportunity for the household workers, but for the daughters of professional men, for young women with possibly a little capital anxious to start out in life on their own, much less is done. Your committee feels that it is of the utmost importance that Canada should encourage to come to its shores women who will include among their numbers those of education and ability.[36]

It can be surmised that the IODE was not down-playing the unquenched demand for household workers, but rather was stressing the need to perpetuate class hierarchies.

The IODE wanted to copy a British scheme for Australian settlement which, assisted by the Victoria League in Australia, encouraged educated women from Britain to settle there. The scheme involved an assisted passage for women aged 18–35 years, and a year of domestic employment at a fixed minimum salary in Victoria, while the women kept in touch with the Victoria League. In contrast to other domestic labourers, it was stated that an 'educated woman in the country districts will often find that she shares the work with the members of the household, and also takes part in their social life'.[37] Such a scheme was considered to be an excellent opportunity for a small number of educated women who desired to go overseas and who were willing to take up domestic work under good conditions. The IODE found it appealing that educated British women might come and live in its communities, since such schemes would offer the 'greatest openings for the chapters to make a definite contribution to the strengthening of the ties which bind the women of the Empire together'.[38] Chapters were urged to study the potential openings in their own localities.

The imperial scale of immigration work involved recruiting from the imperial centre, Britain. Hence, the IODE sought closer contact with the SOSBW and British women's voluntary societies, and again considered the possibility of an office in London. In the words of its immigration convener, Mrs Graham Thompson, 'How much it would help the Order to keep in touch with the movements of imperial women in the Motherland to have its representatives there, with the SOSBW and tap potential British Immigrants at their source.'[39] During a trip to London Mrs Thompson met with Dame Meriel Talbot and Miss Franklin of the SOSBW, and with Lady Cowan of the British Women's Patriotic League.[40] Once again, however, the IODE was a victim of the imperial structure that, ironically, it supported and even perpetuated. The Victoria League in London threatened to get nasty if the IODE opened an office there, making it clear that any activities which seemed like steps towards organization would be considered as an infringement of the understanding between the two societies. So the IODE backed down and concluded that it should continue to focus its efforts on Canada, 'making a tangible contribution at this time to the upbuilding of a British Canada'.[41] Here there was plenty for the IODE to be concerned about.

From disappointment to articulating Anglo-Canadian identity

For all of the efforts to encourage British immigration during the 1920s, it was a time of disappointment for those concerned. The demand for domestic servants and agriculturalists consistently exceeded supply.[42] Marilyn Barber found that, 'because Canadian-born women preferred employment in factories or in the increasing number of offices and shops to domestic work, Ontario housewives increasingly turned to immigration to solve the servant problem'.[43] Once in Canada, however, British girls were not so different from those born in Canada in their aspirations, and did not stay long in domestic service.[44] According to Janice Gothard, there was growing disenchantment among British women with the prospect of paid domestic labour.[45] Of the approximately 100,000 single women assisted under the Empire Settlement Act, around 80,000 of whom went to Canada, few remained in domestic service.[46]

For the IODE, with its preference for British immigrants, the 1920s was a particularly disappointing decade, and that disappointment soon turned to a fear of the 'foreigners' who continued to emigrate to Canada. IODE immigration spokesperson Laura Thompson wrote in 1926:

> Should we now not recognize that Canada's continuance as part of the British Empire may be imperiled by a failure to build up a population resolved to remain loyal to that Empire? Should we now allow ourselves to be timorous as to the possibility of Canada, this great country – being able to provide a livelihood for those British who are already in our midst?[47]

Such an opinion was in line with more general beliefs of the time which, grounded in eugenics and fuelled by declining Anglo-Celtic fertility, in both Britain and Canada, combined to produce a fear of foreigners flooding in from less desirable parts of the world, swamping and destroying British institutions.[48] According to Carrothers, a pro-British immigration academic writing at the time from Saskatchewan: 'it is this foreign-born population that constitutes the greatest problem in Canadian immigration'.[49] An editorial in *Echoes* warned: 'In Canada today seven foreigners arrive for every five British born, and disturbing tales are told of the continental farm labourer who, because of his low standards of living, is willing to work for a pittance, thus displacing Britishers who cannot exist decently on such a wage ... [It] will be difficult for British traditions to survive.'[50]

In this context of growing fears for the survival of an Anglo-Celtic population, it was an important time for the IODE to reassert its preference for 'British stock', forming its beliefs out of the fear of encroaching difference. A speaker at the 1928 National Meeting stated: 'Perhaps no subject before the public today is receiving greater attention of all thinking people than the problem of solving the populating of the great land areas of this vast Dominion.' In advancing the belief that Canada needed immigrants the opinion was voiced that it would 'be best for Canada to bring those of British stock, who would best carry on her traditions, who possessed of these requisites (willing hands and active brains), would not only add to the economic wealth but the social strength of our Dominion'.[51] The assumption was that British migrants were superior to all others, mentally and physically. Furthermore, they would perpetuate Canadian 'traditions' deemed appropriate. In the face of the reality of heavy non-British immigration, the IODE undertook its efforts at canadianization.

Following the pattern established before the war, the IODE's first outreach continued to be the port welcomes, where help was immediately practical and maternal, providing rest rooms for women and food and drink for all in canteens.[52] At Quebec, the largest port of immigrant reception, a postal booth was staffed, and their duties included the distribution of IODE notepaper. Good use was made of these services: in 1930 the postal booth was open for 185 ships and 13,892 letters were posted.[53] As well as ports, train stations were important places where the IODE provided aid for arriving immigrants. In 1930 it was reported that at Bonaventure Station in Montreal, transfer point for the west, Montreal chapters met 171 trains and 25,954 newcomers passed through the rooms where the IODE retained a matron.[54]

In the welcoming work, too, boundaries between voluntary and statal organizations became blurred and the IODE began collaborating with many other societies, such as the Travellers' Aid Society and the Navy League. The IODE was attached to large projects like the Red Cross seaport nurseries in Saint John, Halifax and Quebec. The nurseries were run in cooperation with the Federal Department of Immigration and Colonization, and managed by the Red Cross. *Echoes* in 1927 reported that, in six years, 84,463 infants and children had been cared for at the nurseries, with the IODE's contribution including tea and biscuits for parents.[55] This work depended upon many hours of volunteer labour.

Soon after the First World War the IODE realized that canadianization would be more influential if continued beyond the spaces of ports and stations. The IODE followed eugenic reasoning and urged intervention to improve and absorb the 'racial' qualities of future generations, both physically and mentally. This was particularly important in work with health services. The ease with which immigrants were considered to be successfully assimilated corresponded with the categories of the racial hierarchy. Anxiety was directed towards Asians and African Americans, who were considered unable to be readily assimilated, or canadianized. In 1923 provincial politicians in British Columbia successfully pressured the Canadian Federal Government to stop all Chinese immigration.[56] The IODE's provincial chapter of British Columbia supported this move and urged its national executive to follow suit. A 1923 article on 'the Oriental problem' in *Echoes* stated: 'Eastern Canadians are beginning to realize that Orientals will not fuse in our melting pot ... Let us, in all conscience, stand side by side with our fellow-citizens of British Columbia.'[57]

Consistent with constructions of race, there were strong regional and ethnic differences in how immigrants were treated. Attitudes towards groups of migrants depended on how easily canadianized they were perceived to be. In Ontario and the east, where immigrants were largely British and Northern European, and in marked contrast to its support of bans on Asian immigrants, the IODE organized festive 'Christmas cheer'.[58] According to a 1930 account, parties were given for 800–1,000 girls in different parts of Ontario, 500 new settlers were guests at a 'monster picnic' in New Brunswick and sixty-four Scandinavian families received attention from chapters in New Brunswick.[59]

Although some classes of immigrant were deemed undesirable, looking on the pragmatic side the IODE recognized that it was not helpful to advocate 'wholesale denunciation of the foreigner in our midst', the majority of whom it considered to be industrious people 'doing their duty, as they know it, and filling a great need in the industrial life of our country'.[60] The IODE focus therefore shifted to taking responsibility for the canadianizing of immigrants. Looking back to the pre-First World War years, a member in 1920 noted:

> We did practically nothing. We paid them not nearly the attention that we should have paid to imported cattle. Did we try to understand their point of view, or make them understand ours? No. We made no effort to even teach them our language ... it is just lately that we awoke to the vital importance of educating their children to be Canadians ... If we expect any miracles to be performed among our foreign born, we have got to perform them ourselves.[61]

With such reflections, and with a new zest for intervention, the IODE set out to meet the challenges of canadianization.

Very importantly, through canadianization the IODE was forced to confront what 'Canadian' meant, to move beyond articulating what it was not to expressing just what it was *to* which immigrants were supposed to assimilate. The IODE was still at its most comfortable rattling off mutations of British rhetorics of God, monarch and Empire, and the associated sacred symbols; but increasingly, and because of the immigrant presence, instead of being centred on an imagined Britain, national identity began to locate itself within the space and the people of Canada. What Said has termed *betweenness*, 'overlapping and inter-twined geographies of identity',[62] becomes very apparent here, as definitions of 'Canada' were derived from Britain, but lived in Canada, and mingled with many other influences. Canadianization was initially constructed by the IODE in very practical terms, emphasizing skills such as fluency in the English language and good housekeeping. It was not until later in the century that the IODE was able to articulate a 'Canadian' identity. In the meantime, as a safe fall-back position, cana-dianization was constructed to consist in everything that the alien was perceived *not* to be.

To achieve canadianization, it was believed, immigrants must not be allowed to live in segregated spaces. A growing fear of the segrega-tion of new Canadians was expressed in *Echoes* in 1919: 'In Manitoba about 50 per cent of the population is alien, and in the other Western Provinces the proportion is still higher. Is it any wonder, therefore, that she feels the gravity of the situation and the necessity of speedy action on the part of every loyal Canadian?'[63] In a 1919 address titled 'Canadianize the Aliens' Mrs George H. Smith, national education secretary, presented a large chart of Saskatchewan, showing in coloured blocks the 'different nationalities, origins and numbers of each nationality represented in that Province'.[64] Also with an aware-ness of the importance of space in the assimilation or otherwise of immigrants, in 1920 Ethel Craw argued the risk of spatial enclaves:

> The industrial and agricultural development of Canada, the building of her railroads, and the working of her mines, require an ever increasing supply of unskilled labour from the over-populated countries of Europe and the Orient. But we must provide these toilers with something more than just work for their hands. We must not allow them to live apart in 'Little Russias' or 'Little Italys', never mingling more than is necessary with their Canadian neighbours, nor taking any interest in our national affairs, and cherishing the purpose of returning to their native land when they have saved enough money for their old age.[65]

Segregated spaces, it was argued, could lead to immigrants being 'tainted' with socialism, as Ethel Craw suggested was happening to Finns in Copper Cliff, Ontario.[66] After the war, and mindful of the Bol-shevik Revolution in Russia, there was a strong fear of 'red revolt'.[67] Furthermore, there was fear that immigrants who lived in a block would vote as a block, thus posing a threat to the political system, a concern documented by Howard Palmer with respect to underprivi-leged immigrants of Central and Eastern European origin and Finnish immigrants living in urban centres and mining camps.[68] In 1926 the president of the Order identified a complex non-British threat:

As Daughters of the Empire and loyal Canadians, we should be alive to the serious situation that confronts us in the propaganda that, as the years advance, is being slowly and surely directed at the undermining of the British connection in this Dominion, and the disintegration of those stable elements that have placed Canada in its proud position ... I want to tell you that we have come to a dangerous position. The menace of Communistic and atheistic propaganda is also becoming widespread in every country.[69]

Connecting immigrants with Communism was much more than a fleeting concern, and it would surface again later in the century.

After the First World War, fluency in English was considered to be the most vital component in canadianization. An imperial education, that provided English-language skills and knowledge, was central to the construction of an Anglo-Canadian identity. An article in *Echoes* stated that immigrants must be trained in the 'high ideals' of citizenship. Immigrants should 'learn English, speak English, and think English'. Indeed, it was suggested that if immigrants could be persuaded to undertake 'this heroic method of learning English, nine-tenths of the Canadianizing problem would be solved'.[70] Plans for the canadianization of children extended far beyond English lessons. The IODE subscribed to a complete imperial curriculum that, to borrow from John Mangan, promoted the 'ruling discourse' and legitimized the superiority of its rule.[71] The IODE's national education secretary, Mrs George H. Smith, appealed in 1919 for an 'intensified and broadened Canadianization Campaign', the object of which was to 'banish the old-world point of view, old-world rivalries and suspicions, and make our foreign-born citizens all the way British, in language, thought, feeling and impulse'.[72] Not surprisingly, Smith advocated the teaching of the values of patriotism in the public schools, particularly in outlying districts.

But the IODE experienced difficulties in the instruction of 'patriotic ideals' among ethnic groups. During the 1920s, for example, the IODE questioned the determination of the Doukhobors in British Columbia to educate their children themselves, and resolved to copy schemes underway in Ford and Kitchener to arrange schooling for 'the foreigners in our midst'.[73] Ever aware of the power of segregation, the IODE perceived a threat from sects such as the Western Mennonites who, for religious reasons, attempted to educate their children separately from non-Mennonite children. In this connection the IODE referred to the 'menace to Canadian unity that may arise from the natural tendency of aliens to segregate in unassimilated groups'.[74]

To the grand canadianization programme in schools across Canada the IODE contributed many vigorous and varied ideas: travelling libraries, children's newspapers and the distribution of copies of the

British North America Act to schools and libraries. Prizes were offered for patriotic short stories and one-act plays.[75] The War Memorial Scheme (the focus of chapter six) included a component providing patriotic pictures, lectures and libraries to 'foreign' schools.[76] It was as a part of this canadianization scheme that in 1919 Constance Boulton went on a travelling 'illustrated lectures' tour, undertaken in collaboration with the Navy League of Canada. Boulton visited some thirty-five towns in western Ontario and delivered almost eighty lectures to approximately 30,000 children. She showed pictures of King George, a lion and little cubs to symbolize and naturalize the relationship between the British Empire and the British dominions, and of ships, 'the bulwark of our unity'. Boulton's images and stories were constructed from an imperial narrative firmly founded upon mimicking the imperial centre, Britain. Shifts were occurring, however, in that such imitation produced Canadian heroes like General Currie, and the lectures included tales of the bravery of Canadians and their 'brothers from across the seas'.[77]

In its education programmes, the IODE targeted isolated areas with high percentages of immigrants. In Alberta, especially, it was considered necessary to arouse 'an interest in the British ideals and traditions, which are our common heritage as Canadian citizens, amongst the 60 other nationalities besides the basic racial stocks of British and French origin'.[78] In the face of the perceived immigrant threat, the IODE included French Canadians in its 'basic racial stocks'; a passive inclusion, as at the time French Canadians were not considered a direct challenge to Anglo-Canadian identity. None the less, it was more recognition than previously obtained. With the presence of increasing numbers of non-British European immigrants, French Canadians were re-aligned towards Anglo-Canadians.

The IODE saw that teachers were vital transmitters in the canadianizing of immigrant children in classrooms. It was not alone in that view. In the Prairie provinces, teachers were seen as important in canadianization by a variety of organizations such as the Red Cross and the YWCA.[79] In the 1920s the Province of Alberta IODE held summer school courses in canadianization at the University of Alberta. It also awarded a prize of $150, on the recommendation of the local inspector, to a teacher who had served two or more years in a 'foreign' settlement. Applicants were asked to write an essay of 1,000 words describing their methods of canadianization.[80] A prizewinner working in a Ukrainian settlement articulated her concept of British Canada:

> The problem of the foreigner is a great one; greater than we realize. In
> Alberta we have over 60 000 Ukrainians who occupy, roughly speaking,

a block of land 60 miles square. They have brought with them customs, morals and religions that are in many respects a century behind Anglo-Saxons [sic]. A Ukrainian missionary told me they had no traditions, or what we would call such. They had no King Arthur, or Saint George. The only tradition was oppression.[81]

Ukrainian culture is clearly portrayed as inferior to British culture. The icons mentioned were from British history, and were to be mimicked in Canada.

The potential of the film medium was recognized early on by the IODE. Initially, film substituted for the earlier patriotic entertainments such as musicals and pageants.[82] The IODE brought in experts to advise them on how to use film. Film had the advantage of transcending language barriers. The editor of *Echoes* articulated that significance in 1930, writing that 'the motion picture carries a mutual message in a country where common speech is not an inheritance. Before the "movies" Russian and Scandinavian, Italian and Dutchman, Englishman and Frenchman may sit elbow to elbow and vibrate sympathetically, for all understand the language of images.'[83] From this perspective the IODE advanced the superior merits of British films and petitioned for their purchase and viewing. In 1926 an article in *Echoes* indicated its view in its title: 'British films to the front – getting the soul of England into pictures'.[84] Later, in 1945, in New Brunswick, the Princess Alexandra Chapter showed films about Canada and the royal family at two parties it gave for language students at vocational school.[85]

Into the home

The space of the home, as the place of immigrant women, was also an important focus of canadianization. To promote imperialism, nationalism and social purity, women were considered best able to exert their moralizing influence in the home. Perhaps it was an indication of their own feeling of maternal strength as women that the IODE recognized the importance of immigrant women in settlement, quoting the secretary of state for the dominions saying that 'pioneer wives are the Empire foundation stones', and themselves suggesting at the 1928 National Meeting that

[t]he new settler's success or failure in the new country depends to a great extent on the wife's attitude, whether she can rise above the first discouragements, through failure of the first crops, and other seeming obstacles, and adopt a more optimistic outlook; because we must remember that loneliness in that vast West has been a productive source of many failures in the life of a settler.[86]

[68]

Consistent with its 'racial' preferences, the IODE believed that British women could, with a little training, adapt to become strong and useful, while non-English-speaking women with different cultural values were dangerous. Because of their importance as mothers, such women were considered hostile obstacles to canadianization and were treated with more suspicion than were men.[87] There were occasional voices of sympathy for the hardships that immigrant women faced, as in a 1919 article in *Echoes* that challenged the reader:

> [P]ut yourself in the place of the foreign-born mother – a stranger in a new land, husband and children learning the English language and Canadian ways and gradually growing away from the mother, a keen sense of unwelcome on the part of the native-born, forced by circumstances or the opposition of the native-born to live in unsatisfactory and un-Canadian surroundings.[88]

Other voices questioned whether such 'alien' women were worthy of being naturalized along with their husbands: 'Is she to have full Canadian citizenship because she is the wife or daughter of a naturalized alien, no matter whether she can speak our language or not, or is otherwise qualified?' The immigrant mother could be portrayed as the element most resistant to canadianization. In the words of the IODE's national citizenship and immigration officer, these immigrant women were primitive and 'apparently quite dominated by their men folk, and seem to us to have very little outlook for the future beyond a life of drudgery and repression'.[89]

To alleviate isolation and in the effort to canadianize immigrant women, the IODE was active in home visits, endeavouring actually to gain access to the home and to lead by example. In an article in *Echoes*, 'Reaching women in non-English districts', the suggestion was made:

> Would it not be possible to place women community-workers in these thickly populated foreign districts where teachers' homes have been built by the Department of Education? The community workers could share the homes with the teachers, thus lifting some of the burdens off their shoulders. They would form community centres, visit the women and older girls in their homes, familiarize them with our language, gain their confidence, teach them elementary health conditions and how to care for the sick, and generally help them to adjust themselves to conditions in this country of their adoption. This would at least show the foreign-born woman that we, her Canadian sisters, are interested in her, and sympathize with her. And how far-reaching sympathy is, is it not? Its effect can never be measured.[90]

The article went on to suggest strategies for members to follow. The methods involved establishing, often on false pretences, 'sympathetic points of contact', such as through a 'friendly visit of one woman to another. Treat as if a native-born moving into neighbourhood. Find a sympathetic point of contact – a new baby, a sick child, some flower seeds, a pot of jam' in order to 'get her to help you and unconsciously you help her'.[91] Even the teaching of English was invested with the ulterior motive of improving what was perceived to be the inadequate hygiene of immigrant homes, with the suggestion: 'Ask the women to bring their babies. While you are teaching the women get some tactful young woman who loves children to amuse the babies; perhaps wash them and turn them back to their mothers clean and happy.'[92] There was a strong perception that immigrants were living in unsanitary conditions. In the name of health and citizenship it was the job of the IODE to induct immigrant women within the cult of domesticity.[93] It was suggested to members that they get doctors to help them in improving conditions and that members themselves 'try to improve the living conditions, but do it very tactfully. Sometimes a bouquet or a little picture will lead the foreign-born mother to tidy up a whole room.'[94]

The standards the IODE applied in rural areas reflected the urban aspirations of its members, and were often based on theories far removed from the realities of lived experience.[95] In rural areas the harsh position of women immigrants contrasted with the lives and position of urban and conservative members of the IODE. These were women who had the time to read influential advocate of women's rights Janey Canuck's article on the place of women in Canadian citizenship. Janey Canuck wrote in *Echoes* that 'women are interested in small parks, child-labour, the bettering of conditions in shops and factories, and juvenile courts'.[96] According to the article, women's place in such urban public spaces was from the 'standpoint of the home', while man's place was 'from the industrial side'.[97] Hence, it was the citizenly duty of women to be active in promoting citizenship.

It was with a great sense of citizenly mission that the IODE attempted to influence immigration, and the subsequent life of immigrants. It did so in the places to which it could negotiate access, through its gendered, race and class identities. These were spaces considered by the IODE as dangerous and threatening. For much of the 1920s canadianization was constructed out of British-centred values, imposing an imperial narrative on the space of Canada. Increasing numbers of non-British immigrants, however, demanded that canadianization define more clearly what it meant to be situated in Canadian space. With an imperial narrative still strong, the IODE's response was pragmatic gendered work with immigrants, emphasizing skills above rhetoric. This was also because, with racial prejudices running high, there was scepticism about how successful canadianization could be, and it was still hoped that immigrants would be British.

Notes

1 NLC, IODE Year Book 1925, 30.
2 *Echoes*, 80 (March 1920), 33.
3 See Stephen Constantine (ed.) *Emigrants and Empire: British Settlement in the Dominions Between the Wars* (Manchester: Manchester University Press, 1990).
4 Constantine, *Emigrants and Empire*, 4: the Empire Settlement Act of 1922 was 'an Act to make better provision for furthering British settlement in His Majesty's Oversea Dominions'.
5 Dane Kennedy, 'Empire migration in post-war reconstruction: the role of the Oversea Settlement Committee, 1919–1922', *Albion*, 20: 3 (1988), 403–19, 407.
6 See Una Monk, *New Horizons: A Hundred Years of Women's Migration* (London: HMSO, 1963).
7 Brian L. Blakeley, 'The Society for the Oversea Settlement of British Women and the problems of Empire settlement, 1917–1936', *Albion*, 20: 3 (1988), 421–44, at 415.
8 Kennedy, 'Empire and migration', 415.
9 Bernard Semmel, *Imperialism and Social Reform: English Social–Imperialist Thought, 1895–1914* (Cambridge, MA: Harvard University Press, 1960). Semmel shows the importance of geographer Halford MacKinder in such views.
10 Constantine, *Emigrants and Empire*, 8.
11 John A. Schultz, '"Leaven for the lump": Canada and Empire settlement, 1918–1939', in Constantine, *Emigrants and Empire*, 150–73, at 150.
12 Kennedy, 'Empire and migration', 416.
13 NAC MG28 I 17, 11, 5, 37, Address by Miss Constance Boulton of Toronto on immigration work.
14 *Ibid.*
15 There is a large literature on female domestics. For an overview see Marilyn Barber, *Immigrant Domestic Servants in Canada*, Canada's Ethnic Groups, Booklet No. 16, (Ottawa: Canadian Historical Association with the Government of Canada's Multicultural Programme, 1991).
16 See Kent Fedorowich, *Unfit for Heroes: Reconstruction and Soldier Settlement in the Empire Between the Wars* (Manchester: Manchester University Press, 1995).
17 G. F. Plant, *Oversea Settlement: Migration from the United Kingdom to the Dominions* (London: Oxford University Press, 1951).
18 Schultz, '"Leaven for the lump"', 164.
19 Barbara Roberts, '"Shovelling out the mutinous": political deportation from Canada before 1936', *Labour/Le Travail*, 18: fall (1986), 77–110; *Whence They Came: Deportation from Canada, 1900–1935* (Ottawa: University of Ottawa Press, 1988).
20 Gillian Wagner, *Children of the Empire* (London: Weidenfeld & Nicolson, 1982), xi.
21 *Echoes*, 79 (December 1919), 23. So says Mr Smart, chief inspector of British immigrant children under the Department of the Interior.
22 NAC MG28 I 17, 12, 2, 4, 225.
23 *Ibid.*
24 Joy Parr, *Labouring Children: British Apprentices to Canada, 1869–1924* (London: Croom Helm; Montreal and Kingston: McGill–Queen's University Press, 1981).
25 Alan Gill, *Orphans of the Empire* (Sydney, New York and Toronto: Vintage, 1998).
26 Marilyn Barber, 'Sunny Ontario for British girls, 1900–30', in Jean Burnet (ed.), *Looking into My Sister's Eyes: An Exploration in Women's History* (Toronto: Multicultural History Society of Ontario, 1986), 55–73, at 56.
27 Barber, *Immigrant Domestic Servants in Canada*, 25. For a discussion of the women who migrated to Southern Africa at this time see Cecillie Swaisland, *Servants and Gentlewomen to the Golden Land: The Emigration of Single Women from Britain*

to *Southern Africa* (Pietermaritzburg: University of Natal Press, 1993). For those who migrated to New Zealand, see Katie Pickles, 'Empire settlement and single British women as New Zealand domestic servants during the 1920s', *New Zealand Journal of History*, 35: 1 (2001), 22–44.

28 Barber, 'Sunny Ontario for British girls', 61, and Marilyn Barber, 'The women Ontario welcomed: immigrant domestics for Ontario homes, 1870–1930', in Alison Prentice and Susan Mann Trofimenkoff (eds), *The Neglected Majority: Essays in Canadian Women's History*, vol 2 (Toronto: McClelland & Stewart, 1985), 102–21.

29 LPSC, IODE, *The Ottawa Souvenir* (Elizabeth Tudor Chapter IODE, 1935), 51.

30 Mariana Valverde, *The Age of Light, Soap, and Water: Moral Reform in English Canada, 1885–1925* (Toronto: McClelland & Stewart, 1991), 127.

31 NAC MG28 I 17, 4 April, 1927, Report of president's meeting with Burnham.

32 *Ibid.*

33 NAC MG28 I 17, 4 July, 1928, 154–5, Montreal, Quebec, Manitoba and Alberta have already accepted heavy responsibilities for their present immigration work.

34 Plant, *Oversea Settlement*, 78–80; NAC A–1054 MG28 I 336, SOSBW 2nd Annual Report, 1921, 2. In 1962 the SOSBW became the Women's Migration and Overseas Appointment Society, ceasing operations in 1963.

35 Julia Bush, '"The right sort of woman": female emigrators and the emigration to the British Empire, 1890–1910', *Women's History Review*, 3: 3 (1994), 385–409.

36 NAC MG28 I 17, 4, 2, 8 September 1926, 121.

37 *Ibid.*, 122.

38 *Ibid.*

39 *Ibid.*

40 *Ibid.*, 120.

41 *Ibid.*

42 Marilyn Barber, 'Sunny Ontario for British girls', 56.

43 *Ibid.*

44 *Ibid.*

45 Janice Gothard, '"The healthy wholesome British domestic girl": single female migration and the Empire Settlement Act, 1922–1930', in Constantine, *Emigrants and Empire*, 72–95, at 73.

46 *Ibid.*, 73.

47 *Echoes* (1926–28), 9.

48 See Angus MacLaren, *Our Own Master Race: Eugenics in Canada 1885-1945* (Toronto: McClelland & Stewart, 1990), 29; and Susan E. Wurtele, 'Assimilation through domestic transformation: Saskatchewan's Masonic Scholarship Project, 1922–23', *The Canadian Geographer*, 38: 2 (1994), 122–33.

49 W. A. Carrothers, *Emigration from the British Isles: With Special Reference to the Development of the Oversea Dominions* (London: P .S. King & Son, 1929), 246.

50 Editorial, *Echoes*, 109 (October 1927), 5.

51 NAC MG28 I 17 12, 1, 5, 1928 Annual National Meeting.

52 NLC, *IODE 1900–1925*, 31.

53 *Echoes*, 120 (October 1930), 8.

54 *Ibid.* As a result of the voluntary labour of members at the IODE's rooms only $22.00 was spent on any emergency relief for this large group.

55 *Echoes*, 107 (March 1927), 25: 'What the Seaport Nurseries are doing for Canada and new Canadians'.

56 Howard Palmer, *Ethnicity and Politics in Canada since Confederation*, Canada's Ethnic Groups Booklet No. 17 (Ottawa: Canadian Historical Association with the Government of Canada's Multiculturalism Programme, 1991), 11.

57 O. C. Pease. 'The problem of immigration', *Echoes*, 93 (June 1923), 16.

58 Charlotte Whitton, 'Report of the immigration committee', *Echoes*, 120 (October 1930), 9.

59 *Ibid.*

60 Ethel D. Craw, 'Is naturalization the remedy?', *Echoes*, 82 (October 1920), 44.

61 *Ibid.*

62 Said, *Culture and Imperialism*, 72.
63 Mrs C. C. Hearn of Brandon, Manitoba, 'Canadianization is vital question. Delay and neglect is dangerous – Must extend definite aid to aliens in our midst – Are alien women to have full Canadian citizenship?', *Echoes*, 78 (October 1919), 49.
64 *Ibid.*
65 Craw, 'Is naturalization the remedy?', 44.
66 *Ibid.*, 44–5. Bolshevism was reported as spreading among workers in lumber and mining and railroad construction camps.
67 Daniel Francis, *National Dreams: Myth, Memory and Canadian History* (Vancouver: Arsenal Press, 1997), 36.
68 Howard Palmer (ed.), *Immigration and the Rise of Multiculturalism* (Vancouver, Calgary, Toronto and Montreal: Copp Clark Publishing, 1975), 3.
69 NAC MG28 I 17, 12, 1, 11, 'Insidious propaganda', Minutes of 1926 National Meeting at Admiral Beaty Hotel, Saint John, New Brunswick.
70 'Making Canadian subjects of our foreign population', *Echoes* (December 1919), 79.
71 J. A. Mangan (ed.), *The Imperial Curriculum: Racial Images and Education in the British Colonial Experience* (London and New York: Routledge, 1993), 6. Chapter four examines the construction of the imperial curriculum.
72 *Echoes*, 76 (March 1919), 31–3. Mrs George H. Smith spoke on 5 February to the Toronto Municipal Chapter.
73 BCARS N/I/IM 7P IODE. Provincial Chapter of British Columbia Minutes 1924. Summary of the 12th Annual Meeting British Columbia Provincial Chapter IODE, 23 and 24 April 1925.
74 *Ibid.*
75 NAC MG28 I 17, 3, 1 June, 1925, Suggestions for expansion in the National Educational Department.
76 NAC MG28 I 17, 3, 5 March 1919, The War Memorial scheme.
77 Constance R. Boulton, 'Teaching our children citizenship. Educational work being carried on by IODE bids fair to become one of the most important activities of the Order – What is being accomplished through medium of illustrated lectures', *Echoes*, 76 (March 1919) 55–7. This piece mentions the War Memorial Scholarships and lectureships, selected libraries, and pictures of a patriotic and national character that are to be placed in the 'foreign' schools.
78 'Canadianization work in Alberta', *Echoes*, 115 (March 1929), 7.
79 Wurtele, 1994.
80 *Echoes*, 120 (October 1930).
81 'Canadianization work in Alberta', *Echoes*, 115 (March 1929), 7.
82 See John M. MacKenzie, *Propaganda and Empire* (Manchester: Manchester University Press, 1984), especially chapter three, 'The Cinema, radio and the Empire'. At the January Manitoba Provincial Chapter meeting in 1921 Mrs Valance Patriarche of the Manitoba Censor Board gave an address entitled 'The influence of the motion picture on national life'. Ten years later Raymond Peck, director of Motion Pictures, Department of Trade and Commerce, Ottawa, provided the information for an article in *Echoes* headed 'The educational scope and possibilities of motion pictures'.
83 *Echoes*, 120 (October 1930), 39.
84 Article by William T. Biesel, *Echoes*, 103 (March 1926), 10.
85 PANB MC 200 MS 45/2.
86 NAC MG28 I 17, 12, 1, 5, 13.
87 *Ibid.*
88 'What a woman can do in canadianization. A few suggestions for personal service – Neighbourliness the keynote – Teach English – Other ways and means of helping along this great work', *Echoes*, 79 (December 1919), 35.
89 *Ibid.*
90 *Ibid.*
91 *Ibid.*
92 *Ibid.*
93 McClintock, *Imperial Leather.*

94 *Echoes*, 79 (December 1919), 21.
95 For a discussion of such contradictions in views of motherhood in Quebec, see Andrée Lévesque, *Making and Breaking the Rules: Women in Quebec, 1919–1939* (Toronto: McClelland & Stewart, 1994).
96 Mrs Arthur Murphy (Janey Canuck), 'Canadian citizenship', *Echoes* 78 (1919), 53.
97 *Ibid*.

CHAPTER FOUR

Exhibiting Canada: Empire, migration and the 1928 English Schoolgirl Tour

In the late summer of 1928, twenty-five young women aged 17–18 years, representatives of sixteen élite English public schools,[1] assembled with their parents on the departure platform at Euston Station in London, to begin a two-month tour of Canada. From London they took a train to Liverpool, and then went by sea to Canada. Figure 4.1 outlines the Canadian itinerary. The girls had been carefully selected. Nominated by their respective headmistresses, and having survived final selection by a sub-committee of the SOSBW, they were wished *Bon Voyage!* by no lesser a personage than Secretary of State for the Dominions Colonel Amery.[2]

Each of the parties involved in organizing the tour, from the IODE and the SOSBW to the Canadian and British Governments, had its own particular great hope for the tour. Such enthusiasm on an imperial and a national scale contrasted with the media attention. A wide selection of Canadian newspapers in the 1920s had been full of articles discussing the pros and cons of immigration to Canada, yet coverage of this tour in the Canadian mainstream press was limited to a few group photographs of the prim young English schoolgirls, and the details of their itinerary were placed mainly on the social pages.[3] I have found no mention of the tour in the left-wing press of the time: the opportunity to use the tour to critique Canadian labour and immigration policies was apparently passed up.[4] The media's coverage, such as it was, of the tour was confined to reports of the activities of a women's club movement, which seems indicative of a view of immigration as a male-led, employment-related, affair, while women's involvement was restricted to the 'private sphere' of hospitality.

This chapter provides a case study of how the reality was not so simple. The IODE collaborated with the SOSBW in this impressive cross-Canada tour. In its organization, itinerary and subjects, the tour provides a vivid snapshot of the IODE's ideal Canada. The itinerary

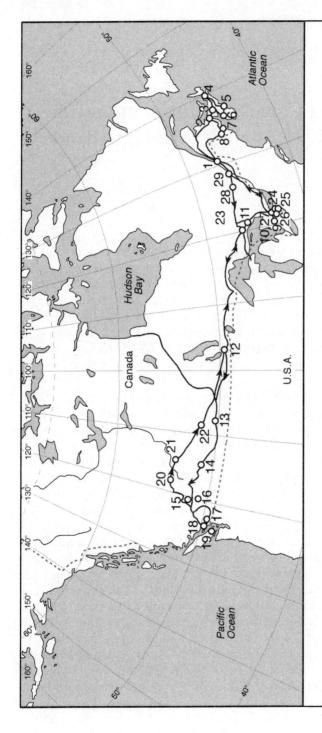

→ ← Direction of travel

1. Ar. Quebec - Saturday, Aug. 11. A drive to points of interest, Indian Lorette, Quebec Bridge, etc. Tea given by Mrs. Ross, Vice-Regent, Shadacona Chapter.

Sunday, Aug. 12.—Special service at Cathedral. Visit to Montmorency Falls. Luncheon given by Mrs. Firmiss, Regent of the Municipal Chapter of Quebec. Afternoon spent at tennis. Tea at Quebec Golf Club, guests of the Municipal Chapter of Quebec.

9. Ar. Woodstock - noon of Friday, Aug. 24. Lunch at Woodstock Golf Club and drive about the town.

10. Ar. Toronto - Saturday, Aug. 25— evening. Visit in the evening to the Canadian National Exhibition, entertainment at dinner by the Directors of the Exhibition.

Sunday, Aug. 26—Supper at the Toronto Hunt Club, guests of the National President, Mrs. John A. Stewart.

18. Ar. Vancouver - Thursday, Sept. 20. Visits to University of British Columbia, lumber mill and a fish cannery, Stanley Park, etc.

19. Ar. Victoria - Saturday, Sept. 22— morning. Visit the Archives. Tea at Molton Coombe—guests of Mrs. Curtis Sampson, Provincial President.

Sunday, Sept. 23—Young people's service, Cathedral.

26. Ar. Hamilton - Monday, Oct. 8— a.m. Lunch at Tamahaac Club. Drive around city. Motor to Brantford—Visit His Majesty's Chapel of the Mohawks, the Bell Homestead, where the telephone was invented, and the Bell Memorial. Motor to Galt—Tea, as guests of the Galt Chapters.

Arrive Guelph— Visit to the Ontario Agricultural College. Dinner —guests of the Guelph Chapters.

2. Ar. Amherst - Tuesday, Aug. 14. Visit Fort Beauséjour, and short lecture on history of the district. Lunch at Golf Club.

3. Ar. Truro - Wednesday, Aug. 15. Tea at Miss Whidden's. Drive to various points of interest. Dinner at Golf Club.

4. Ar. Sydney - Thursday, Aug. 16. Breakfast at the hotel. Visit to Louisburg and district. Luncheon and civic welcome extended at the hotel. Trip on Sydney Harbor on Dominion Iron and Steel Company launch. Swim and tea at Miss K. McLennan's, Petersfield.

5. Ar. Halifax - Friday, Aug. 17 — morning. Breakfast served by the C.G.I.T. of Halifax and Dartmouth. Visit to Provincial House and City Hall. Drive to Memorial Tower. Guests of Mrs. Morrow, Provincial President, at lunch at Saraguay Club. Drive to the Citadel and dockyard. Tea at Government House. Picnic supper—guests of the H.M.S. *Shannon*, Laura McNeil Grant and Robin Hood Chapters.

August 18 — Motor to Lunenburg, Bridgewater, etc. Supper—guests of the Y.W.C.A. at their camp at Hubbard's Cove.

August 19 — A morning watch service. Trip round the Harbour — guests of the military authorities.

6. Ar. Annapolis - Monday, August 20. Visit Fort Anne.

7. Ar. Saint John - Monday, August 20— afternoon.

Tuesday, Aug. 21 — Drive to Hampton. Lunch at Wayside Inn. Guests for tea of Mrs. Walter Allison and Duke of Rothesay Chapter at Mrs. Allison's house, Rothesay.

Wednesday, Aug. 22 — Visit to points of interest in Saint John. Lunch at Riverside Golf Club.

8. Ar. Fredericton - Wednesday, Aug. 22— evening.

Thursday, Aug. 23 — Drive about Fredericton to points of interest. Lunch at Golf Club. Golf, tennis and drive. Tea at Experimental Farm.

Monday, Aug. 27 — Friday Aug. 31. NOTE.—Party divided into two— 15 girls and Miss Thompson, guests at Miss Edgar's camp, Glen Bernard, Sundridge, Ont. 10 of the girls and Miss Galt, guests at Miss Hamilton's camp, Tanamakoon, Algonquin Park.

11. Ar. North Bay - Friday, Aug. 31— evening. Dinner and theatre party guests of the Samuel de Champlain Chapter.

12. Ar. Winnipeg - Sunday, Sept. 2 — evening. Monday, Sept. 3 — Motor to Headingly to Sir James Aikens' farm. Evening, musical, guests of Assiniboine Chapter.
Tuesday, Sept. 4 — Motor to Old Fort Garry—picnic at Little Britain.
Wednesday, Sept. 5 — Motor to Portage la Prairie, guests of Prairie Gateway Chapter.

13. Ar. Regina - Friday, Sept. 7— morning.

Sunday, Sept. 9 — Visit to parks and drive through surrounding country.

14. Ar. Calgary - Monday, Sept. 1— afternoon. Tuesday, Sept. 11 — Drive to the E.P. ranch. Lunch with the Misses Brown.
Tea at Oktoks, guests of the Colonel Wyndham Chapter.

Wednesday Sept. 12 — Luncheon, guests of the Chapters. Visit to Calgary Museum. Tea, guests of Mrs. W. R. Hall

Thursday, Sept. 13 — Visit to the oil fields. Tea, guests of Mr. P. Burns at his Bow Valley Ranch.

15. Ar. Vernon - Saturday, Sept. 15. Luncheon and drive.
Drive to Kelowna—guests for night of Jack McMillan Chapter.

16. Ar. Penticton - Sun. Sept. 16. Two days spent in visiting surrounding country, orchards, etc.

17. Ar. Chilliwack - Wednesday, Sept. 19. Guests for the night of the Municipal Chapter of Chilliwack. Visit surrounding farming country.

Monday, Sept. 24 — Motor to Sidney. Luncheon—guests of the Allies Chapter. Visit Mrs. Butchart's gardens, where afternoon tea will be served. In the evening, a swimming party and dance.

Tuesday Sept. 25 — Drive to Ladysmith. Lunch, as guests of the Porter Chapter. See the Chemainus Saw Mill in operation. Guests for the night of the Chapters in Nanaimo. Leave for Jasper Park, Wed. Sept. 26.

20. Ar. Jasper - Thursday, Sept. 27.

Friday, Sept. 28 — Drive, swim, possibly a Picnic. Jasper.

21. Ar. Edmonton - Saturday, Sept. 29. Leave Edmonton, Sunday, Sept. 30—p.m.

22. Ar. Saskatoon, Monday Oct. 1 —a.m. Leave Saskatoon, Monday, Oct. 1 —p.m.

23. Ar. Sudbury - Wednesday, Oct. 3—p.m. Breakfast—guests of the Nipissing Chapter. Visit to International Nickel Company Shelter. Lunch at Copper Cliff Club. Drive to Coniston to Mond Nickel Company's plant and tea at Coniston. Dinner at Mrs. W. C. Morrison's and reception at Mrs. Crawfords.

Ar. Toronto - Friday Oct. 5 —a.m. Swim and luncheon at Granite Club—guests of the Municipal Chapter. Drive around city and visit to I.O.D.E. Preventorium. Tea at the Parliament Buildings—guests of Mrs. Ferguson, wife of the Premier of Ontario. Supper and dance at Mrs. Burden's, Regent of the Municipal Chapter of Toronto.

24. Ar. St. Catherines - Saturday, Oct. 6— a.m. Luncheon and drive and visit Welland Canal.

25. Ar. Niagara Falls - Saturday, Oct. 6— p.m. Conducted tour of the Falls and dinner, as guests of the Provincial Hydro Commission. Guests of the Clifton and Niagara Rangers Chapters, Niagara Falls, over night.

Ar. Grimsby - Sunday, Oct. 7—a.m. Tea and reception at Deer Park Golf Club. Visit Vineland Experimental Farm. Guests over night of the Chapters at Grimsby and Beamsville.

27. Ar. Toronto—Monday, Oct. 8—p.m. Party divided into three. 9 girls with Miss Thompson, to Montreal to spend six days at McGill University. 8 of the girls, with Miss Galt, to Kingston. 8 girls remain in Toronto, in the personal charge of the Committee.

28. Ar. Ottawa - Sunday, Oct. 1 —a.m. Visit to Parliament Buildings and other points of interest. Visit Government House.

29. Ar. Montreal - Monday, Oct. 15 —p.m. Leave Montreal, Monday, Oct. 19. Sailing on the Duchess of Atholl.

Figure 4.1 Itinerary of the 1928 English Schoolgirl Tour of Canada

formed a narrative of superior British-based culture, economy and politics in a modern resource-rich, technologically advanced, democratic Canadian nation. The schoolgirls were considered highly desirable 'British stock', of the respectable classes and positioned to transmit back to Britain an appropriate image of Canada. They were themselves simultaneously on display, setting an example to which Canadians should aspire. Complicating the events was an entanglement in the post-war immigration interests of Britain, as well as of Canada at large.

Empire unity

The tour was part of the British Government's Empire settlement scheme of the 1920s, as outlined in the previous chapter. The tour organizers, however, were operating on a much grander level than simply expecting that the twenty-five schoolgirls would themselves emigrate. Related to immigration, Empire unity was the theme behind the organization of educational excursions for representatives of vibrant British youth. The badges given to the girls by the SOSBW, as well as the minutes of the SOSBW, refer to the tour as simply an 'oversea tour', without specific reference to Canada. Commenting on the reasons, as she understood them, for the tour, Betty Bidder, a member of that group of schoolgirls, recalls: 'We were all issued with a badge before we left and I still have mine and, in fact, have even found it. I see it was from the SOSBW, which I think stood for the Society for the Overseas [sic] Settlement of British Women. Perhaps this indicated that Britain wanted to get rid of us rather than Canada wanted us as immigrants.'[5]

That the tour was intended to encourage Empire unity is supported by memories of the tour. Beatrice King, another of the girls on the tour, offers this contemporary view: 'I don't think there were any real feelings that we were expected to emigrate. It was I think purely to enlarge our outlook and to show us what a truly marvellous country Canada was. You could not fail to see this.'[6] Neither Betty Bidder nor Beatrice King emigrated to Canada. Beatrice King considered emigrating after the Second World War , but was put off by stories that jobs and housing were hard to find. Betty Bidder has a grandson living in Toronto. She compares the spirit of the tour with that of 'overseas experience' trips undertaken today by young adults throughout the Western world: 'My grandchildren go all over the world as a matter of course, but in 1928 our trip was looked on as a great adventure.'[7] Empire unity, however, was strongly connected to migration. Avril Maddrell argues that the British school curriculum, for geography in particular, played a part in encouraging migration. The 1928 Schoolgirl Tour took place in the context of school texts that, Maddrell suggests, imparted information about different parts of the Empire and linked to migration through the travel of schoolchildren.[8]

The idea for Empire tours had begun in the early 1920s when, following a visit to England by the Young Australian League, a reciprocal visit to Australia was sponsored by the Church of England Council of Empire Settlement. There were grand plans to send 200 boys from English public schools on tours of the Empire.[9] Along with the headmasters of public schools, Colonel Amery was on the schools' Empire tour committee, thus connecting the tours to 'oversea settlement'.[10] Between 1927 and 1939 around twenty tours were organized, and small groups of public schoolboys travelled to South Africa and Rhodesia, Canada and Newfoundland, New Zealand and Australia, India, East Africa, the West Indies and British Guiana.[11] Similar tours by schoolgirls during the same period have received no attention until now. Of the four schoolgirl tours between 1928 and 1938, the 1928 tour of Canada was by far the most extensive. Due to the onset of the Depression, the next tour was not until 1934 when, from 2 August until 14 December, twenty-five schoolgirls went to Australia and New Zealand. That tour, like the one in 1928, was led by Miss Thompson, with the Victoria League hosting the girls. The girls travelled via the Panama Canal and Fiji, and returned via Ceylon and Suez.[12] Plans for a 1935 tour to South and East Africa were abandoned because of the Abyssinian Crisis.[13] In 1936 there was a third tour, for six weeks, on which, again under the supervision of Miss Thompson, twenty-six girls visited eastern Canada.[14] From April until the end of July 1938, a fourth tour visited South Africa and Rhodesia.[15]

It was in 1927 that the Oversea Settlement Committee of the Colonial Office suggested to the SOSBW that it consider the possibility of a tour to Canada for English schoolgirls. As the SOSBW contemplated which women's organizations it would approach for help in Canada, an IODE national executive officer, Miss Arnoldi, surreptitiously visited the SOSBW offices as part of a visit to England.[16] Through Miss Arnoldi, the SOSBW asked the IODE if it would cooperate in a tour and a situation agreeable to both parties was worked out. Enthusiasm was subsequently gauged from the IODE's cross-Canada membership, the response being one of 'hearty endorsement'.[17] The IODE had the additional intention that, after the tour, having worked positively with the SOSBW, it would become the sole representative of the SOSBW in Canada, and thus extend its influence over female emigration to Canada. The outcome of these hopes unfolds in the next chapter.

The IODE attempted to centre the tour's focus on Canada, with Empire unity as a peripheral, though important, concern. For the IODE, the tour was clearly intended to be more than an educational excursion. At the end of the 1920s, the IODE was desperate to attract British immigrants. Members of the IODE countenanced the possibility of these girls, and others like them, emigrating to Canada. When one of the girls wrote to the IODE, after the tour, saying, 'I shall probably be coming to Canada to live before long because Dad is so interested in my account of the trip that he has made up his mind to go and see the country for himself', the editor of *Echoes* commented: 'From the foregoing it is evident that the visit of the English schoolgirls to Canada will have a far reaching effect, not the least of which will be the encouragement of British migration to this Dominion.'[18]

On the party's return to Britain, the interests both of the IODE and of Empire unity found outlets in talks given by the girls at their schools and in radio broadcasts. When Beatrice King returned to her school she was 'asked to tell about 100 of the senior girls all about it'.[19] In a radio broadcast, Miss Thompson, director of the tour and member of council of the SOSBW, commented on 'the wonderful hospitality of our hostesses'.[20] Each member of the touring party stayed as the guest of approximately twenty-two families around Canada: 'We liked Canada and I hope some of us may go back again. We are all ardent propagandists for the Great Dominion.'[21]

Gender, race, class and environment on the propaganda tour

The historical record of the tour is formed by the girls' diary entries, which were subsequently published in *Echoes*, a radio broadcast made upon return to Britain, and by my correspondence with two of the touring party, the content of whose replies, of course, reflects their lifetimes' memories (though its energy and enthusiasm continues to portray the hopes at the time of the IODE). Both the published diary entries and the broadcast can be considered 'propaganda'; in John MacKenzie's sense of 'the transmission of ideas and values with the specific intention of influencing the recipients' attitudes in such a way that the interests of its authors will be enhanced'.[22] I suspect that the girls were willing to please tour organizers and so accentuated positive images. Further, in publishing the diary entries *Echoes* chose extracts that suited its purposes. Likewise, the radio broadcast was carefully managed. Considered as propaganda, it revealed a colonial discourse that emphasized the interests of the tour organizers. My correspondence with the women who were on the tour as girls attempts to move beyond the propaganda; but, as with all of the interview-based material in this book, information recalled through lifetimes of experiences is influenced by the present, and must be treated as such.

Significantly, the tour captures a 1928 moment in the narrative of hegemonic Anglo-Canada. To adapt Edward Said's perspective, the strength of the tour was found in the power to block the formation of 'other' narratives. Emphasizing the similarities between the dominion and the 'mother country', the IODE hoped, would encourage British citizens to emigrate to familiar territory. It was felt to be all-important during the tour that the schoolgirls should be given 'an intimate insight into all that was best in our Canadian life'.[23] The rhetoric of the British race as one big family was taken to great extremes. It was the IODE's purpose throughout the tour to 'make the girls seem like extended family members', so that they would 'have the point of view of relations visiting their own people and seeing the inside of our Canadian homes and the atmosphere and sentiment of Canadian life'.[24] The girls were to see and feel Canada at its best. As Betty Bidder recalls: 'As far as I remember, I felt like I was to be an ambassadress for Canada, and was expected to tell everyone back in England what a wonderful country it was. I had no trouble in doing this at home and at school but do not flatter myself that it had a great deal of effect.'[25] To the IODE, the schoolgirls epitomized the ideal Canadian, and they were exhibited to Canadians as model citizens. One of the IODE organizers proudly asserted in her post-tour report:

> Twenty-five nicer and more attractive young people it would have been hard to find and their warm appreciation of what was done for them and their intense interest in Canada and what she had to show was very refreshing. Their personal feeling towards the Order before they had finished their tour was a very noteworthy feature of their Canadian impressions.[26]

The schoolgirls had identities as 'daughters' of the 'mother country' and future mothers themselves. In his examination of female personifications in the 'white' British colonies during 1886–1940, Dominic Alessio suggests that women were constructed as 'agents of civilization', their role moving beyond the symbolic to that of active racial and moral agents.[27] Anna Davin articulates the view that such maternal civilizing work was deeply infused with race ideology and population dynamics.[28] In line with such work, the schoolgirls were openly referred to as fine 'British stock', the carriers of racial purity, the reproducers of the next generation. There was a high value placed upon the redemptive, feminine, civilizing effects which it was believed that motherhood could have on a nation.

While containing remnants of an ideal of Victorian imperial motherhood, the tour took place in the context of the new modern era for women. The girls' bobbed hairstyles and Mary Jane shoes, and their love of outdoor pursuits signalled the new freedom of movement for women. Meanwhile, the educational component of the tour had been recently deemed suitable for young women. The girls presented a spectacle that was a part of the modern 1920s, years captured in Veronica Strong-Boag's *The New Day Recalled*.[29] In more practical terms, their transportation by automobile and motor coach, as well as by rail, during the tour was also new and modern. The great distance to be covered was ambitious and made possible only by new technology in transportation. Similarly, in Britain the radio broadcast that told the story of the tour was further evidence of the utilization of new technology. Overall, from the context of the 1920s, and on a small scale, the tour offers an insight into the modernization of imperialism and nationalism themselves. And upper-class Anglo-Celtic femininity was an important part of such modernization. In *Forever England* Alison Light shows, through literary sources, how English culture and patriotism became bound up with domesticity and 'the private' at this time.[30] The tour was another representation of such modernity.

The desirability of the girls was embedded in naturalized notions of race, health and sexuality. There was a strong connection between the perceived health of the girls, the health of the British race and the health of Canada as a place. Right from the beginning of the tour's organization the SOSBW showed a concern for the health and fitness of the girls. Much care was taken by the IODE in the appointment of Miss Galt, a nurse who travelled with the girls and looked after their health. There was a clear sporting link in that the tour's director, Miss Thompson, had previously taken a team of English hockey players abroad. In planning the itinerary much attention was given to sports and recreation with hints of the eugenics of a healthy body as essential to the 'superior breeding stock' of a healthy nation. This included comments that the girls had gained weight during the tour and would have to lose it by exercising on board ship on the way back to England.

Underlying references to the health and beauty of the girls was the assumption that the Canadian environment was suitable for British immigrants as distinct from those considered members of 'lesser races'. Morag Bell has chronicled the links between geography and imperial emigration.[31] Racist ideologies constructed a variety of environments throughout the British Empire as healthful for Anglo-Celts. As previous chapters have shown, Canada was portrayed as a healthy place, a northern environment of strength where 'British stock' thrived.[32] To advance the Canadian climate as being easy for British immigrants to acclimatize to, the Canadian winter was downplayed in all aspects of the tour. The October 1928 editorial in *Echoes* proposed that there would be no suggestion of a 'cold Canada' in photographs or memories.[33]

Great effort was made to naturalize the Canadian environment as a place with a suitable landscape for 'British stock' to inhabit. The schoolgirls had travelled through the 'marvellous' coastal scenery of Nova Scotia, and the Annapolis Valley was described in the broadcast as 'a fruitful, peaceful tract of country, reminding one of old-fashioned pictures of the promised land'.[34] In the diary entry of Sheila Keane her first glimpse of the Rocky Mountains was recorded: 'they looked too marvellous for words, with the sun shining on their snow-capped peaks. I don't think any of us thought they would be quite so wonderful, or would seem so extraordinarily near.'[35] Of Niagara Falls, Mary Short noted in her diary entry: 'it was thrilling to think that we were at last at the foot of the Falls of which we had heard so much. The volume of water and the wonderfully coloured rainbows impressed us enormously.'[36] Vacationing in the 'contact zone' of Niagara Falls, located in, as Dubinsky terms it, 'anachronistic space' replete with race and gender, was downplayed in favour of memories of natural beauty.[37] Images of the landscape of Canada have stayed with Betty Bidder over the years. As she recalls: 'I have very vivid memories of many beautiful places from Niagara to the Rockies. Some are so well known that they must have survived unspoilt; Niagara, Banff, Lake Louise, Jasper Park.'[38]

The girls actually spent time living 'in nature'. The wilds of northern Ontario were chosen for a week-long stay in log cabins. Audrey Fletcher recorded her elation: 'as soon as our baggage arrived we rushed to put on breeches or gym tunics so that we could feel we were really campers'.[39] It was reported in the broadcast of the girls' camping experiences in northern Ontario: 'we slept in log cabins on the shores of a perfect lake, and bathed, canoed, rowed, walked (or hiked) held sing-songs round camp fires, ate corn off the cob, hot dogs and all kinds of strange but pleasant foods, and in fact, had the time of our lives. Canadians certainly do know how to make the most of their glorious Summer.'[40] Here, race and sexuality appeared natural in what was considered the most healthful of environments, the idealized epitome of Canadian space.[41] The girls' enjoyment of their surroundings, where they frolicked and were at one with nature, reinforced their suitability as Canadian immigrants.

The twenty-five schoolgirls were mostly upper-middle class, and had each paid the substantial sum of £100 towards their transportation; the remaining costs were met by the fundraising of the IODE. A few had had their passages paid for by their schools. This was the case with Beatrice King, who recalls:

> My school, Christ's Hospital, founded by Edward VI, son of Henry VIII, in 1552, very kindly sent me, as I had really left school and was waiting to start a teachers' training course in January 1929. Miss Thompson had wanted this school to be represented. All the other schools were for fairly wealthy girls. My father was a parson with a big family and *not* wealthy![42]

Because class difference operated in a more fluid way in Canada, the girls probably experienced a broader spectrum of society than that which they were used to in England. Where possible, it was arranged for the girls to meet Canadians of their own age and social position, 'for the personal friendships that may thus arise are all a great strengthening of ties between the two countries'.[43] Betty Bidder recalls:

> Our hostesses were unfailingly generous and kind and were from all possible walks of life. On our arrival, we would see a bunch of women of all ages backed by a row of cars varying from a shining new Packard (no Cadillacs that I remember) to a Model T Ford, and the hostesses and their homes covered the same range. I am sure I sampled everything from a millionaire's house to working-class cottages; we probably were most comfortable in the middle-class professional homes from which we came but I hope we behaved reasonably well in any of them.[44]

After the tour there were frequent references by the SOSBW and the girls (and by the IODE itself) to the wonderful hospitality of the IODE and the lengths to which it had gone during the tour. Beatrice King remembers the IODE members as 'kind and entertaining'.[45] As she recalls: 'Then we stopped at small stations and were given a great welcome and given pamphlets, souvenirs, fruit, etc. This made us feel like royalty. We took turns to thank them. Then on we would go.'[46] Even breakfast was often preceded by welcoming speeches, to which the girls took it in turns to reply: 'Being one of the youngest, my turn did not come around for a third time, for which at the time I was grateful.'[47] The social schedule was hectic and tiring: 'Sometimes I fear', recalls Betty Bidder, 'we must have seemed very off-hand, if not downright rude; a diet of almost uninterrupted sight-seeing does tend to cause mental indigestion, and I can remember saying that if I have to admire another town hall I shall scream.'[48]

Privileged class position allowed access to official space. The girls were the guests of many prominent Canadians. The welcome extended in Duncan, British Columbia, was typical of the pomp and circumstance surrounding the tour. Cicely M. Nelson noted in her diary: 'we had a royal welcome – it is simply wonderful the way so many people turn out to see such flying visitors! We put a wreath on the war memorial and then we sang the national anthem. The Mayor extended a welcome to us and everybody seemed so pleased to see us that we were only sorry we could not stay longer.'[49] The tour itinerary was full of dinners and luncheons with mayors, lieutenant-governors and members of Parliament, making for a highly pressured itinerary. Legislative buildings across Canada, attributed to British-styled democracy and justice, and the connection to constitutional monarchy were emphasized, with royalty given a prominent position wherever possible. For example, there was a visit to the Prince of Wales' ranch near Calgary. Of Regina, Pamela Butcher wrote: 'in the afternoon we visited the Parliament Buildings, which were very fine. We were pleased to see a photograph of little Princess Elizabeth hanging on the wall there.'[50] Rosamund Upcher commented that the Parliament Buildings in Ottawa 'were very interesting, especially the peace tower, and we all thoroughly appreciated the privilege of being allowed to see the memorial chamber, which is most unusual'.[51] It commemorates, of course, Canada's loyal support for the Empire in the First World War.

At various moments during the tour, appeal was made to domesticity: the girls were shown domestic science rooms, attended a household economics lecture and handicraft fairs, and were given feminine presents such as toiletries. But because they were British and of privileged class their gender did not exclude the girls from the more masculine and public spaces. In fact, as representatives of modern womanhood, they were shown examples of Canada's present competence and of the country's commercial promise. At the National Exhibition in Toronto the girls were presented with a full Empire narrative. Schoolgirl Phyllis Carter noted in her diary:

> We were taken to the Empire Marketing Building, which was beautifully laid out. We were particularly interested in the lovely models of animals and scenes of different parts of the Empire. We rushed around the Ontario Building and saw all of the natural resources in the Province. Then we dashed through the agricultural section. Afterwards there were bands and fireworks.[52]

Empire unity was made visible in the relationships of trade in natural resources. There appeared to be no end to the diversity and richness of the resources that Canada contained. In British Columbia they

> were shown over some huge lumber mills, some of the biggest in the World, I believe. It is marvellous what can be done with an enormous tree in a few minutes, and rather sad in a way. A mighty tree trunk is dragged in from the river, and in a few moments cut up almost as though

it were butter, the whole thing being done by one man directing a vast mass of machinery.[53]

In Sudbury, Muriel Brown showed an understanding of the production of nickel: 'we all agreed that to visit Coniston is the best way to learn the "Mond Process" for nickel – much better than consulting a Chemistry text book'.[54] In Calgary they took in 'the modern city' and the surrounding oil wells 'with strange jets of gas spouting over the countryside'.[55]

Throughout the tour the agricultural resources and wealth of Canada were emphasized by visits to a wide variety of experimental farms and orchards. At Regina the girls visited the Grain Exchange and participated in the Harvest Thanksgiving: 'One has, of course, heard descriptions over and over again of Canadian wheat fields, and it is impossible to convey an adequate impression to you.'[56] In the fruit-laden Okanagan Valley the girls 'ate more peaches than one could have believed possible' and met many English settlers, reinforcing the notion of the bountiful life in a Canadian environment that was put forward as suited to British immigrants above all others.[57]

Progress and modernity in the developing dominion

All development was linked to Canada's position in the British Empire. As Miss Thompson stated, the 'idea was that the girls should learn something of the past history of Canada, as well as gain an impression at least of its present position and future development'.[58] They were shown 'our historical beginnings in Quebec and the Maritimes' and then moved through the country as 'our civilization moved West', and capped it all off with a week's visit to the universities to obtain 'a more intimate knowledge of the young people of their own age'.[59] There was an emphasis throughout the tour on familiarizing the girls with the heroes and great men who had helped to build Canada, with continual reference to grand narratives of conquest and domination. In Quebec City, with no guilty feelings about how French Canadians might view the site, they visited the exact landing place of General Wolfe, the British hero who captured French Canada for Britain in 1759. That is not to say that there was no recognition of a French Canadian presence, but rather that the visit was an input considered in relation to the hegemonic status of British Canada. Tensions were to be glossed over, or treated as rousing patriotic events in the formation of an overall grand narrative. In the Maritimes at Fort Champlain, the girls learned more of French–English rivalry, and in Winnipeg they received lessons on the 'thrilling history' of the pioneers of the Hudson's Bay Company.[60] Given the huge diet of British influence, it is not surprising that an unintentional side-effect was to emphasize difference. Recalling the tour, Beatrice King wrote that her favourite parts were 'Montreal or Quebec, as they had such a French influence, and the history involved with these two'.[61]

Unlike the heroics, economic merit and cultural supremacy of the British and the French, native peoples were to be marvelled at for their continued use of what were judged primitive ways of the past. In Chilliwack, British Columbia, evidence of the extent to which Canada's place in the Empire had supposedly infiltrated the native mind was recorded: 'We visited an Indian school, and it was interesting to see the children show us England on the map, and on being asked, the (to us) somewhat puzzling question "what is the other name of that country?" to hear them all respond without hesitation, "Our Motherland". What a queer world it is!'[62] Assimilation was at once inevitable and quaint.

At the end of the tour there was time for the girls to reflect upon and consolidate their experiences. The girls were split into three groups, each to spend a week at one or other of McGill, Toronto and Queen's Universities, where special courses on Canadian history and literature placed an emphasis on imperial progress, modernization, the superiority of Britain and a strong Canada within the British Empire. The courses arranged for them helped the girls in 'focusing some of the ideas they had collected throughout the tour'.[63] Cicely M. Nelson wrote about her courses at McGill: 'Dr Cyrus Macmillan gave us two lectures on "Canada in Literature" which made us realize, I think for the first time, that Canadians are just as much heirs of Shakespeare as English people and that what we all really ought to work for is Empire literature.'[64] The courses summarized the narrative of the tour more generally as a portrayal of what Canada had been, presently was and might be, shown to those who were ideally sought to create it. This was to be a Canada that mimicked Britain, and where all difference was subsumed into a strong modern nation within a united Empire.

The 1928 English Schoolgirl Tour of Canada demonstrates how the IODE created a narrative of Canadian history within the larger narrative of the Empire. The tour possessed all the qualities of the IODE's earlier pageants and entertainments, making Canada seem as delicious as Okanagan peaches. Further, the IODE's position in promoting Canada, from within the Empire, saw it utilizing British interests for its own benefit. The schoolgirls themselves became part of the narrative, and themselves provide insight into who was considered a desirable immigrant. As the girls discovered the Canadian environment and society, their multiple identities demonstrated the intersections of gender, class and race. The tour reveals the intricate politics of colonial identity in the interwar years where the everyday, the Canadian national and the British imperial divides were transgressed. Such politics were contingent upon the assumption by both the Canadian and the British government that Canada was best populated by British immigrants. The itinerary of the tour and the schoolgirls themselves document the production of British Canada within the larger narrative of the Empire. As the girls discovered the Canadian environment and society, they were simultaneously displayed and naturalized as the most suitable 'stock' to populate Canada. Their British and Anglo-Celtic status allowed access to a surprisingly masculine itinerary of commercial 'progress' and development.

The 1920s saw nationalism and imperialism modernize, with the schoolgirls' experiences tied up in an era of technological improvement. If the hegemonic narrative represented in the tour was powerful, it was also more complicated than it appeared, being continually reconstituted and re-created in interacting spaces that cross-cut gender, race and class, as well as official boundaries. Most immediately, owing to the gendered maternal importance of women in both nation and Empire, it was the voluntary labours of the white Anglo-Celtic Canadian IODE at the 'periphery' that were responsible for the conduct of the tour. Representative of Anglo-Canadian hegemony, the IODE had the economic, social and cultural connections to plan and execute the tour. It also possessed an unfailing desire to populate Canada with British migrants, and was complicit in British plans for Empire settlement. As well as supporting the Empire's unity, the IODE placed high hopes that on a micro level the tour would directly encourage British migration to Canada. In this sense the tour was a desperate measure by those with the resources to assert their vision, and it was testimony to the extensive effort that the IODE would expend in its attempt to populate Canada with British immigrants. It was an important moment, but one that would fade quickly as the Great Depression changed expectations and possibilities.

Notes

1 'Public school' in Britain refers to private fee-paying schools, as opposed to the 'free' schools of the state system. The schools were: Bishop Fox's School, Taunton; Cheltenham; Christ's Hospital; Grassendale; Huyton College, Liverpool; Royal School, Bath; Rodean; Sherborne; St Mary's, Calne; St George's, Harpenden; St Paul's; St Felix; Wycombe Abbey; Watford Grammar School; and Woodford Green School. Most of the schools were in the south of England. *Echoes*, 114 (December 1928), 9.
2 'The story of the English School Girls' Tour (taken from the diaries of the girls)', *Echoes*, 114 (December 1928), 6.
3 *Globe and Mail*, 24 August 1928, 18 and 20; *Daily Province*, 21 September 1928, 12,

and 23 September, 2; *Regina Leader Post*, 6 Sept 1928; *Daily Colonist* (Victoria), 23 September 1928, 7.

4 Leftist newspapers examined in reaching this conclusion included: *Alberta Labour News*; *Canadian Labour Press*; *Hamilton Canadian Labour World*; *Canadian Trade Unionist*; *La Vie syndicale*; and *Young Worker*.

5 Correspondence with Betty Bidder, 27 July 1994.

6 Correspondence with Beatrice Scarr, 20 June 1994.

7 Correspondence with Betty Bidder, 27 July 1994.

8 Avril M. C. Maddrell, 'Empire, emigration and school geography: changing discourses of imperial citizenship, 1880–1925', *Journal of Historical Geography*, 22: 4 (1996), 373–87.

9 J. A. Mangan, *The Games Ethic and Imperialism Aspects of the Diffusion of an Ideal* (Middlesex: Viking, 1985), 29. See also J. A. Mangan and Roberta J. Park (eds), *From 'Fair Sex' to Feminism: Sport and the Socialisation of Women in the Industrial and Post-Industrial Eras* (London and Totowa, NJ: Frank Cass, 1987).

10 Mangan, *The Games Ethic*, 29.

11 *Ibid.*, 30.

12 SOSBW 15th Annual Report (1934), 16; and 16th Annual Report (1935), 10.

13 SOSBW 16th Annual Report (1935), 11.

14 SOSBW 17th Annual Report (1936), 10–11.

15 SOSBW 19th Annual Report (1939), 16.

16 NAC A–1054 MG28 I 336, 18. SOSBW 8th Annual Report (1927). From SOSBW records in the Fawcett Library (now the Women's Library): 'Readers will doubtless be familiar with a scheme under which a party of public schoolboys visited Australia in 1926. The remarkable success of that tour led to a suggestion being put forward by the Oversea Settlement Committee that the SOSBW should explore the possibilities of arranging one for girls from secondary schools.'

17 NAC MG28 I 17, 4, 2, 43, 2 November 1927, IODE National Executive Minutes.

18 Editorial, *Echoes*, 114 (December 1928), 5.

19 Correspondence with Beatrice King, 20 June 1994.

20 *Echoes*, 114 (December 1928).

21 *Ibid.*

22 John MacKenzie, *Propaganda and Empire: The Manipulation of British Public Opinion 1880–1960* (Manchester: Manchester University Press, 1984), 3.

23 NAC MG28 I 17, 12, 1, 84, IODE National Meeting Minutes 1929.

24 *Ibid.*

25 Correspondence with Betty Bidder, 27 July 1994.

26 NAC MG28 I 17, 12, 1, 84, IODE National Meeting Minutes 1929.

27 Dominic David Alessio, 'Domesticating "the heart of the wild"', 249.

28 Anna Davin, 'Imperialism and motherhood', *History Workshop*, 5 (1978), 9–64.

29 Veronica Strong-Boag, *The New Day Recalled: Lives of Girls and Women in English Canada 1919–1939* (Markham, London, and New York: Penguin, 1988).

30 Alison Light, *Forever England: Femininity, Literature and Conservatism between the Wars* (London and New York: Routledge, 1991).

31 Morag Bell, '"The pestilence that walketh in darkness"'.

32 This is a common myth in Canadian identity. See Carl Berger, 'The true north strong and free', in Peter Russell (ed.), *Nationalism in Canada* (Toronto: University of Toronto Press, 1966), 3–26.

33 Editorial, *Echoes*, 113 (October 1928), 5.

34 *Echoes*, 114 (December 1928), 9.

35 *Ibid.*, 21. Sheila Keane's diary, entry for 14 September, Banff and Lake Louise.

36 *Ibid.*, 22. Mary E. Short's diary, entry for Toronto–Niagara.

37 Karen Dubinsky, 'Vacations in the "contact zone"', 262. Also see Karen Dubinsky, *The Second Greatest Disappointment: Honeymooning and Tourism at Niagara Falls* (Between the Lines: Toronto, 1999).

38 Correspondence with Betty Bidder, 27 July 1994.

39 *Echoes*, 114 (December 1928), 7. Audrey Fletcher's diary.

40 *Ibid.*, 9.
41 Karen Dubinsky, *Improper Advances: Rape and Heterosexual Conflict in Ontario, 1880–1929* (Chicago and London: University of Chicago Press, 1993), 148. Dubinsky suggests that at the time northern Ontario was considered a 'superior physical environment'.
42 Correspondence with Beatrice Scarr, 20 June 1994.
43 NAC MG28 I 17, 12, 1, 1929 National Meeting Minutes.
44 Correspondence with Betty Bidder, 27 July 1994.
45 Correspondence with Beatrice King, 20 June 1994.
46 *Ibid.*
47 *Ibid.*
48 Correspondence with Betty Bidder, 27 July 1994.
49 *Echoes*, 114 (December 1928), 22; Victoria–Jasper, 25 September.
50 *Ibid.*, 6.
51 *Ibid.*, 23, Rosamund Upcher's diary.
52 *Ibid.*, 7, Phyllis Carter's diary.
53 *Ibid.*, 9, broadcast.
54 *Ibid.*, 22, Muriel Brown's diary.
55 *Ibid.*, 9, broadcast.
56 *Ibid.*
57 *Ibid.*
58 *Ibid.*
59 NAC MG28 I 17, 12, 1, 1929 National Meeting Minutes.
60 *Echoes*, 114 (December 1928), 9; broadcast.
61 Correspondence with Beatrice King, 20 June 1994.
62 *Ibid.*
63 *Ibid.*
64 *Ibid.*, 23, Cicely M. Nelson's diary.

CHAPTER FIVE

Britishness and Canadian nationalism: Daughters of the Empire, mothers in their own homes, 1929–45

During the Depression and the Second World War the IODE's vision for Canada was influenced by Britain's weakening position in relation to a strengthening Canada. Although the influence of investments and popular culture from the USA was increasing at that time, British immigrants were still valued as superior to those of other races and the IODE promoted its own version of British-influenced arts and culture. Through booklets, work in schools and radio broadcasts the IODE created heritage and tradition. Largely unaware of American or French Canadian presences, the IODE continued to negotiate access to spaces where it could reinforce its own construction of a British Canadian identity. During the Second World War, when Canada came to Britain's aid, stringent organization led to a massive contribution to the war effort by large numbers of IODE women. The IODE used its maternal position to reinforce allegiance to Britain, but its perception was ever more Canada-centered. With women's increasing status in society, the IODE's war work was ever-confident and impressive. Although undertaken in a different time, it was work that was still grounded in a maternal identity which drew upon notions of female imperialism developed at the beginning of the century.

Making a British Canada during the 1930s

Soon after the Schoolgirl Tour the IODE asked the SOSBW if it could become the Society's sole Canadian representative in Canada. The situation became tense when the SOSBW turned down the request. The SOSBW condescendingly wrote to the IODE: 'We are glad that in spite of the inability of the IODE to correspond officially with the SOSBW, we may still count upon their kind help in various directions. We owe a debt of gratitude to the Order in relation to the Schoolgirls' Tour, and should greatly regret a severance of connection with such good friends.'[1]

Why did the SOSBW refuse sole-agent status to the IODE? Although the IODE was clearly spectacularly competent at organizing events such as the Schoolgirl Tour, and was otherwise of great use to the SOSBW, it is important to remember that the IODE was one of many women's and immigration organizations active at the time. In declining to place its eggs in just one basket, the SOSBW hoped to draw upon groups such as the YWCA, the Salvation Army, the WCTU, the Girls' Friendly Society, the British Oversea League and the Navy League. Competition between these groups saw them vying for attention and was beneficial to the SOSBW. Further, due to hierarchies of Empire, the SOSBW displayed a mixture of condescension and wariness towards the IODE. Given the Victoria League's reticence towards the IODE, it is not surprising that the SOSBW also felt that the IODE needed to be kept in its place. Hence it continued to acknowledge the IODE's status as a 'friend', rather than recognize it as an equal. Despite the IODE's special efforts, there would be no special treatment for the Order from London.

Rejected, the IODE expressed an increasing pragmatism in its attitude towards Britain and seemed tired of trying to encourage British immigrants on idealist grounds. The 1929 transfer of the canadianization work to the immigration committee of the Order was an acknowledgement that there would have to be even more active canadianization, as well as securing British immigrants.[2] When SOSBW representatives, Miss Franklin and Miss Hargreaves, visited Canada in 1930 to meet with the IODE about the immigration of educated girls and to reconsider the IODE as the Society's sole Canadian agent, the IODE was sceptical. The Order told Miss Franklin that a survey in the late 1920s for the placement of educated British women had produced disappointing results. And with more girls graduating from higher education within Canada, the Order no longer thought that large-scale interim domestic work for British immigrants would be viable.[3]

The IODE's cautiousness was not surprising given the onset of the Great Depression. The Depression forced radical reconsideration of Empire settlement schemes and according to Dane Kennedy effectively 'killed the grand emigration plans of Amery and Milner, the Dominions having no interest in adding to their unemployment'.[4] At the end of the summer of 1930, R. B. Bennett, the new Conservative Prime Minister, cut off immigration. With thousands of Canadians unemployed, the IODE grew more wary of immigrants, especially those from the British 'lower classes'. Although it was opposed to cutting immigration altogether, the IODE was suspicious that Britain was using Canada to alleviate its own domestic problems.[5] When the Empire Settlement Act came up for renewal in 1937, the IODE recognized that Britain 'with its large number of unemployed is extremely anxious to place these people in the Dominions'.[6] The IODE felt that Canada could afford to 'select prospective settlers with the greatest care' so that they 'are not to become failures or add further to the relief rolls'.[7]

Despite such scepticism, however, in general, the IODE's preference for British immigrants and a British-based society remained unchanged. In a 1938 Vancouver radio broadcast, IODE member Mrs Hodgson stated: 'British settlers are badly needed in Canada today for its future well-being and in order that our British heritage and traditions may forever remain part of our national pride. It is hoped that our government will soon see its way clear to open the gates of Canada to selected settlers from the British Isles.'[8] A booklet prepared in 1939 titled 'Canada within Empire' shows how little, in some ways, ideas had changed since 1900. Canada's vast spaces were united not by features of their location in Canadian space, but instead through a connection to the British Empire:

> [T]he great distances separating the peoples of the various provinces, the lack of a national educational policy, the racial and religious differences all make it difficult to achieve a conscious national unity, but a knowledge of our common heritage within the Empire, the principles of justice and freedom, should form a basis for mutual understanding and cooperation.[9]

The symbols of Canadian identity to be taught to immigrants were still defined through the subjugation of difference; the symbols of the flag, the coat of arms and the monarchy were mentioned, and Great Britain was still presented as 'the mother country'. Aside from the considered five races of the English, Welsh, Scottish, Irish and French Canadians, there was a significant discounting of other ethnic groups in Canada.[10] Despite promises that assimilation would permit others to participate as citizens, it was only by taking on a new identity that immigrants might belong; ultimately they were striving towards something in which they would never be able to participate fully, despite the claim of 'ideals dear to all Canadians'.[11]

At this time, as during the century more generally, education was an area of sustained effort by the IODE, which realized the importance of education in promoting its ideals and was quick to see the importance of textbooks and libraries for schools. Work on 'the imperial curriculum', of racial images and education in the British colonial experience, has highlighted the function of education, curriculum and textbook in 'shaping imperial images of dominance and deference'.[12] Education often overlapped with canadianization, especially when the objective was to educate new Canadians in the ways of good citizenship. Such work involved English lessons in order, as the Provincial Chapter of British Columbia put it in 1928, to break down barriers to the 'foreigners in our midst' being instructed in 'patriotic ideals'.[13] Calendars, pictures and other symbols of national and imperial attachment were constantly provided to schools by chapters across the country, a practice that has continued to the present.[14] The IODE was well represented on education boards, as a contemporary Regina member recalls: 'We were on every education board in Saskatchewan, we were always invited to be on it, because we had input and we did our research and we knew what we were talking about'.[15]

The IODE was directly influential in the classrooms thanks to the large number of teachers who were members. One such member recalls her experiences of teaching in the 1930s, and what she now perceives was a challenge to a British-influenced curriculum. Here, the connection of patriotic work in the classroom to fighting in war is strongly articulated:

Working with children in my day, you automatically taught patriotism. I don't think things were always rosy, because before I was married in 1934, I remember one Friday afternoon everything was done and I had a bright class of boys ... they'd call them junior high today – they were ready for high school. And I said, 'Right, now you can have a concert', and they always loved a concert and I always tried to get my children to speak on their feet; I thought it was very important for them to be able to stand up in front of people and express themselves. So they would elect a chairman and the kids had to do what the chairman told them to do – if it was to speak for three minutes on daylight saving and so on – and in-between that we'd sing songs ... we were singing 'Rule Britannia, Britannia Rules the Waves'. So there came a knock at the door, and it was the principal of the school, the first time that I'd ever seen the man, and I said, 'What do you want?' And he said, 'We're not allowed to teach those war-mongering songs any more.' This is 1934. I said, 'Oh, who says so?' He said, 'The Department of Education.' That was at the beginning of what we are now in, bilingualism and multiculturalism and so on, you know.

Four or five years later, I stood on the platform of the CPR [Canadian Pacific Railway] Station, out the back of town here, and the train was leaving for Halifax. It was a train full of soldiers, and the boys were on board and the IODE was there with our baskets, and we had kleenex (tissues) and candy and cigarettes, and things you give young people going away. And there were three or four of those boys there who had gone to school with me and [who] I knew, and they knew me, and I said to one of them (he used to caddy for me at golf, boy he was a good golfer!), I said, 'Honey, have you any idea what you're going to fight for, besides a pay cheque?' And he turned around, and he looked at me for a few minutes, and he said, 'They didn't give us much chance to learn, did they Mrs Baker?' I said, 'No, they didn't. And,' I said, 'it's just sad to be leaving that way.' And that was my one feeling that I had to that 1939 war. I blame Canadian schools for the watering down. You know, right now we take our Canadian troops and we put them off in Cyprus or we put them off in Somalia or somewhere else, and they haven't had any – and I'm going to use the word – INDOCTRINATION to give them a reason why, as a Canadian, they should be there. And I think that's wrong. That's like me giving you a loaded gun and saying go kill anyone you want to. You don't have to have a reason, and I don't think it's right.[16]

The 'indoctrination' referred to was the narrative of Anglo-Canada that the IODE actively promoted through education. In the 1930s education that emphasized strong attachments to the British Empire provided a precursor to participation in the Second World War.

Working for victory

Contemporary members are quick to recall the IODE's contribution to the Second World War. The belief that war was central to the IODE's identity is expressed in the recollection of a Fredericton, New Brunswick, member:

> The First World War, yes, that's when the IODE really flourished, because there was a need in every field, for veterans and veterans' children, and sending things overseas and raising money to help with the overseas projects. Tag days, and everyone was so patriotic that the IODE really flourished. Of course that's why we were established in the very beginning.[17]

With the proximity of the war there came the accompanying sense among members that it was during war that the IODE was of 'greatest importance'.[18] Both in sources from the time and in recent accounts, it is clear that the IODE considered its work important, an indicator of women's recognition of their work as a vital part of the war effort. As women's place in Canadian society by the Second World War was not characteristically one of meekness, neither was the IODE's war work. Yet the IODE's contribution was influenced by enduring ideological beliefs about women's place from the past.

The Second World War saw the IODE contributing to the war effort through a wide spectrum of identities and spaces. Of particular importance in the IODE's work was a complex maternal identity. On one level maternal identity was played out on the 'home front', with women making up for absent men. It was with women's blessing that 'the men who sail in little ships through treacherous waters endure with fortitude and patience the trials through which they must pass because of what they learned of these virtues at their mother's knee'.[19] From the domestic site of the home, the IODE intervened and constructed places as mothers. On a wider – metaphorical – level there was the rhetoric of 'Canada prides herself on having been on the side of the motherland and since war began has paid her way, has the largest volunteer fighting force in the World, the largest small arms factory in the Empire, and has been privileged to share in the great glories as the daughter who is mistress on her own house.'[20] Maternal identity was complex and replete with contradictions. Such a situation led to the IODE's presence in many different places and levels during wartime.

The IODE advanced particular constructions of motherhood in order to justify its contribution to the war effort. In *Echoes* in 1942 there was reference to the role of the mother in international relations:

> Who has such valuable training in a kind and just diplomacy as the Mother of a family? Who so impartial when judgement is required? Who so anxious to distribute fairly the material benefits at her disposal? I beg of you mothers, carry this spirit of tolerance and understanding to every member of the human race, and we shall have new International Relationships.[21]

Maternal sacrifice was construed as international in influence, representing supreme moral fortitude. As mothers, the women of the IODE occupied a domain of grief and sorrow. It was a domain that was sustained by the 'hands-on ... useful work' of aiding the war effort.[22] When such maternal identity was combined with Canadian and British identities the effect was a rousing female imperialist assertion of patriotism. An example of these identities working in combination was provided at the IODE National Meeting in 1940, where the President Mrs Horkins remarked:

> The exercise of mutual tolerance is of vital importance. Many women are experiencing pangs of deep sorrow at the present time. They have had to say good-bye to either a husband, a son, a brother, a sweetheart or a nephew. They are worried and their nerves are on edge. People are likely under stress of great emotion to lose the large perspective. We should think of this before criticising too severely. Canadians have inherited a splendid past from their British ancestors and it is within our power to hand down to our descendants equality and freedom, together with selflessness, co-operation, and mutual tolerance.[23]

In keeping with the spirit in which the IODE was formed, her words also appealed to race and British ancestry. As 'Daughters of Empire', Canadian IODE members had a part to play in helping the women and children of Britain. Of the women of the Empire, Horkins noted in her speech a year later: 'Their spirit and their sacrifice in this terrible war is the wonder of the world. Every day, with unflinching courage and nearly always with a smile, they say farewell to the faces which they have loved, not long since, but have lost awhile.'[24] Again, mothers must make sacrifices for national and imperial victory. As Horkins contended:

> The blood-stained year of 1941 has brought manifold sufferings – sufferings before unknown – but the fortitude of the women has been unequalled in all the annals of history. These indeed are the times that try women's souls, but all honour to the women of England, to the women of all the united nations, so goes the toast, without their courage we should be lost.[25]

Canada's contribution was put in a context of loyalty to Britain and to the allies of Britain and Canada. It was not enough for women to feel the horrors of war; they must also work for victory.

The vital input of women's voluntary work was recognized by the IODE. In her book *Canadian Women in the War Effort*, Charlotte Whitton wrote of women's home responsibilities: 'These responsibilities had – and still have – a value, in the national economy, of millions of dollars in the "non-gainful" occupation of hundreds of thousands of Canadian homemakers whose inability so to keep the gears of home life meshing would mean the complete collapse of the home front behind all war effort in the Dominion.'[26] At the same time as it was linked to the nation, women's work was considered to be the most suited to household and personal service, considered by Whitton as the 'most *natural* and accessible area of women's effort'[27] (original emphasis). Reinforcing women's place in the home was a conservative statement for Whitton to have made, herself a 'new' professional woman. Yet, Whitton recognized that IODE members' collective contribution would be through maternal work, not through the activities of a minority of professional women. Whitton was able to separate her own life story from the lives of women more generally, as she generally perceived them.

As mothers collectively, the IODE 'adopted' ships and military bases, stating that 'the authorities have found the interest taken by a civilian group in a ship and its sailors to be very beneficial to the morale of the men and now desire every ship to have a sponsor or "fairy godmother"'.[28] Between 1942 and 1950, 357 ships were adopted by IODE chapters.[29] Items sent to the ships varied from patriotic pictures of the king and queen to coffee percolators, clothing, boxing gloves and ashtrays.[30] Being fairy godmothers was a complex project for the IODE. Shipments went missing and ships put in requests for items that their superiors did not want them to have. Caught in the middle, IODE chapters were chided by the navy. A letter to the IODE from the navy regarding the PWSC *Winnipeg* inquired: 'May I ask if you are putting sweaters in the ditty bags? This is contrary to the understanding reached with the Dominion Council of the Navy League and a policy which I am satisfied is unwise. Many of the men receiving ditty bags have all the sweaters they need while other men are in great need of these sweaters.'[31] The softer, spoiling side of motherhood did not fit with the navy's ideals of equality.

The IODE was particularly strong in work with the navy and people working at sea. This was because the navy fell into a less clear-cut official category than the army and airforce, and as a result, received fewer provisions. Two substantial IODE projects in this area were the operation of a canteen in Halifax and a seaman's mission in Saint John, New Brunswick. A contemporary member recalls the mission, and members' efforts to entertain and provide for the seamen:

> It's still on Prince William Street, and that's where the seamen would come in during the war when they were on leave or had a break from their ship; and the IODE entertained almost every night of the week during the war, with dances, and serving refreshments, coffee. For years we made socks and things that they would need on board ship, heavy mittens, socks, and we made ditty bags.[32]

Again, the IODE was offering maternal help to refresh and bolster seamen.

As it had been during the First World War, knitting was a significant activity of the IODE. Knitting patterns were circulated for members to follow. 'We all knitted', says a member who lived in North Bay, Ontario, during the Second World War: 'It was to send overseas. I pity who ended up wearing it: I didn't know what in the name of goodness I was doing!'[33] As a 'reserve army of labour' women were frequently called upon to supplement government clothing supplies. One member recalls that the coastguard and merchant marines had no government-provided uniforms: 'They weren't volunteers, but they weren't actually part of service ... [but] they did an awful lot of work getting the convoys across to England'. She helped a woman who used to make vests out of scraps of fur donated by furriers: 'I was a little girl, and we didn't have sitters in those days, and so mother dragged me along and I used to help her match the pieces of fur to make up these vests for the merchant marines, and it was great fun and we'd get different patterns.'[34]

That kind of work took place at 182 Lowther Avenue, the Toronto national headquarters of the IODE. Figure 5.1 shows members at work

Figure 5.1   Second World War IODE members at work in the packing room at 182 Lowther Avenue

in the packing room. Recalling headquarters during the war the same member talked of making layettes to send to bombed-out families in England:

> They had a stable[s] at the back and those were the working and packing rooms during the war. And it was busy practically eighteen hours a day, people packing and working. I used to carry our sewing machine on a streetcar down to this place. We lived a fair distance away, but they only had one sewing machine and if you want to get any work done you need a lot of them.[35]

With a lack of infrastructure and the high demand for aid, resourcefulness was essential.

Given the IODE's strong background in education and libraries, and its history of patriotism, the Department of National Defence had confidence in the IODE, and suggested that it supply books to the troops.[36] The campaign for library books was regarded as a contribution to Canadian citizenship. A pamphlet produced in support of the book campaign boldly asserted: 'Books banish boredom! Books boost morale! Books

Figure 5.2   IODE Second World War service library display at the Canadian National Exhibition

uplift and educate!'[37] Building upon its roles as mothers and educators the IODE gained access to this space of citizenship formation. Figures 5.2 and 5.3 show the IODE's display at the Canadian National Exhibition in 1941, and members preparing books. The IODE attempted to control the kinds of books that should and would be read by troops, stating that 'cash is wanted as the IODE has preferred buying power and through experience knows the type of books the service people like'.[38] Troops were perceived as at once defending Canada and reinforcing a sense of attachment to the Empire. Figure 5.2 features a poster that appeals to a pristine Canadian landscape, linking reading to the strong, healthy homeland. Such rousing patriotic hopes contrasted with the dirt and death of war, and with the other materials that troops read, such as information from the Canadian Communist Federation (CCF) and pornography. None the less, the IODE was well organized in this respect, and was determined to go about its work.

The IODE was just as vigorous and firm in the prosecution of its war effort in the Second World War as it had been in the First. Whereas it

Figure 5.3   IODE Second World War service library

began the First World War by donating a battleship, the IODE began the Second by donating a Bollingbrooke bomber. Figure 5.4 shows the bomber being presented to the Royal Canadian Airforce. In 1940 the IODE raised $100,000 within six weeks for the Bomber Fund, and an additional $130,000 was sent directly to the Lord Beaverbrook Aircraft Fund in England.[39] Clearly, the Order's cross-Canada structure and organization, set up in the years before the First World War, were still working effectively. Sometimes provincial, municipal and local chapters initiated their own projects, while at other times, such as in the case of the Bomber Fund, there was an appeal made to all chapters by the National Chapter in Toronto.

The war accentuated the IODE's attitudes towards race. In 1942 the IODE campaigned for the forced internment of 'enemies' living within Canadian territory. At the 1942 National Meeting a motion from the Alberta Provincial Chapter was passed:

> Whereas in this time of war there are enemies of the British Empire within our borders, be it resolved that a petition be sent to the government of Canada at Ottawa from the IODE petitioning them to deprive enemy aliens and subversive naturalized Canadians (who have been nat-

Figure 5.4   Presentation of the Bollingbroke bomber by the IODE to the RCAF

uralized during the past five years) of their liberty, and place them in concentration camps for the duration of the war. CARRIED.[40]

In the context of war, such harsh words lacked the hope of canadianization that was evident in the interwar years. Old racist attitudes surfaced in the IODE's call for internment. The British Columbia Provincial Chapter, for example, asserted in 1944 'that the dual nationality of the Japanese will never allow them to become assimilated into Canadian life'.[41] Individual members and local chapters varied in their sensitivity; national and provincial levels were especially rigorous. Rumoured reports of weakness towards internees made it into the national minutes. The national executive in Toronto, having been informed that on the Prairies chapters were supplying magazines and cigarettes to 'enemy aliens' in internment camps, responded: 'This action is being severely criticized by Canadians outside the Order.'[42] The suspension of democratic values, so important to the IODE, is understandable only in so far as the IODE deemed such action necessary to promote the goal of victory.

The Second World War saw Canada, through its contributions to the war effort, move to a stronger position as a nation. As British cities were devastated by the bombing during the Blitz, Canada's position of strength became very apparent. As IODE President Horkins noted at the outset of the war, in 1939:

We have many things to be thankful for in Canada – our granaries are full of wheat, our sheep are grazing on the hillsides and our birds are still singing. So far there is no danger of the horrors of bombardment or the heart-rending uncertainties which confront non-combatants in war. Think of these blessings! And let us pray as we never prayed before: 'Oh God, make wars to cease!'[43]

In this speech there was an increased awareness of Canada *in* and *for* itself, and of a Canadian environment and resources that were strong and important. Britain was still to be admired, and the courageous reaction of British citizens was used further by the IODE to glorify British identity. Later on, in 1941, Horkins noted: 'We should be proud to give as well as to lend help to those who are all "in the front line", and whose endurance and heroism compels the homage of the world.'[44] Britain was still the 'spearhead of modern civilization' and the 'solid bastion of democracy'.[45] With this example before them, the IODE perceived a strong place for a Canadian nation to perform the duty that is 'of paramount importance to us as Canadians: it is to give our time, our money and our brains to help win this war'.[46] And here women as mothers had an important part to play as Daughters of the Empire, and mothers in their own homes.

The IODE was active in helping with British war guests in Canada. The symbolic connection between Briton's homes and the Empire as a home was frequently expressed in IODE rhetoric. National War Guest Convener Edith Angas reported in 1941:

These are Britain's mothers and children who have come to us for shelter. Hitler with his bombs may destroy her homes, but he cannot destroy the love that has been fostered in those homes, nor break the ties of love which bind this Empire; he may break in pieces the lovely churches of the Motherland, but he cannot break the faith that has been nurtured in those churches, nor kill the spirit which is born of faith.[47]

As well as providing such temporary shelter, the IODE saw the opportunity during war to recruit 'new' Canadians considered to be eligible. Thus British women who were marrying Canadians were sent wedding dresses by IODE members. In Fredericton, New Brunswick, a member recalls: 'There weren't any wedding dresses, so IODE rounded up a number of wedding gowns in different sizes, sent them off to Britain, and loaned them to the girls so that they would be married in a proper dress.'[48] The name of the provider was fixed to the outfits 'so that the thanks of those to whom these dresses are loaned may go to the donating chapter'.[49]

The enthusiasm with which war brides were welcomed was reminiscent of the 1928 treatment of the English schoolgirls. These women being 'secured' were believed to be 'a fine type of English or Scotch settler whose influence will be felt all over the Dominion'. With military efficiency IODE officers urged: 'our machinery must be set up immediately, so as we may not lose the opportunity of contacting further arrivals'.[50] The Canadian Government also took active steps to get the war brides to Canada. This was the first time that the Canadian Government provided 'home to home' transportation for the dependants of its servicemen.[51] To help the women to adapt, the IODE in 1944 produced a welcome booklet titled 'From kith to kin': 'So you will find us different, but thanks to our fine British institutions we dwell together, bounden subjects, loyal to one Crown, but Canada is proud of her full-drawn strength and rights within the household of British nations.'[52] Here was evidence of the identities that the IODE valued, those of mother, Canadian and British subject with membership in the big home of the British Empire.

Preparing for peace

At the end of the Second World War the IODE actively supported the return to the home of women who had been in paid employment. The IODE had supported women in the army during the Second World War, justifying its arguments by the British example. Despite the challenges war seemed to offer to patriarchy, the IODE, as representatives of the mainstream, did not intend to overturn the division of labour in Canada. As early as 1943 the IODE was corresponding with the Government's Advisory Committee on Reconstruction in developing a plan to deal with 'problems that will arise, on the conclusion of hostilities, in connection with the re-employment, readjustment and rehabilitation of women now engaged in war occupations'.[53] The IODE appeared initially surprised that the sub-committee on postwar problems of women foresaw women as being so disruptive, and stated: 'it is also regrettable that the members of the sub-committee seem to take it for granted that all women (married and single) in war occupations will seek employment in the postwar period'.[54] The IODE believed that women should be encouraged to return to their homes because 'the preservation of home life was of the utmost importance to the nation'.[55] Such opinion supports the argument of Ruth Roach Pierson, that wartime meant temporary practical work change for

Canadian women, and not a fundamental ideological shift in attitudes towards women and work.[56]

Thus the IODE continued to align itself with motherhood, a position of vital importance in its war efforts, and believed that a woman's place was in the home. Such rhetoric masked real changes in women's lives that had happened during the first half of the century. Particularly for Anglo-Celtic middle-class women, the postwar Canadian social context was very different from that of late-Victorian Canada. Their entry into higher education and the professions, and the achieving of the vote were real achievements that also contributed to a more confident position in society. After the limited federal suffrage granted to women in 1917, suffrage was extended in 1918 to each female citizen, and in 1919 women could stand for the House of Commons. Manitoba was the first province to grant women the right to vote, in 1916; and during the following years provincial women's suffrage was granted across Canada, with the last province being Quebec, in 1940. In 1929 the Person's Case declared that women were persons and so were eligible to sit in the Senate. During the interwar years, women began to enter public office. Louise McKinney was elected to the Alberta Legislature in 1917, and in 1921 Agnes MacPhail became the first woman elected to the Canadian House of Commons.[57] In education, women played a prominent part, and gained a footing as professors in the universities, IODE members Wilhelmina Gordon and Mary Bollert among them. In public service and in welfare agencies, women were present as bureaucrats, the most notable IODE example being Charlotte Whitton, who would go on to become Canada's first woman mayor.

The Second World War accentuated the contradictions between feminism and patriotism. On the one hand, women proved their equality with men. During the war, once again women had shown that, in the absence of many of Canada's men, they were capable of keeping the country going, whether in the home or in gendered male occupations. Women's auxiliaries in the services nudged women toward equality in combat, and the IODE's rhetoric often displayed a strong militaristic bent. Yet, on the other hand, owing to the female imperialism that underpinned it, the IODE was able to simultaneously emphasize motherhood *and* women's place as 'honorary men' in strategic war matters. Such were the contradictions of being a group of women negotiating a position in a patriarchal war. Older ideas of maternal sacrifice remained at the same time as narratives of the active combat with the enemy gained strength. Meanwhile, the IODE's metaphorical conception of home as nation and Empire became, during the Second World War, more assertive, more confident, more proven and more Canadian in its focus. From its members' place as mistresses in the home, the IODE had negotiated access to different spaces in order to be Daughters of Empire, representing a strong, loyal Canadian identity. During the peacetime which followed, the IODE participated in powerful and innovative war memorialization.

Notes

1 NAC MG28 I 336 A–1054, SOSBW 1929 10th Annual Report, 32.
2 NAC MG28 I 17 12,1, 6, 1930 National Meeting Minutes.
3 *Ibid.*
4 Dane Kennedy, 'Empire migration in post-war reconstruction: the role of the Oversea Settlement Committee, 1919–1922', *Albion*, 20: 3 (1988), 403–19.
5 John A. Schultz, 'Canada and Empire settlement 1918–1930', in Stephen Constantine (ed.), *Emigrants and Empire: British Settlement in the Dominions Between the Wars* (Manchester: Manchester University Press, 1990), 150–73, at 168.
6 *Echoes*, 146 (March 1937), 51: 'Only last January the British House of Commons approved a resolution which would enable the Government to contribute 75% of the cost of any migration scheme, against 50% at present.' This was a preliminary step to extend the expiring 1922 Empire Settlement Act for fifteen more years.
7 *Ibid.*
8 NAC MG28 I 17, 19, Radio scripts of broadcasts on IODE history and work for radio programme *Vancouver AM*, 1938.
9 NAC MG28 I 17, 40, Misc. IODE, *Canada Within The Empire* (Toronto: IODE, 1939), 5.
10 *Ibid.*, 18.
11 *Ibid.*, 5.
12 J. A. Mangan (ed.), *The Imperial Curriculum: Racial Images and Education in the British Colonial Experience* (London and New York: Routledge, 1993), is a collection of essays focusing on 'the function of education, curriculum and textbook in shaping imperial images of dominance and deference' (p. 1). For a discussion of Canadian textbooks, see Timothy J. Stanley, 'White supremacy and the rhetoric of educational indoctrination: a Canadian case study', in J. A. Mangan (ed.), *Making Imperial Mentalities: Socialisation and British Imperialism* (Manchester: Manchester University Press, 1990), 144–62.
13 BCARS N/I/IM 7P, IODE Provincial Chapter Minutes, 15 October 1928.
14 NAC MG28 I 17, 9, 6 May 1964. By 1965, the IODE calendar, started by National Education Secretary Wilhelmina Gordon, had been in existence for forty years. In 1964 the IODE printed 37,000 calendars for schools. The calendar is still produced.
15 Interview, 18 April 1994: Regina, Saskatchewan.
16 Interview, 21 October 1993: Fredericton, New Brunswick.
17 Second interview, 25 October 1993: Saint John, New Brunswick.
18 Interview, 23 October 1993: Fredericton, New Brunswick.
19 NAC MG28 I 17, 6, 11, National Meeting, presidential address by Mrs Horkins.
20 NAC MG28 I 17, 6, National Meeting, 31 May 1944.
21 'Women and international relations', *Echoes*, 168 (autumn 1942), 14.
22 Interview, 9 October 1993: Campbellford, Ontario.
23 NAC MG28 I 17, vol. 12, part 2, National Meeting (1940), presidential address by Mrs Horkins.
24 *Ibid.*
25 NAC MG28 I 17, vol. 12, part 2, National Meeting (1941), presidential address by Mrs Horkins.
26 Charlotte Whitton, *Canadian Women in the War Effort* (Toronto: MacMillan, 1942), 1.

27 *Ibid.*, 4.
28 NAC MG28 I 17, 23, 15 March 1943. Mrs Angas reports that in the records of the Department of National Defence, Naval Service, there are fifty-one ships without sponsors.
29 NAC MG28 I 17, 23, Adoption of ships 1942–50.
30 *Ibid.*
31 *Ibid.*, Letter to IODE Coordinator Mrs Richardson.
32 Interview, 25 October 1993: Saint John, New Brunswick.
33 Interview, 8 November 1993: Kingston, Ontario.
34 Interview, 4 November 1993: Ottawa, Ontario.
35 *Ibid.*
36 *Ibid.*
37 NAC MG28 I 17, 23, Adoption of ships, 1942–50.
38 NAC MG28 I 17, 23, 5, Armed Services libraries campaign, 1943–45.
39 Whitton, *Canadian Women in the War Effort*, 31.
40 NAC MG28 I 17, 6, 30 May 1942, National Executive Minutes. The motion was from Alberta IODE.
41 NAC MG28 I 17, 6, 6 September 1944.
42 NAC MG28 I 17, 5, 3 July 1940, National Executive Minutes.
43 Mrs Horkins, 'A message to the members of the Order', *Echoes*, 156 (autumn 1939), 3.
44 Mrs Horkins, 'How much we many owe that dauntless few', *Echoes*, 162 (spring 1941), 3.
45 NAC MG28 I 17, 12, 2, 11, 1940 National Meeting, presidential address by Mrs Horkins.
46 Mrs C. H. Wilson (national war service convener), 'Are we facing the facts?', *Echoes*, 162 (spring 1941), 5.
47 NAC MG28 I 17, 12,2, 79, 1941 National Meeting.
48 Interview, 23 October 1993: Fredericton, New Brunswick.
49 NAC MG28 I 17, 6, 6 September 1944, National Executive Minutes.
50 *Echoes*, 174 (February 1944), 2.
51 Ben Wicks, *Promise You'll Take Care of My Daughter: The Remarkable War Brides of World War II* (Don Mills, Ontario: Stoddart, 1992), 40.
52 RCSL Charlotte Whitton, *From Kith to Kin* (1944), 14.
53 NAC MG28 I 17, 6, 6 October 1943.
54 *Ibid.*
55 *Ibid.*
56 Ruth Roach Pierson, *'They're Still Women After All': The Second World War and Canadian Womanhood* (Toronto: McClelland & Stewart, 1986).
57 See J. Arthur Lower, *Canada: An Outline History*, 2nd edn (Toronto: McGraw-Hill Ryerson, 1991 [1973]), 281–5 for a summary of the development of Canadian women's rights. Provincially, women gained the right, respectively, to vote and to be a candidate in the provinces as follows: British Columbia 1917, 1917; Alberta 1916, 1916; Saskatchewan 1916, 1916; Manitoba 1916, 1916; Ontario 1917, 1919; Quebec 1940, 1940; New Brunswick 1919, 1934; Prince Edward Island 1922, 1922; Nova Scotia 1918, 1918; Newfoundland 1925, 1925. Quebec's slowness is attributed to an extreme conservatism that was influential in social, political and religious matters during the interwar years. *A History of the Vote in Canada* (Ottawa: Minister of Public Works and Government Services Canada, 1997), 64–8.

CHAPTER SIX

'Other than stone and mortar': war memorials, memory and imperial knowledge

Through its war memorials, the IODE has used memory to produce identity, instilling a shared sense of the past and defining aspirations for the future.[1] In recent years historians have placed renewed emphasis on the role of memory in the making and re-making of history. Raphael Samuel's innovative work has destabilized memory as fixed or singular, and has brought into question the structure of history as a discipline.[2] For my particular purposes, how war is remembered is important as it can reveal much about imperial and national identity, patriotism and citizenship.[3] Whereas early work on war and memory, in particular Paul Fussell's 1975 *The Great War and Modern Memory*, argued for the disruptive effects of war and the dawning of new eras, recent interpretations emphasize the conservative effects of war, and its forcing, to borrow Jay Winter's phrase, of a 'walking backwards into the future'.[4] The IODE, as a conservative organization, was ever careful to emphasize continuity with past traditions, and its ideology emphasized service and sacrifice in order to preserve freedom and democracy. Yet, in memorializing war, the IODE has also repeatedly demonstrated its capacity for insight, initiative and innovation, exerting efforts well beyond the erecting of stone memorials. From the changing design of the memorials through the twentieth century can be gained a clear view of a shift away from constructing Britain as Canada's imperial centre to a focus on Canada itself. This was mirrored in the considerable transformation of memorialization, which, through a powerful combination of practicality and emotion, the IODE used to introduce innovations in Canadian education and welfare.

Gendering the memorialization process

The IODE was involved in memorializing Canada's part in war through gendered feminine activities concerned with the care and nurture of the national family. To follow Anne McClintock, 'nations are frequently figured through the iconography of familial and domestic space'.[5] As the South Africa War ended, one of the first projects of the IODE was to establish the South Africa Graves Committee which worked with the Guild of Loyal Women of South Africa (GLWSA) to locate and mark the graves of fallen Canadians. The IODE was concerned that the Canadian Government was showing insufficient respect for the Canadian war-dead; those 'sons of the British Empire' whose heroic sacrifice must not be forgotten and whose dependants must be cared for with dignity.[6]

The problem was not confined to the Canadian war-dead. Soldiers from all parts of the Empire lay unidentified in South Africa. It was not long before the newly formed Victoria League attempted to take control of the project – from London. However, because the IODE and the GLWSA were older than the Victoria League, with the project well under-way as the League formed, on this issue the League had no choice but to cooperate. The IODE continued to correspond with the GLWSA, and sent money for it to set about finding, recording and, eventually, marking all of the Canadian graves – and nearly all of the other imperial forces' graves. It was the GLWSA which put in the hard work, and the women of the IODE and the Victoria League who provided lists of the fallen and helped with essential funds. The exercise was probably the most truly collaborative venture that these dispersed female imperialists would ever attempt. By 1910, the League was amalgamating the various branches of the GLWSA, and, given the opportunity, would have done the same in Canada.

To perpetuate the memory of the war-dead, the IODE contributed to a variety of stone memorials. The total number of war memorials throughout Canada is estimated at 1,300.[7] Jonathan Vance suggests that women's organizations, including the IODE, were responsible for as much as one-third of Canada's civic war memorials.[8] Of commanding physical presence, these monuments were positioned in diverse landscapes, from public squares to quiet cemeteries. As in other ventures, the IODE collaborated with different interest groups, local, national and international. Figure 6.1 shows the IODE assembled, in May 1939, on the eve of the Second World War at the Cenotaph outside of City Hall in Toronto. Paying homage to Canada's war-dead at stone memorials has always been an important part of the IODE's official ceremonies. Laying wreaths at war memorials, for example, was performed on Remembrance Day and as a part of its National Meeting held annually in the spring.

Memorialization was also achieved through the process of *naming*. Many IODE chapters were named after war heroes or military contin-

Figure 6.1   At the Toronto Cenotaph, 1939 National Meeting

gents, while others took the names of battalions to which they were attached. Special 'memorial chapters' were formed, such as the Silver Cross Chapter in Ottawa, membership of which was restricted to those women to whom the Silver Cross had been awarded in memory of husbands, sons or daughters who had made 'the supreme sacrifice' during the First World War.[9] Members of chapters have unfailingly placed wreaths on memorials, cared for the families of dead (and returned) women and men, donated money, food and toys to soldiers' families, and visited veterans' hospitals.

Such benevolent feminine care saw the IODE acting as replacement breadwinners and fathers, and making up for the lack of state intervention. The ethic of care and responsibility was particularly innovative in the area of education. The Elizabeth Tudor Chapter, for example, comprised largely of 'new' professional women, focused its effort on educational work among the children of ex-soldiers, so that they were 'assisted in placing their feet upon what is hoped will be the pathway of success'.[10] After the First World War the IODE offered bursaries to children whose fathers and mothers were killed or totally disabled in the war. The IODE bursaries started off valued at $250 for four years, and 249 were given out in total.[11] An architect of this work in the interwar years was Wilhelmina Gordon, one of the first women lecturers (she taught English) at Queen's University in Ontario. In 1920, Gordon wrote that 'veteran's sons and daughters who were mentally fit and eager to go to college had almost nowhere to turn for help now that their fathers were no longer able to provide for them'.[12] Her words exemplified the political connections between the IODE and federal government, as her thinking was closely in line with that of her brother-in-law W. F. Nickel, a prominent member of Parliament who was also outspoken on opportunities for children of the war-dead. Nickel is on record as having said that 'if there is one thing more than another that a child is entitled to whose bread-winner is taken away it is a fair chance in life'.[13]

Memorializing education

The IODE's national bursary scheme for children who had lost a father was part of a grander and more ambitious project, the IODE's First War Memorial. Towards the end of the First World War, the IODE started planning for a memorial in *other than stone and mortar* that should be ... [a] tribute to those who had sacrificed their lives'[14] (emphasis added). By this time a governmental agency, the Imperial War Graves Commission (IWGC), had taken over the responsibility for marking graves.[15] What had been a women's voluntary work initiative during the South Africa War was now taken up by government. As a result, the IODE embarked on new kinds of commemorative projects which would give a sense of the past and define Canadian aspirations for the future. The First War Memorial involved three educational ventures: bursaries, to make sure that dependants of the war-dead would not be disadvantaged; the distribution of patriotic educational material; and postgraduate scholarships. In an open letter to members from the IODE national press and publicity committee in 1919 the plan was sweepingly set out as 'a most extensive and varied scheme of Patriotic Educational Propaganda, designed to cover every phase of education, and from which Canada nationally should, as the years go on, reap a rich harvest in sound patriotic citizenship'.[16] Looking to the future through investing in children was a strong postwar concern across Canada, as it was in other countries whose soldiers had fought in the war and which were keen to rebuild and mould their sense of nationhood.

The educational memorial was 'undertaken with a view to instilling an intelligent patriotism into the minds of the young people of Canada and the building up of a sound Canadian citizenship'.[17] Such patriotism was to be achieved through placing in 1,000 schools a series of war memorial pictures, reproduced from the war artists' record of the part played by Canada, as executed under the direction of the Canadian War Records Office in London.[18] Jonathan Vance considers the pictures 'entirely traditional', as well as illustrating a 'view of the war that was already deeply ingrained in the education system'.[19] His argument is that Canada remembered the First World War by emphasizing traditional values, continuity and the positive results of the war experience. The rhetoric of the IODE lends support to this argument. The IODE's ambition was that the pictures would constantly remind Canadian children of 'the heroic deeds of the men and women, whose sacrifices saved the Empire and its cherished institutions'.[20] Individual chapters raised money to purchase the pictures, which were centrally ordered through the IODE's national education secretary.

These pictures from the First World War were part of a broader vision that the IODE held for the Canadian nation, in which the experience and culture of Anglo-Celtic Canada would triumphantly dominate, blocking out other narratives and universalizing the experience and culture of Anglo-Celtic Canada. In that sense the pictures enforced the dominant culture, along the lines examined by Iris Marion Young – the denial of difference – and by Edward Said – the workings of imperialism.[21] In addition to the First World War scenes, the collection of suitable representations included heroes and heroic deaths, such as *The Death of Wolfe* in the British conquest of Quebec by American artist Benjamin West. Writing on Canadian national dreams, Daniel Francis calls this picture 'a monument to historical fabrication'.[22] Indeed, in such collections French Canadian and aboriginal figures appeared only in support of myths of mainstream Anglo-Canadian identity. Nor was the construction of memory limited to visual representations. Books were purchased as part of the educational memorial, and the IODE intended to provide every school in Canada attended by children of foreign-born citizens with a full set of the 'Daughters of the Empire Historical Library', in the conviction that the foreign-born, unless appropriately educated, would threaten Canadian beliefs.[23] Along with the pictures and books, the IODE offered illustrated lectures to the children of Canada on the history and geography of the Empire.[24]

Towards the end of the Second World War the IODE mapped out its Second War Memorial, by expanding activities in relation to the bursaries, the scholarships and the educational materials. To IODE members 'there seemed no finer or more fitting way to honour the memory of those who gave their lives in the Second World War than in making possible a richer, more abundant way of life for their children'.[25] Due to increased governmental intervention in areas of previous IODE initiative, such as grave marking and assistance with education for dependants of the war-dead , more importance was placed on general nation building and in the creation of collective memory. Among the Canadian public there was an even greater dissatisfaction with stone and mortar commemorations, and a call for useful memorials such as parks, hospitals, homes for the elderly and the wounded.[26] In this same vein – the combining of innovations of the Second War Memorial with useful and nation-building memorials – was the extension of the IODE's postgraduate scholarships. In Canada in general, the postwar years were a time of growth both in the universities and in the civil service, and well-qualified people were in demand. With the State offering basic educational assistance, such as allowances for dependants of the war-dead, the IODE focused on useful projects that aimed to ensure that postwar Canada would have a supply of highly educated citizens able to serve Canada both locally and on the world stage.

The War Memorial Scholarships were supported by a Canada-wide endowment fund. A large fundraising campaign was undertaken by chapters throughout the provinces. As distinct from the bursaries, which were based largely upon need, scholarships were awarded for academic excellence, and the primary concern was to select the most able and promising available graduates of Canadian universities. They were offered 'with quiet pride' as 'a tribute to those who envisioned a better world, a peaceful homeland and [who] were willing to take up the struggle to ensure its future'.[27] The scholarships were distributed evenly among the provinces for postgraduate study in the 'mother country'.[28] Table 6.1 shows the distribution by sex and province. The IODE sought individuals who could be further trained in the ways of useful citizenship, and it considered that British universities could provide an education superior to that available in Canada. This is not to say that Canada was not proud of its own universities. Indeed, during the 1928 Schoolgirl Tour, McGill, Queen's and Toronto Universities had been showcased. Yet, along with other countries in the British Commonwealth, Anglo-Canada looked up to educational opportunities offered in Britain.

The committee of selection for the War Memorial Scholarships was instructed by the IODE National Chapter to prefer, other things being equal, a 'returned man' or an immediate relative of a man who served in the war,[29] and this was apparent in the large share of scholarships awarded to individuals with relatives who were killed or permanently disabled on overseas service: of the 115 First War Memorial Scholars, 28 had fathers who served, 14 had brothers who served and 45 themselves served in either the First or the Second World War – those

Table 6.1 First War Memorial Scholars by province

Province	Women	Men	Total	% of total
Alberta	9	7	16	14
British Columbia	5	7	12	10.5
Manitoba	0	13	13	11
New Brunswick	0	9	9	8
Nova Scotia	3	11	14	12
Ontario	4	10	14	12
Prince Edward Island	2	9	11	10
Quebec	3	9	12	10.5
Saskatchewan	1	13	14	12
Total	27 (23.5%)	88 (76.5%)	115	

Source: Record of Post-Graduate Scholars for the IODE First War Memorial

serving during the Second World War had their First War Memorial awards deferred until after the war in order for them to join the war effort.[30] Scholarships designated for returned soldiers potentially discriminated against women. The IODE, however, actively supported education for women, as well as the presence of women in politics and non-traditional occupations. As table 6.1 shows, in the First War Memorial, 23.5 per cent of the recipients were women. Considering the lower participation rates of females pursuing graduate degrees at the time, this was quite an achievement, and it can be asserted that the IODE effectively contributed to getting women into positions traditionally associated with masculine power and influence.

The acceptance of diversity in the selection of War Memorial Scholars was more contentious. Focusing on educational forms of memorial allowed the officially non-denominational IODE to instigate a project that allowed for religious differences. This explains in part why the IODE was a leader in the trend towards practical expressions of memorial during the early part of the century. But as the IODE was in fact an overwhelmingly Protestant organization, its claim to non-denominational status masked real biases. Trouble arose in 1925 in Prince Edward Island when the religion of a candidate came up for discussion. One member complained that it was not fair that IODE money should go to educate nuns and priests, whereupon National Education Secretary Wilhelmina Gordon warned the Island members to settle their differences swiftly, or risk having their local control over selection taken away.[31]

Table 6.2 UK institutions attended by First War Memorial Scholars

University	Men	% of total scholars
Oxford University	39	34
University of London	31	27
London School of Economics	21	18
Cambridge University	15	13
University of Edinburgh	6	5
University of Liverpool (Marine Zoology)	1	1
University of Aberystwyth (Agriculture)	1	1
British post-graduate medical school and National Neurological and London Hospitals	1	1
Total	115	

Source: Record of Post-Graduate Scholars for the IODE First War Memorial

In practice, the selection process allowed ample scope for the screening out of candidates of difference, since it involved subjective judgements about the character and good citizenship of applicants. Local committees were comprised of IODE members and university professors. The selection process reflected the Anglo-Celtic membership of the committees as well as the Anglo-Celtic make-up of Canadian university students. The majority of names that appear in the record of War Memorial Scholars are Anglo-Celtic, which is hardly surprising; but the ethnicity of recipients changed over the years and, little by little, more Canadians of non-Anglo-Celtic backgrounds were awarded scholarships. There was a perception here that such students had assimilated the values of Canadian citizenship, meeting the requirements of the Anglo-mainstream educational narrative.

Imperial knowledge and colonial identity

By modelling the War Memorial Scholarship on the Rhodes Scholarship, and by sending Canadian graduates to British universities, the IODE expressed a firm colonial agenda.[32] Consistent with a sense of Canada that was derived from Britain, the IODE First War Memorial

Scholarships encouraged study at the centre of the Empire so that students would return to the periphery imbued with imperial ways. The topics studied reflected the IODE's agenda.[33] Scholars were to study topics of history and economy of relevance to the British Empire. The First War Memorial Scholars were concentrated in four institutions. As table 6.2 shows, 92 per cent went to London, Oxford or Cambridge University, and the London School of Economics, 5 per cent going to Edinburgh. In 1925, War Memorial Scholar James Stuart Martell responded to Gordon's question about the value of studying in Britain:

> The IODE student in Britain should, and I think does, return to Canada with a truer understanding of the British people, a wider conception of the World Empire, and a clearer vision of Canada as a nation rather than a particular province. Absence from one's country is usually conducive to patriotism and the Canadian who returns to Canada after a year or so abroad is often a truer Canadian than when he left.[34]

This was what the IODE wanted to hear. Martell went on to complete a PhD at London University, and then returned to Halifax, Nova Scotia, where he worked in the public archives and gave occasional lectures in schools. Unfortunately, he died in 1946, only a decade after his return.[35]

There was much working-through to be done in the early years of the War Memorial Scholarships. Until 1926, due to a lack of money, the funding for scholars was awarded to provinces in alternate years. The inferior status accorded by British universities to Canadian degrees created problems, because Canadian students in Britain were often required to complete a gruelling qualifying year and IODE support was only for one year. Many returned to Canada not with a postgraduate degree but with a diploma or a second Bachelor's degree. As Alberta's first War Memorial Scholar (in 1924) recalled, seventy years later:

> London University didn't recognize an Alberta BA, so I had to take the last year of their BA course, which meant British history from year one, and I had to write the finals, all of the finals – except that they excused me the language ones, Latin and Anglo-Saxon – [but I had to do] all the rest of them, and that meant hours and hours and hours of lectures in addition to working on a thesis. And I chose the thesis of [The] Evolution of Indian-Native Policy. So I had lectures at Bedford College, and I was registered at King's College in the Strand, and I was at University College; and I did the postgraduate work at Bedford. I was doing research in the British Museum and taking lectures in the Mallot Building ... Well, it was just for one [year] and you couldn't re-apply for it. So I didn't finish. I stayed on for a while because I still had family. I was born in Britain.[36]

The problem of scholars returning to Canada without a postgraduate degree was resolved in 1928, by making scholarships more easily renewable and recognizing that the students were victims of an imperial prestige that the IODE sought to perpetuate.[37] The Alberta scholar's choice of topic, native Indian policy, was an engagement with the study of Canada. This was a hope of the IODE, that scholars would apply British ideas to Canadian topics.

The Memorial Scholarship programme continues to the present. It is often in connection with this programme that students looking to fund their postgraduate studies first come to hear about the IODE. Although the scholarships still exist as a memorial to past wars, the military service of the applicants themselves is now of less importance. This obviously makes demographic sense. Out of over 400 Second War Memorial Scholars to 1990, 18 men and 1 woman had been on active service during the Second World War, three men had served in peacetime, and a considerable number had been involved with war administration through work in government departments.[38] IODE members repeatedly expressed concern that the selection criteria should not be structured to favour male relatives. In the 1950s they challenged the initial priority accorded to men,[39] fearing that deserving women students would be overlooked in favour of male relatives who were also eligible for government rehabilitation programmes.[40] By 1990 the share of scholarships awarded to women had risen to one-third (118 women out of a total of 406[41]), well above women's national postgraduate participation rates.

The IODE's position on educating women is fascinating. During the 1920s prominent members who were themselves highly educated had been involved in the instigation of the War Memorial Scholarship. Mary Bollert, who was dean of women at the University of British Columbia and president of the CFUW from 1926 to 1928, Charlotte Whitton and Wilhelmina Gordon were all instrumental. The presence of educated women among the IODE's membership meant that ideas about the education of women which were real concerns of the CFUW during the 1920s were influential in the IODE's work.[42] Yet, overall, for the IODE patriotism came first, and the scholarships were memorials that favoured returned servicemen and topics in line with an 'imperial curriculum'[43] of a kind with the narratives present in the IODE's war memorial pictures and with traditional history, politics, science and medicine. This is to say that the IODE believed in equality between men and women in education, but at the same time had greater faith in the establishment of the educational system than it did in a group such as the CFUW.

CFUW was dedicated to improving the position of women in all areas of the university, from students to academics. Geneva Misener, professor of classics at the University of Alberta, considered gifts and loans a practical way of helping women students into postgraduate education.[44] In 1919 CFUW established a Women's Travelling Scholarship, with a yearly value of $1,000, to be tenable in a British university.[45] Interestingly, although CFUW had the feminist rhetoric, in action it was the IODE that quietly went about awarding War Memorial Scholarships to women. Although the IODE's overarching justification was patriotic, and supportive of dominant constructions of Anglo-Canada, underneath there was a gutsy pro-woman element. By the 1950s, with an imperial curriculum that was losing its rigidity, members of the IODE were able to make stronger demands that men were not to be officially favoured over women.

As the British Empire was transformed into the Commonwealth,[46] the postgraduate scholarship programme adjusted its vision. Whereas the scholarships were initially for topics on Empire history and economy, in 1972 the terms of reference were broadened to include 'any subject vital to the interest of the Commonwealth'.[47] The opportunity ceased to be a pilgrimage to Britain, and the scholarships became tenable in any Commonwealth country, to be used wherever the educational opportunities were of greatest utility to Canada. For the Second War Memorial Scholarships, the same four institutions, London, Cambridge and Oxford Universities, and the London School of Economics, still dominated, receiving over 60 per cent of the scholars, but there was an increasing diversity in the institutions attended by the scholars, with over fifty-five universities in Britain attended up to 1990. The increasing number of scholarships used within Canada signalled a more positive appraisal of the Canadian education system. The University of Toronto received 6 per cent (twenty-three) of the Second War Memorial Scholars. Queen's and McGill Universities, along with the University of Toronto, arguably the more 'established' of the Canada's universities, received the next highest numbers.[48] Through the 1960s, the number of Canadian universities attended by recipients increased. This process mirrored the diversification in the British universities that scholars attended during the 1950s. Such diversification was a further sign of the rejection of a narrow colonial knowledge.

It was the unabashed hope of the IODE that its scholars should become the 'makers of Canada'.[49] It was hoped that they would return home after their studies to become active Canadian citizens. Where possible, the IODE formed networks to find employment suitable for these scholars. Such networks also served to warn against those scholars who did not live up to expectations. Wilhelmina Gordon was not slow to send letters if she thought that unfavourable information about scholars should be made known. In 1931 she wrote to the principal of Manitoba College in Winnipeg, warning him that a candidate for a post at the college was known to have been in debt during his time in Edinburgh, a debt which the IODE had covered for him, and that he had a problem with drink.[50]

Overall, however, praise was heaped upon the IODE War Memorial Scholars, and they have indeed assumed posts of responsibility and leadership in all parts of Canada. Their number includes cabinet ministers, a former speaker of the House, ambassadors to Spain, Morocco and New Zealand, a Canadian trade commissioner in Hong Kong, doctors, psychiatrists, clergymen, lawyers, chief reporters and war correspondents with the Canadian Broadcasting Corporation, and newspaper editors, geographers, historians, archivists, chemists, and others in many facets of industry.[51] The largest number (approximately one-third), have, however, followed careers in higher education. On the surface, these scholars can be perceived as having beautifully fulfilled the ambitions of the IODE. By educating yet other generations in the ways of citizenship, they represent the ultimate in perpetuating the memory and ideal of Canada which the IODE feels it has had a hand in creating. Of course, the IODE has no control over the beliefs of recipients or the direction of their thoughts after receiving a scholarship. Interestingly, some scholars have produced work that critiques the very values espoused by the IODE. This has not become an issue for the IODE, which appears happy to claim some of the credit for scholars in prominent positions, and to leave their politics alone.

The IODE was founded during times of war, and we have seen how the IODE has remembered and enshrined the virtues of Canadian identity through its initiatives during the twentieth century in the memorialization of war. The IODE's War Memorials attempted to ensure a sense of the past and to influence the future people and place of Canada. While emphasizing continuity and tradition in ideology, in practice initiative and innovation have been the order of the day. The IODE has been a step, or even a war, ahead of both the British and the Canadian government in its grave-marking scheme and its bursaries for dependants of the war-dead/veterans and its postgraduate scholarships. It has been skilfully effective in its undertakings, from its gendered position in caring for children through to knowing how to make the most of privileged connections. The subjects, the places of study and the recipients of War Memorial Scholarships all represent the changing production of Canadian identity, demonstrating the transition from mimicking an imperial centre to its standing alone as a nation centered in Canadian space. The IODE has known how to utilize education and encourage young minds to perpetuate imperial and national ideology based upon memorialization.

Notes

1 James Fentress and Chris Wickham, *Social Memory* (Oxford and Cambridge, MA: Blackwell, 1992), 25.
2 See Raphael Samuel, *Theatres of Memory*, vol. 1: *Past and Present in Contemporary Culture* (London and New York: Verso, 1994).
3 See Katie Pickles, 'Edith Cavell – heroine. No hatred or bitterness for anyone?', *History Now*, 3: 2 (1997), 1–8.
4 See Paul Fussell, *The Great War and Modern Memory* (Oxford and New York: Oxford University Press, 1975); and Jay Winter, *Sites of Memory, Sites of Mourning: The Great War in European Cultural History* (Cambridge and New York: Cambridge University Press, 1995).
5 McClintock, *Imperial Leather*, 357. See also Marina Warner, *Monuments and Maidens: The Allegory of the Female Form* (New York: Atheneum, 1985).
6 For a treatment of memorials in Canada, see Brian S. Osborne, 'Canadian nation building: a monumental approach to landscapes of power', Paper presented at the 9th International Conference of Historical Geographers' pre-conference symposium, 'Landscape and identity', 28–30 June 1995, Garden Hotel, Singapore.
7 Robert Shipley, *To Mark Our Place: A History of Canadian War Memorials* (Toronto: NC Press Limited, 1987).
8 Jonathan Vance, *Death So Noble: Memory, Meaning, and the First World War* (Vancouver: University of British Columbia Press, 1997), 208.
9 LPSC, F5012 1934 I34 booklet, *The Imperial Order Daughters of the Empire: Chapters of the Order* (Ottawa, 1934), 47.
10 *Ibid.*, 51.
11 Queen's University Archives (hereafter QUA), Wilhelmina Gordon Collection, Box 4/13 IODE correspondence; NAC RG38, 358. In its 1919 Pension Act the Government of Canada allowed for the continuation to the age of 21 for a child taking a course of instruction.
12 QUA, Wilhelmina Gordon Collection, Box 4/13, IODE correspondence. Dr W. Gordon, 'The First War Memorial: a brief account of its early history' (1954), 1.
13 Desmond Morton and Glenn Wright, *Winning the Second Battle: Canadian Veterans and the Return to Civilian Life 1915-1930* (Toronto: University of Toronto Press, 1987), 53.
14 IODE, *Record of the Post Graduate Scholarship Holders for the Years 1945–1990 of the First and Second War Memorials Instituted by the National Chapter of Canada IODE* (1990), Foreword.
15 See Michael Heffernan, 'For ever England: the Western Front and the politics of remembrance in Britain', *Ecumene*, 2: 3 (1995), 293–323.
16 NAC MG28 I 17, 23, IODE, Open letter to the Regent, officers and members, Toronto 15 September 1919. Signed Annie Bethany McDougald, Laura J. Thompson, Constance J. Laing, all of the national press and publicity committee.
17 LPSC, LP F5012 1945 I34, 'The Imperial Order Daughters of the Empire – what it is and what it does', 10.
18 QUA, Wilhelmina Gordon Collection, Box 4/13, Misc. 1919–1950s.
19 Vance, *Death So Noble*, 240 and 241.
20 NAC MG28 I 17, 23, 8, 'War Memorial Fund 1919'.
21 See Iris Marion Young, *Justice and the Politics of Difference* (Princeton, NJ: Princeton University Press, 1990); and Said, *Culture and Imperialism*.
22 Daniel Francis, *National Dreams: Myth, Memory, and Canadian History* (Vancouver: Arsenal Press, 1997), 20.
23 QUA, Wilhelmina Gordon Collection, Box 5/13, pamphlet concerning canadianization.
24 Details of this part of the War Memorial were introduced in chapter three.
25 May Kertland, *IODE. The Third Twenty-Five Years* (Toronto: G. Best Publishing, 1975), 62. Over the years 1950–65, 293 bursaries were awarded to the value of about $0.5 million.

26 Arnold Whittick, *War Memorials* (London: Country Life Ltd, 1946), 1.
27 Foreword, by Cecilia Furness, national officer and War Memorial secretary, to IODE, *Record of the Post-Graduate Scholarship Holders for the Years 1945–1990*.
28 IODE, *Record of the Post-Graduate Scholarship Holders for the First Twenty Years of the First War Memorial Instituted by the National Chapter of Canada* (1945).
29 QUA, Wilhelmina Gordon Collection, Box 4/13, 21.7.20, 2, letter from Gordon to Miss Laing.
30 *Record of the Post-Graduate Scholarship Holders for the First Twenty Years of the First War Memorial*.
31 QUA, Wilhelmina Gordon Collection, Box 4/13, File M, 1924–26, 18 April 1925, letter to Gordon from Hazel MacMillan, convener of the Prince Edward Island War Memorial committee, 9 May 1925. Correspondence from Gordon to MacMillan.
32 *Ibid.*, IODE, 10 August 1920, Prospect and retrospect, Toronto: IODE national educational committee, 5.
33 For a contemporary general discussion, see J. A. Mangan (ed.), *The Imperial Curriculum: Racial Images and Education in the British Colonial Experience* (London and New York: Routledge, 1993).
34 QUA, Wilhelmina Gordon Collection, Box 4/13, 26 March 1935, letter from James Stuart Martell in response to questions that Gordon had put to students concerning the benefits of overseas study.
35 IODE, *Record of the Post-Graduate Scholarship Holders* (1990).
36 Interview, 27 April 1994: Edmonton, Alberta. The interviewee was an IODE Memorial Scholar in 1924.
37 QUA, Wilhelmina Gordon Collection, Box 4/13, File on bursary holders 1924–27, 18 May 1926. The Provincial Chapter of British Columbia passed a resolution that scholars in Britain needed two years to attain a degree, and the nine annual post-graduate Scholarships would be made biennial and of $2,800 in value.
38 IODE, *Record of the Post-Graduate Scholarship Holders* (1990).
39 NAC MG28 I 17, 11, 30 May 1952, Minutes of a meeting of the War Memorial committee to deal with First War Memorial business at Niagara Falls. 'The question was raised as to whether there was a tendency to award the Post-Graduate Scholarship to the candidate who had seen military service in World War II, on the grounds of sentiment, rather than to the candidate who scholastically showed the most promise.'
40 Morton and Wright, *Winning the Second Battle*.
41 IODE, *Record of the Post-Graduate Scholarship Holders* (1990).
42 See Katie Pickles, 'Colonial counterparts'.
43 See Mangan, *The Imperial Curriculum*, chapter five, for discussion of the imperial curriculum.
44 NAC MG28 I 196, vol. 31, Chronicle, 1931–34.
45 NAC MG28 I 196, Minutes of CFUW 1919 meeting.
46 See W. David McIntyre, *The Commonwealth of Nations: Origins and Impact, 1869–1971* (Minneapolis: University of Minnesota Press, 1977).
47 Kertland, *IODE. The Third Twenty-Five Years*, 62.
48 IODE, *Record of the Post-Graduate Scholarship Holders* (1990).
49 Mrs Detwiler in Foreword to IODE, *Record of the Post-Graduate Scholarship Holders for the First Twenty Years of the First War Memorial* (1945), 2.
50 QUA, Wilhelmina Gordon Collection, Box 4/13, Correspondence 1930–31, 6 March 1931, letter to Principal MacKay, Manitoba College.
51 Kertland, *IODE. The Third Twenty-Five Years*, 63.

CHAPTER SEVEN

Conservative women and democracy: defending Cold War Canada

In 1947 a Canadian cartoonist penned a cartoon during the IODE's National Annual Meeting in Halifax. 'Removing the Red stain – a noble work of mercy' displayed a mother figure sweeping away Communism from her comfortable sphere of apron and broom. In the accompanying article, 'The IODE fights Communism', the national president of the IODE asked C. Bruce Hill of St Catharine's, Ontario, president of the Canadian Chamber of Commerce, what women might do from their family position to fight war? In reply Hill suggested that women as mothers should exercise extreme care as to what their children were taught both inside and outside of the home. To fight Communism, a woman could 'keep herself informed on national and world matters and she can be careful of the organizations she, herself, joins'. On top of that advice it would be useful to teach children 'pride in and loyalty to the traditions of democracy of the British Empire and their application to Canadian life today'.[1]

Such advice illuminates the importance of women to postwar Canadian citizenship. Citizenship was a place that was gendered through an appeal to women's enduring domestic positioning. While the postwar years saw women's place idealized, as wives and mothers women were simultaneously accorded a part to play in promoting good citizenship. The IODE believed that Communism within Canada posed a severe threat to Canadian citizenship, and its women and mothers sought to rigorously 'sweep away the Communist stain'. It did this through its work in the areas of education, media relations, civil defence, immigrant training and citizenship courts. Such work continued the IODE's mission for a British-influenced Canada.

The IODE's reaction to the Cold War reflected a forced reconsideration of Canadian identity. While the IODE promoted democratic principles of progressive conservatism, its methods and its attitude to Communists were influenced by an individualism and a politics more often associated with the USA, and with an ideal of home and motherhood as 'private' gendered spaces. Communist threats to democracy, real or imagined, forced the IODE to consider what was 'Canadian' and to redefine Canada through the difference that it sought to destroy. This process involved moving away from attachments to Britain and towards an identity located in Canadian space. The IODE's work with immigrants and citizenship demonstrated this shift, articulating a clear and confident vision of Canadian citizenship that, although still influenced by Britain, was less dependent on the rapidly devolving Commonwealth. With the increased emphasis on individualism, home and gender played an important part in producing Canadian identity. Masculinist conceptions of democracy, however, have not considered how such spaces were vital components of citizenship.

The new enemy: Communism as a threat to democracy

The assumption of the citizen as male has dominated much of the thinking on Cold War democracy, serving to exclude women from public recognition and to focus their concern upon the separated 'sphere' of 'the home', one that has little or no place in mainstream accounts of the Cold War.[2] To the contrary, historians such as Elaine Tyler May refute divisions between political and family values, and instead reveal connections between gender, family and national politics. During the Cold War the IODE, as a group of conservative women, operated between and across constructed public and private spheres. Caught up in an era in which 'family values' predominated, the IODE evinced women's essential place in the home and their moral influence as mothers. At the same time, the IODE confidently intervened in matters of national and international concern, perceiving a growing threat not only to Canada but to world peace itself: 'Over the entire past decade there has brooded the shadow of imminent catastrophe should a World War develop and our increasing national awareness has been tempered by the tensions of a World divided into mutually suspicious armed camps.'[3] Indeed, so great was the perceived threat that the IODE went into an attacking mode, akin to its activities during the world wars.

Throughout the Cold War the IODE advocated strategic voting as a tactic against Communism. The vote had not been available to members in the early 1900s, but by the 1950s it was a tool that women were keen to utilize. It is worth noting, however, that during this period not all Canadian women had the vote, as native Indian women were still excluded. Not surprisingly, the IODE urged members to vote for progressive conservatism. The reasons for abandoning its hitherto non-partisan stance, and instead urging members to use their votes 'wisely', at once engaged with the constructed public level of politics and the private gendered domestic realm. Indeed, it was perceived that the

> most powerful weapon that Canadian women have today against Communism is *the vote*. Some of us do not realize that we now have more than fifty per cent of the voting power in the Dominion. Think of it! But the mere casting of a vote is not enough. We should have definite information about the candidate for our support – his or her former affiliations and real aims and objects. Failure to make certain about such matters has already made possible the entry of pro-Communists into our parliaments.[4]

It was as women, yet women motivated by concern for the nation, that the IODE abandoned its non-partisan stance. And although times had, since the IODE's beginnings, dramatically changed for women, old ideas were re-presented. For example, on the one hand the language that the IODE used was redolent with Edwardian maternalism, while on the other it was infused with the postwar rhetoric of participatory citizenship. The motion was passed at the1948 National Meeting that as 'immediate concerted action is imperative', every member of the IODE must be 'urged to take an active and intelligent interest in the selection of candidates for Municipal, Provincial and Federal elections and use her vote to influence toward the defeat of Communism'.[5] The following year, members pledged to fight the 'menace of Communism in Canada'. IODE National President McCurdy was quoted as saying: 'Who can measure the power and influence of 32,000 women in Canada, speaking out and acting in unison when they felt that the principles for which they stand are threatened?'[6] The request was reiterated in 1957 by the editor of *Echoes*:

> As every member of the Order is aware, the IODE is non-political and non-sectarian. In these words of comment there is no intention to extol or to condemn any shade of political opinion – other than Communism which we heartily condemn – or any party represented in Parliament ... Let us also make sure that each of us may be equally proud of the part we as individuals play in the fields of municipal, provincial and national government in electing those who will form and carry out the policies that will shape the future destinies of our country and in the training of our children in the responsibilities of citizenship.[7]

There was no place for Communism in the kind of citizenship sought by the IODE. As a women's organization, the IODE expressed concern for children, a concern which had everything to do with politics and was not confined by public and private borders, but one which justified the IODE women's place as mothers in politics.

When women's historians of the postwar era in North America have questioned the image of women's place in the home, right-wing women have thus far been excluded from consideration. Many of the members of the IODE were, in fact, women leading lives closest to the 'suburban ideal' that contributors to *Not June Cleaver*, a study of women and gender in the USA during the postwar years, set out to complicate: they were white middle-class housewives, with time to devote to women's organizations.[8] These were women who upheld conservative family values, who from their beliefs crafted a specifically female anti-Communism. Primarily, the IODE saw Communism as a threat to its conception of democracy, an important defining component of its Canadian identity. Democracy was viewed by the IODE as embedded in government, constitutional monarchy and the right to vote. 'Pure democracy' was 'a society consisting of a number of citizens who assemble and administer the government in person'.[9] It rested upon the four freedoms – freedoms of worship and speech, and freedom from want and fear. The IODE modelled its concept of democracy on its perception of British democracy, and patriotically stated that it was 'owed to the Motherland to keep Canada free'.[10] The words of the provincial president of Ontario in her 1949 annual speech captured that sense of strong attachment to Britain: 'Therefore, may I say that the undeviating purpose of our Order is to foster and maintain our Dominion and maintain for our Dominion and our Empire our way of life, our freedom of choice and, as a matter of fact, all that we connote or imply in our meaning of the word Democracy.'[11] Britain's battered post-Second World War economic position and the movement towards independence of Commonwealth countries were put aside as the IODE glorified British tradition and empire building with statements such as: 'The hall-mark of British justice and British law is indelibly stamped on the parliaments of all free nations everywhere. England has stood alone, defending the gates of freedom with head bloody but unbowed, longer than any other nation, either recorded in history or now extant.'[12] This was hyperbole, considering the aid recently given to Britain in the Second World War, but it had a logic necessary for the continuation of colonial attachments that set Britain apart as the example to be emulated.

The IODE's version of conservatism was backward looking, retaining many of the features of nineteenth-century conservatism, and not displaying the pragmatic components of postwar Canadian conservatism more generally. The IODE's democratic sentiments were grounded in a Tory politics moulded around the time of Canada's confederation. The ideology for this form of democracy was derived from a combination of Bossuet, Burke, Bentham and counter-Reformation Catholicism, eighteenth-century English Tory conservatism, and nineteenth-century English utilitarianism.[13] John Conway notes that 'British conservatism and its expression in Canada in the nineteenth and twentieth centuries are based upon an organic rather than an individualistic concept of society'.[14] This conservative democracy stressed that the goals of society could not be achieved in one generation: 'Change, to be fruitful, must be brought about slowly, so that the desires of one generation will not obliterate its obligations to secure the good for its successors.' In contrast, American liberalism was based upon a belief in unending progress, with Americans placing value on individualism and individuality above community.[15] Whereas American assent had to be constantly renewed, Canadian assent was personified by the monarch and modified as need arose by the crown in Parliament; hence the IODE's continuing emphasis on Canadian constitutional monarchy and its institutions. For all that postwar Canadian conservatism more generally was descended from such politics, it was nevertheless pragmatic and quick in down-playing the British connection.

On the contrary, the IODE consistently expressed clear organic sentiments, emphasizing the importance of training future generations in its construction of Canadian identity. In the Cold War it was against the Communist threat rather than the USA that these beliefs were directed. For example, proselytizing Communists were portrayed as making full use of the comprehensiveness of their doctrine, so that what they preached appeared to be *the* means of putting the world to rights; therein lay the appeal of its missionaries' message. In contrast, the democracy promulgated by the IODE may have seemed to lack such appeal, especially for the young, because it characterized the society in which they had been brought up – it was what they were used to. *Echoes* put the issue in these terms:

> One great difficulty for the mother or the teacher in combating Communist influence is the fact that the Communist missionaries make the one irresistible appeal to the black and white tones of Communism seem to offer a simple, direct answer to 'what's wrong with the world'. In this situation, even the mother finds herself regarded as a reactionary, and her thinking dismissed because she 'belongs to another generation'. And there is another complicating factor: that political science and economics classes did not concern themselves as extensively with Communism in mother's and father's day as they do now ... Democracy is the fruit of many generations of living and experience. Yet Democracy must be presented to the young in a vital, exciting form if they are not to veer off into the modern political pitfalls.[16]

Communists were perceived as threatening women's domain and portraying women who defended 'democratic' values as reactionary. Eradicating Communism was therefore the concern of women. In 1951 in *Echoes* a powerful 'warning' appeared, arguing that 'to break up our free society from within is the main objective of the enemy. Compassion and human feeling are ruthlessly exploited and THE YOUNG ARE UNREMITTINGLY PURSUED'[17] (original emphasis). The warning was directed at the National Federation of Labour Youth which was enlisting youth for apparently 'praiseworthy' purposes, 'the better to receive Communist poison later'.[18] With youth perceived to be under attack, it was an appeal to motherhood that the IODE used to fight Communism.

Postwar maternal politics

The IODE engaged with the perceived 'masculine domain' of democracy and politics not in spite of its status as an organization of women and mothers, but because of that fact. The connection between the space of the home and democracy was clearly put in 1942:

> Democracy, like so many saving graces, has its beginning in the home. Consequently women have a special responsibility. In the home members of the family must learn to live co-operatively; they must learn discipline, tolerance, unselfishness, self-restraint and, above all, consideration for the rights of others. These are the first principles of democracy. Building for democracy is a task for the women of Canada. If we have vision, we shall succeed.[19]

Women were called upon for their qualities as women, to defend and promote democracy. They should do so from their position in the home, defending their families, a frequent appeal made to IODE members during the Cold War. In order to uphold democracy women should exercise their capacity as care givers and moral watchdogs to children and youth. As the editor of *Echoes* alerted the readership in 1951:

> Have you ever wondered how you would behave if any enemy started dropping bombs on Canada and kept dropping them, forcing you and your family and your neighbours to live close to death, perhaps for a matter of years? That is something that did not happen to us in World War I and World War II. But it happened to other people and it is almost certainly that we will have to face if World War III develops. There may be no war – we pray there will not be – perhaps no bombs will fall. Yet today in a grim world, tense with dread, we have the need for clear-eyed courage, steady thinking, unshaken faith. We need civilian morale *now*, war or no war, and we need women able to create and maintain it. We who love Canada can so serve her now.[20]

Through women's capabilities as care givers and nurturers, the task of upholding democracy was theirs. It is interesting that the IODE used maternal identity in support of its politics. At the same time, other North American women, also claiming to be 'ordinary housewives', and who, like IODE members, were largely affluent, white and educated, called for peace in the name of motherhood. Women Strike for Peace began in the USA in 1961 when an estimated 50,000 women walked out of their kitchens and left their jobs to protest against escalating militarism.[21] Like the IODE, they claimed to be saving children, but from nuclear war, not a Communist threat.

The IODE considered youth to be the most vulnerable and likely targets of Communists. Its fear was fuelled by the moral scare and 'delinquency panic' of the 1940s and 1950s.[22] It was the place of IODE members as mothers to intervene and rescue children from Communist influences. Democracy at once had everything to do with the home as well as with the nation. A reprint by *Echoes* of an editorial from the *Vancouver Province* was indicative of the perceived threat to Canadian youth. In this editorial a mother told how she had lost her son:

> From a tractable boy he has become a defiant, unmanageable youngster. All the good old Canadian traditions have gone by the board. Canada, according to him, is a nation of war-mongering capitalists. I am, he says, an ignorant illiterate, when I attempt to argue with him. These children are not old enough to remember when Canada was a sweet and pleasant land. They see their parents harassed by prices and taxation which make even necessities hard to obtain. Communists are appealing to the youth of our country as Hitler appealed to the youth of Germany. Through fun ... parties at which their insidious propaganda can be disseminated. If reputable political parties are doing nothing to catch and hold the loyalty of young Canadians, Communism is. In another four or five years these youngsters will be old enough to vote. God help Canada then![23]

Women's intervention, it was believed, would be most successful through the education of youth. An article in *Echoes* in 1948 stated that the perceived Communist threat to youth was particularly the concern of Canadian women because 'the training of youth, in the home and in the schools, is particularly the responsibility of women. And a heavy responsibility it is.'[24] Fear in the schools was intensified by the belief that North Americans had a complacent lifestyle that left opportunity for the Communist peril to strike. The construction of just who the Communists were had plenty to do with Canada's southern neighbour.

The IODE's notions of democracy were challenged and altered by the Cold War, with important consequences for its construction of

Canadian identity. Arguably, the events of the Cold War led Canada to 'choose' to be positioned next to the USA, turning away from Britain and looking to occupy its own respected place on the world stage.[25] This was a shift away from a stronger colonial attachment to Britain, leading to tension between British democratic values and the values of an American individualism situated across the border. Such tensions were played out in the IODE's definition of the Communist threat and in its methods of 'combating' Communism.

Three major types of Communist, all seen as challenging Canada, were constructed by the IODE: Communists in the Soviet Union; Communists in Canada; and immigrants from countries under Soviet influence. Where the Soviet Union was concerned, the IODE believed it to be at the opposite pole to that of 'British democracy'. 'The Russian State is omnipotent', the IODE argued; individual human beings were unimportant, and 'a Communistic government is inevitably a tyrannical one'.[26] Communism was seen as a force undermining Christianity, the churches and morality. *Echoes* in 1948 published a drawing with the inscription 'An indication of Communist publicity. Communist workmen throw an effigy of Jesus Christ and of the Sacrament into a garbage pit.'[27] This cartoon simultaneously rejected Soviet industrialization and atheism. The presence of a toppled liberty bell indicates that this cartoon was a direct import from the USA. Ironically, it is American republicanism that is under threat here, and not the Canadian body politic. It appears that the cartoon was a hasty import.

The Soviet Union was deemed evil, but who were the Canadian Communists threatening from within? Merrily Weisbord has suggested that 'the mythology of Communism had always been inextricably bound up with the Soviet Union, the prime example of a Communist State'.[28] As was the belief of the Canadian and United States' governments and many other organizations during the Cold War, the IODE equated all progressive organizations with the Soviet Union, thus discrediting and silencing them as traitors. Purported links to the Soviet enemy were sufficient grounds to denounce Canadian Communist Party members, trades unionists and 'peaceniks'. As Whitaker and Marcuse have suggested, the Cold War in Canada had an enormous impact upon progressive indigenous politics, which was 'rendered so difficult by the false choices apparently imposed by the rigidities of the Cold War'.[29]

So powerful an aura did the IODE build up around its imagined enemy, and so great was the fear generated among members, that the Order was not often called upon to define clearly the characteristics of Communists. Rather, in sweeping statements, as was generally the case during the Cold War, it was common in one sentence to uncritically condemn Communists alongside Fascists. For example:

> At one time it was fashionable to dismiss the Communist party throughout the world as a group of blundering malcontents, just as it was once fashionable to tag the National Socialist Party in Germany with the same label. But the Nazis demonstrated that they knew a great deal about introducing propaganda into the education of youth – the Communists are equally expert in this field.[30]

The reference to Nazi Germany solidified the image of Communists as being to the Cold War what Germany was to the Second World War.

The peace and trades union movements in particular fell victim to this generalized attack. For Canada, the Cold War began with the riveting Gouzenko trial, where scientists and Communist politicians were subjected to humiliating detainment and trial after the defection of a Russian cipher clerk, Igor Gouzenko. Gouzenko revealed a supposed Soviet espionage system that was using Canadian civil servants to supply secret and other confidential information concerning atomic power to Soviet intelligence. Twelve Canadians and a British civil servant were detained by the Royal Canadian Mounted Police, and a special Royal Commission was set up.[31] The reverberations for left-wing movements were debilitating.

Further to sparking the attack on Canadian Communists, the Gouzenko affair contributed to the silencing of peace activism.[32] Labelling scientists as Communists, as was done with the Canadian Association of Scientific Workers, was an effective way of calling a halt to the international control of atomic power.[33] Likewise, in the USA, scientists working towards international control of atomic weapons were silenced. The international control movement collapsed; the nuclear arms' race began.[34] As Denis Smith has put it, the Cold War was off to a frightening start and 'fear was malignant: henceforth it paralysed thought, sustained ignorance, and bred intolerance'.[35] The after-shocks of the Gouzenko affair reached all left-wing organizations, as a broad-based highly ideological attack enforced a 'ready acceptance of the logic of guilt by association'.[36] Those with left-leaning politics were not the only ones to suffer. In an era that promoted the home and heterosexual family life as being at the heart of security, those who fell outside of the confines of the nuclear family, especially homosexual women and men, were subject to intensive persecution.[37] Although the Canadian Government and public opinion were sympathetic when Canadian scholar and diplomat Herbert Norman committed suicide in Cairo in 1957, for those deemed 'security risks' because of their politics and/or sexuality there was much 'witch hunting' within the Canadian civil service.[38]

As the IODE was usually quick to emphasize Canada's political differences from the USA, there was the potential for Canadian conservatism, on anti-American grounds, to resist the hysteria of American anti-Communist tactics. Whitaker and Marcuse argue that this possibility did not materialize. Instead, the conservative press tended to strike a generally pro-American line, with anti-Communist arguments well received by conservative Anglo-Canadians. Whitaker and Marcuse argue for a shift in Canadian conservative thinking from anti-Americanism to anti-Communism by 1948. With hindsight, the activities of the IODE, as representative of 'the deepest blue sections of tory opinion' – those with 'empire emotions' – to a certain extent support Whitaker and Marcuse's argument, especially in the tactics used against Communism.[39] Yet in democratic ideology there remained a strong presence of 'British heritage', the influence of which led to a distinct Canadian Cold War identity.

During the Cold War the IODE displayed a strong sense of mission in crushing difference, notably in denouncing the peace movement. Here, a framework of domesticity and gender relations was not always a necessity. A vivid example was the IODE's reaction to the visit of the Very Reverend Hewlett Johnson, the dean of Canterbury. The 'Red Dean' was worrisome because as 'a tireless apologist for the USSR' his cross-country speaking tour of Canada in 1948 'attracted large "respectable" audiences and inspired the formation of groups that became local branches of the Peace Congress'.[40] Sponsored by the Toronto Peace Council, the dean's cross-Canada itinerary included Vancouver, supposedly under the auspices of the Vancouver branch of the Council of Canadian-Soviet Friendship.[41]

The IODE used its influence to try to deny the dean entry to Canada. An emergency meeting of national officers in Toronto resulted in a message to acting Prime Minister Louis St Laurent, describing the dean as 'a supporter of the doctrines of Communism emanating from Russia'.[42] An editorial in the St Catharines's Standard supported the IODE's call, stating: 'The IODE doesn't want him admitted to Canada at all, and that patriotic body of women is quite right. Communism cannot be combated if we entertain and encourage it right at home.'[43] Other newspaper reports called upon supporters of the dean: 'It is profoundly disturbing', reported the Vancouver News Herald, in a statement made by Reverend J. Gregory Lee of St Peter's Anglican Church in Ottawa, 'to find a body like the IODE in company with the Mosley fascist group of Great Britain, who recently sought to prevent the Dean speaking before an East London audience.'[44]

The IODE's reaction to the dean's visit was fuelled by a fear that Communists would infiltrate the Church. Although the IODE prayed for peace, it branded the peace movement as Communist, in contradiction of Canadian democracy. Later, in 1955, the IODE national executive's minutes denounced a 'new Communist snare', warning Canadians not to sign petitions of the Canadian Peace Congress.[45] Siding against the Soviets, the IODE's view was boldly stated in *Echoes*:

HERE IS THE TRUTH: – Ever since 1945 the free West has been endeavouring to outlaw the atom bomb for purposes of war and to reduce progressively all other armaments in the only practicable and indeed possible way, that is by international agreement under the United Nations with impartial international inspection in all countries concerned. The Soviet Union's refusal to accept inspection has been the insuperable barrier to progress in all negotiations so far. A recent suggestion of a Soviet change of attitude on inspection has not yet been converted into a concrete proposal. Meanwhile Soviet propaganda continues to misrepresent the situation, pretending that they alone are prepared to ban atomic weapons. The fact is that Soviet policy has been the only obstacle in the way of world disarmament.[46]

Following this reasoning, Canada had no choice but to support nuclear armament, and supporting peace rallies and international cooperation was futile, treasonous and encouraging to Communism. In 1958 when the United Church tabled a resolution to support a 'ban the bomb' parade around Toronto's streets, the IODE responded that the 'reds' were 'taking in' the churches.[47]

Enemy immigrants and canadianization

Along with Soviets and left-wing Canadians, immigrants as a group were considered Communists or potential Communists. Immigrants from 'red' countries, who would arrive in Canada and spread their anti-democratic ways, were cautioned against. In 1946 the Province of British Columbia IODE tabled a motion that led to the resolution by the national executive:

[B]e it resolved that the Canadian Government, when considering the future immigration policy for Canada, be urged to give preference to settlers of British origin and people of Allied countries, restricting admission of people of enemy countries until such time as Nazi and other anti-democratic doctrines shall have been eradicated, and assurance can be given that such immigrants will subscribe to our democratic ideals.[48]

This is in line with Franca Iacovetta's suggestion that 'responses to new immigrants after the Second World War were still conditioned by strident anti-Communism and an overriding desire to preserve and promote as much as possible the Anglo-Celtic, northern, white 'character' of the Canadian population'.[49] Indeed, the IODE's traditional preference for British immigrants recalled earlier racist positions when it argued that it was owed 'to pioneers of the country that future generations will be predominantly white and predominantly BRITISH'[50] (original emphasis). These sentiments represented Canadian official policy. In 1947 Mackenzie King made the famous, much-quoted, statement that the Government would attempt to foster the growth of the population of Canada through the encouragement of immigration and that 'the people of Canada do not wish, as a result of mass immigration, to make a fundamental alteration in the character of our population'.[51]

Under the 1947 Immigration Act there was practically free entry for people from Britain, Australia, New Zealand, South Africa, Ireland and the United States. Citizens of other, 'non-entry', countries were eligible only if they had special skills that were in demand, as in agriculture, mining, and lumbering, or if they had adequate means for their own support.[52] The skills in demand would permit the taking on of persons displaced by the Second World War, and hence serve the purpose of moving Canada to a more prominent position in international affairs.[53] According to Robert Harney, displaced persons provided ideal, almost chattel, labour, and their recruitment satisfied Canada's reputation 'for high moral purpose among the community of nations and its image of generosity of spirit in providing access to a land of second chance'.[54] In this vein, Canada admitted an increasing number of refugees – between 1946 and 1966 more than 300,000.[55] There were special arrangements for those displaced persons possessing skills in demand, with agriculture and resource labour being high priorities; for example, Polish and Italian ex-servicemen received special treatment on such grounds.[56]

Given the numbers of refugees arriving in Canada following the Second World War, the call for 'British stock' was all the more urgent. The IODE carefully monitored displaced persons and, according to its persistent hierarchies of race, classified the types of occupation to which refugees were most suited. In 1946 the unmarried Polish war veterans, stereotyped as strong and rural, were noted as having been tested for physical fitness and farm experience. Finnish men, associated with the sea and the forests of Scandinavia, were thought to be suited to work in lumber and fishing, with Finnish women, cast as clean and orderly, fit for domestic service.[57]

The IODE was particularly concerned about the arrangements for young displaced women. In 1947, it reported that 2,000 displaced girls, out of a projected 10,000, were due to arrive in Canada. On 19 October 775 persons were due, including 100 girls for domestic service, the rest going into lumber camps in Ontario. After strict medical examinations, the girls would be sent to positions as domestics at prevailing wages for at least one year.[58] The IODE suggested that members canadianize these new arrivals and make arrangements 'for social teaching of our language and facts of our country'.[59] Here the IODE displayed much continuity with its work during the first half of the twentieth century. Although there was a perceived need for protection of immigrant girls, domestic service was still considered to be their ideal occupation. Meanwhile, instruction in the English language and canadianization were the ongoing strategies for assimilation.

The IODE was quick to dissociate groups of Eastern European immigrants to Canada from Communism and quickly aided them in canadianizing. That there was need for such rescue work was a common belief in Canada, one that was advanced by the media. Hungarians, for example, were shown as emigrating to escape the dreaded clutches of Communism. A newspaper report in 1956 stated: 'Hungarians hate the colour red, symbol of Russian oppression. This is one foible discovered by social groups working with the largest contingent of refugees yet arrived from the Communist-suppressed country. Red means Russian, and the refugees don't want to be confused with their oppressors.'[60] In Alberta, the Saint Margaret of Scotland Chapter IODE, founded in 1955, demonstrated the efforts made by the IODE to canadianize newcomers from Communist countries. With an all-Hungarian membership, the chapter made a tenuous yet bold connection between Saint Margaret and Hungary. There were contested claims as to the identity of Margaret, but linking Hungary and Scotland emphasized the similarities between the two 'heritages' and legitimized the place of the Hungarian 'new' Canadians.[61] Chapter members' activities in canadianizing immigrants included acting as interpreters for immigration authorities, working at the emergency clothing bank, and assisting with English classes. Through the Red Cross, the chapter supplied medicine to Hungary, and during the Hungarian Uprising they met each group of refugees arriving in Calgary.[62]

It was common for the IODE to portray immigrants from Eastern Europe as fleeing from the perils of Communism to the democracy and freedom of Canada, where complacent citizens took democracy 'for granted'. This problem of complacency was articulated in a 1948 statement sponsored by the special IODE committee set up to study ways and means of combating Communism:

> The trouble is, most of us take democracy for granted. The young men and women coming into Canada these days from the displaced persons

camps of Europe don't take democracy for granted. Some of the young women who have become domestics in Canadian homes were daughters of well-to-do families, university-educated, products of cultured homes. They were hunted out of those homes, they lost their families because of totalitarianism. That they were rescued at all is because of democracy – democracy which won the war and now is sending aid to the suffering.[63]

As the IODE had sent aid to Europe during the First and Second World Wars to fight the Axis powers, it afterwards sent aid to fight Communism.[64]

The IODE was involved with every stage of the process for integrating immigrants from arrival to full citizenship. A statement at the National Meeting in 1959 by the immigration and citizenship convenor ran: 'I cannot stress strongly enough the term integration. In it lies the clue to the successful absorption into Canada of the immigrants who come to our shores, and to their happiness in their new homeland. Our work must thus be directed toward facilitating and hastening this process of integration.'[65] As Canada became central to the IODE's vision, there was, as well as the importance of 'skills', a clearer and more important emphasis on citizenship values. Out of the perceived threats posed by the Cold War, the IODE was forced to articulate a Canadian identity, grounded in Canadian space. The IODE began to give more attention to Canadian values than to perceived racial origins.

With the diminished importance of the turn-of-the-century-constructed racial hierarchy, the potential for the canadianization of all immigrants increased, and when combined with an articulated sense of Canadian identity, together with the sense of Communist threat, there was much work to be done. In 1951, for example, the IODE was instrumental in setting up the publication *Canadian Scene*, a bimonthly non-profit information service which distributed press releases in the languages of the major immigrant groups. IODE members Mrs Osler and Mrs Jennings were acting on fears that foreign-language newspapers were teaching Communist doctrine[66] to 'the tens of thousands of Europeans who enter Canada each year'.[67] The immigrants, it argued, were regarded by Communists as 'fertile ground for their ideological distortions', and *Canadian Scene* was created to provide an alternative – 'a clear and interesting picture of what is going on in this country, emphasizing the institutions of democracy and inculcating a feeling of national pride in their new homeland'.[68] In an attempt to control the ethnic press, 'as a perfect means for creating good Canadian citizens', *Canadian Scene* allowed the IODE to exert a degree of control over the content of immigrants' papers and to re-formulate Canadian identity.[69]

The articulation of a Canada-centered identity also emerged in the IODE's work in welcoming immigrants. The initial port contact provided the opportunity to combine welfare work with canadianization, and the IODE used the demand for its gendered work to hand out literature. In the late 1950s, for example, 992 'new' Canadians entering Canada through the Port of Saint John, New Brunswick, were met by IODE members who offered flags, treats, toys, books, socks and mittens to the children.[70] In 1955, Mrs G. L. Hamilton of Windsor, Ontario, national immigration and canadianization convenor, claimed that in the previous year members spent 2,030 hours working at the docks. They handed out 1,204 lbs of biscuits, served 65,000 cups of coffee and 25,280 glasses of milk.[71] The objective of this work was that 'the Daughters of the Empire, as first ranking women's patriotic organization, can and should by example awaken every Canadian citizen to the contribution they can make towards building a strong and noble national future through Assimilation and Canadianization'.[72] From the end of the Second World War through to the end of the 1960s adults were given booklets such as 'Ten steps to Canadian citizenship' and 'This Canada of ours', 500 copies of which were produced for the IODE by the Royal Bank of Canada.[73] At this time, the reading matter was approved by, and often produced in collaboration with, federal government. In 1953 'close liaison' was kept with the Department of Citizenship and Immigration, in Ottawa. The IODE saw its position as 'providing the medium for the distribution of government literature prepared by it for the newcomer'.[74] Work at the ports and stations of Canada continued as a staple activity of local IODE chapters until aviation took over. It was not until the 1959 National Meeting that the suggestion was made that the IODE should try to 'cover the airports'.[75] New technology was bringing the IODE's days of port and station welcomes with coffee, milk, biscuits and patriotic literature to an end.

Through its citizenship work, the IODE was promoting harmonious family life. The provision of home comforts and arranging for the individual 'adoption' of some families may have been left to women's voluntary labour, but happy families were considered central to national well-being. In a 1966 address to Toronto's Saint George Chapter, Dr Robert Kreem, social worker and director of the International Institute, an agency for immigrant aid, emphasized the importance of family as well as financial comfort in the adjustment of immigrants to life in Canada.[76] In the postwar years, along with other women's organizations such as the YWCA and the WCTU, the IODE continued to support the integration of immigrants into Canadian home life. The IODE swept up after immigrant families which were unable to fend for themselves. In one instance, a Toronto chapter paid the grocery, gas and heating bills of a young Portuguese mother whose husband was in a Toronto hospital suffering from tuberculosis.[77] Canada, it was believed, could only benefit from propping up immigrant families in the absence of the male parent, supporting the status quo and fostering peaceful family life.

In the 1950s citizenship courts became a focal point of IODE efforts. As an example of typical chapter activities for the lead-up to these courts, in a 1955 meeting of Calgary's municipal chapter Mrs C.E. Gray spoke on the work being done with new Canadians. A Miss Halstead had offered to teach the new Canadians basic English, and Mrs Marshall was to assist by serving coffee during the lessons. Plans were also being made to improve the courthouse procedure when new Canadians acquired their citizenship. Books and Christmas cards were still needed, and the Rupert Brooke Chapter had donated six pictures to the reception centre.[78] In canadianizing new citizens, education and the English language were considered vital.[79] Through the contact provided in the preparation for a citizenship court, the IODE was able to give English lessons and teach 'Canadian values'. The IODE helped immigrants with preparation for court, in filling out citizenship forms where there was no official help,[80] and held classes with new applicants on the rights and privilege of being a Canadian citizen.[81]

At the citizenship courts the IODE created a special place in the post-ceremony receptions. Its stated aim was to provide new Canadians with an experience such that they might 'remember the day on which [they were] given ... citizenship not as a humdrum one on which [they] had to attend at court, but as a proud, bright and festive milestone in [their] life'.[82] The IODE felt that it was fulfilling its mission when individuals wrote to the Order to say, for example: 'My wife and I will never forget the wonderful reception we had from the IODE the day we took our citizenship. The warmth and kindness of that reception will have a great influence on us for the rest of our lives.'[83]

In citizenship court receptions the IODE negotiated between the spaces of refreshments and citizenship. In return for its gendered catering services, the IODE was permitted to hand out patriotic propaganda. Amongst the greeting cards, calendars and maple-leaf pins distributed in New Brunswick during the 1960s were tea cups and saucers with the IODE crest on them, with the purpose of triggering drinkers' memories as to the message of the IODE.[84] In Saint Andrews, in 1966, the Passamaquoddy Chapter presented each of six new Canadians with a crested cup and saucer, and, centred on the refreshment table, a large cake covered with small Union Jacks.[85] Overall, the courts represented a festive and proud moment for the IODE and

Canadian identity. It was an identity that, although firmly influenced by Britain, was now produced in Canadian space.

Part of this more confident Canada-centered identity can be read from the certificates of naturalization that were handed out at citizenship ceremonies. Figure 7.1 is one of the certificates given out during the 1940s in New Brunswick. The responsibilities and privileges of citizenship were more clearly articulated in the post-Second World War years than previously. Yet there was no sense of conflict with the British tradition or recognition of French Canada, and no indication of the move to American individualism which appeared, as we will see, in other areas of the IODE's work. Here the British body politic of constitutional monarchy and the 'ancient liberties of the British peoples' were articulated.

Ironically, the IODE's confidence came at a time when the percentage of British immigrants in Canada's total immigrant intake continued to decline. According to Anthony Richmond, of the 2.5 million immigrants who entered Canada between 1946 and 1965, one-third were from the United Kingdom. The number of British immigrants reached its peak in 1957, after which it was eclipsed by other groups.[86] Furthermore, in situating Canadian identity in North America, the IODE was employing anti-Communist strategies of the USA to uphold these British-based democratic values.

Combating Communism USA-style

The IODE's tactics for combating Communism were heavily influenced by the USA's. In 1948 the IODE set up a special committee to 'combat Communism'. Made up of representatives from four of the major committees of the Order – the national educational, Empire study, *Echoes* and film committees – this task assigned to this new committee was to make 'an intensive study of the whole subject of Communism and to disseminate, as much as possible, correct information to members of the Order'.[87] Despite its ardent statements, such as 'we who believe in Democracy are honestly shocked at the regimentation of minds and affront to human dignity imposed upon citizens of dictator governed states, whether Communist, fascist or modern feudal in form',[88] the IODE's tactics bore a striking resemblance to those that the IODE accused Communists of using. 'The Alert Service', for example, which was run from a Toronto office, was an IODE-funded service started in 1950, with the intention of 'helping Canadians to equip themselves to meet the propaganda and infiltration efforts of Communists'.[89] In this office Marjorie Lamb was responsible for the writing and printing of 'alerts': 'pamphlets written in plain

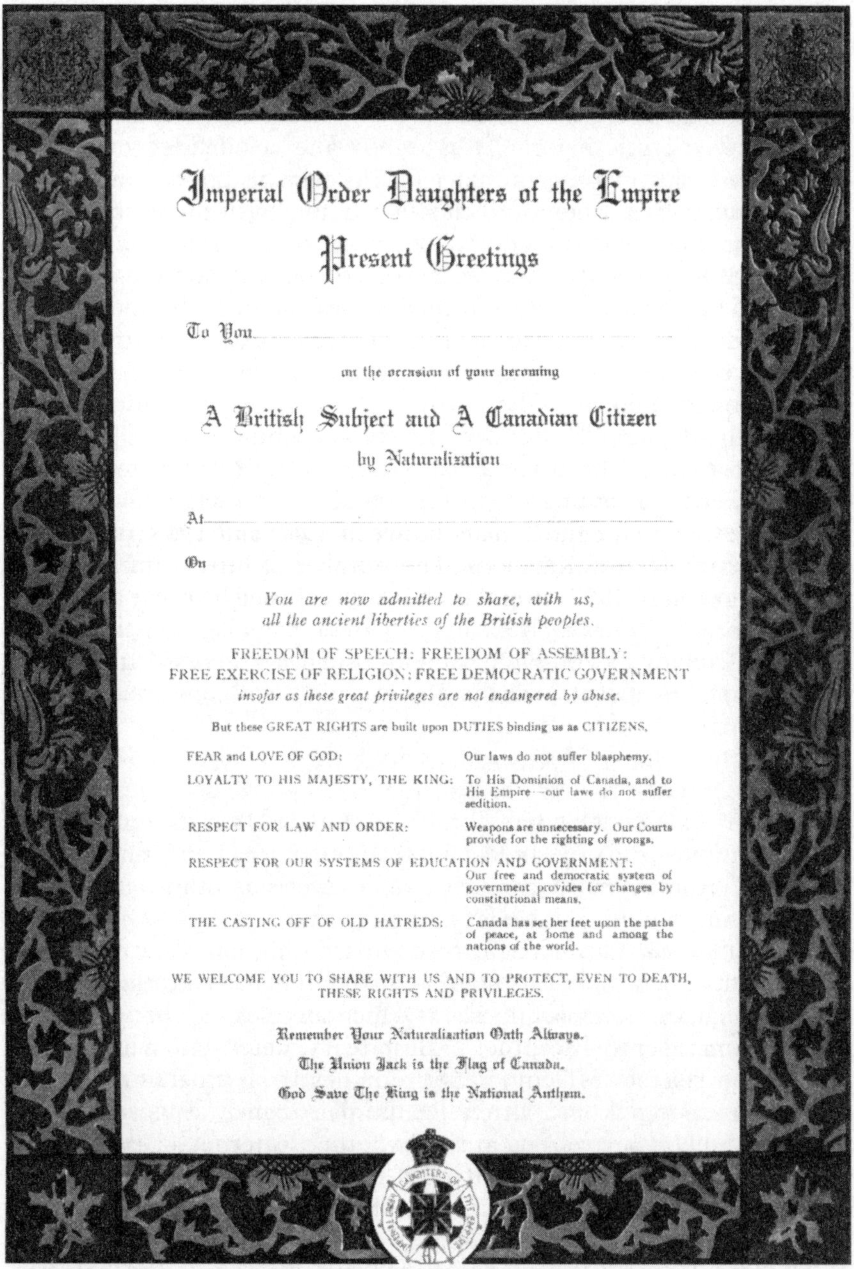

Imperial Order Daughters of the Empire

Present Greetings

To You ....

on the occasion of your becoming

A British Subject and A Canadian Citizen

by Naturalization

At ....

On ....

You are now admitted to share, with us,
all the ancient liberties of the British peoples.

FREEDOM OF SPEECH: FREEDOM OF ASSEMBLY:
FREE EXERCISE OF RELIGION: FREE DEMOCRATIC GOVERNMENT
insofar as these great privileges are not endangered by abuse.

But these GREAT RIGHTS are built upon DUTIES binding us as CITIZENS.

FEAR and LOVE OF GOD:	Our laws do not suffer blasphemy.
LOYALTY TO HIS MAJESTY, THE KING:	To His Dominion of Canada, and to His Empire—our laws do not suffer sedition.
RESPECT FOR LAW AND ORDER:	Weapons are unnecessary. Our Courts provide for the righting of wrongs.
RESPECT FOR OUR SYSTEMS OF EDUCATION AND GOVERNMENT:	Our free and democratic system of government provides for changes by constitutional means.
THE CASTING OFF OF OLD HATREDS:	Canada has set her feet upon the paths of peace, at home and among the nations of the world.

WE WELCOME YOU TO SHARE WITH US AND TO PROTECT, EVEN TO DEATH, THESE RIGHTS AND PRIVILEGES.

Remember Your Naturalization Oath Always.

The Union Jack is the Flag of Canada.

God Save The King is the National Anthem.

Figure 7.1 Post-Second World War IODE citizenship certificate

English to keep Canadians accurately and constantly informed about the policies and operations of Communism, and to devise and encourage sound methods of combating Communist subversive above-ground tactics in Canada'.[90] Marjorie Lamb was written about as being 'both nationally and internationally recognised as a qualified expert on Communist above-ground activity in this country and on methods of countering it'.[91] A trained interior decorator, with an education in Canada, England and France, and former president of Altrusa International, she was reported to have developed her momentum for combating Communism in 1926 while she was studying at the Sorbonne in Paris.[92] The alerts took the form of simply typed texts of approximately four pages, which could be readily copied. Titles in 1962 included 'Communism and you', 'Communist organizations', 'Communist literature and propaganda' and 'Conspiratorial Communism'.[93] The IODE was active in distributing the alerts nation-wide, first to its own members, for discussion at meetings, then to school libraries, church groups and industries. At election times it was anticipated that members would distribute the alerts to areas with Communist candidates.[94] It appears that the IODE's ideas for these alerts came directly from the USA. Guy Oakes has written about 'Alert America' and the 'Alert America Convoy', a comprehensive information service that distributed pamphlets, dramatized the Soviet threat and convinced Americans that civil defence was necessary for survival.[95]

IODE propaganda, while overall emulating that of the USA, simultaneously forced the IODE to consider and define more clearly than previously what constituted 'Canadian'. The IODE was quick to recognize the power of the media in getting its ideas across. In 1948, National President Mrs New set out four objectives of the IODE with regard to the 'complete eradication of Communism in Canada'.[96] The IODE wanted the Government to make information about Communist activities available to the press and to translate information for foreign language newspapers. The IODE recommended that members across Canada set up listening committees to 'determine whether the cause of democracy is being undermined by radio programmes', and the CBC was urged to 'make fuller use of commentators and newscasters who will impress upon the public a greater realization of the menace of Communism'.[97] With its history of encouraging British-influenced Canadian arts and culture, the IODE was active in submitting a brief to the 1951 Royal Commission on National Development in the Arts. Meanwhile, at the local chapter level school prizes in arts and music continued across the country.

Attempts to influence the media were made by the IODE throughout the 1950s. In 1955 the *Edmonton Journal* reported that the IODE was 'out to combat communism in Canada'. The paper reported that, at its National Annual Meeting in Winnipeg, the IODE had decided that it wanted the CBC to broadcast fuller reports on Communist activities to Canadians.[98] In 1957, the special committee to combat Communism was re-titled the 'democratic action committee'. Its purpose was 'to mould the thinking of our people along democratic ways and thereby instil true patriotism'.[99] The goal was to be achieved through comic books and cartoon stories dealing with Communism (similar to then-popular versions of biblical stories in comic-book form); youth programmes would work through schools.[100] In 1959, the IODE was still voicing its opinion that there was not enough awareness of propaganda that threatened Canadian institutions: 'Books, press, radio, TV, stage and screen advertising, and even on occasion the pulpit have become the tools of propaganda. While we worry about survival in case of atom bomb or guided missile attack, we may scarcely be conscious of the danger we run of losing our precious right of independent judgment.'[101] Pushing for Canadian content was all the more urgent, given the pertinence of Whitaker and Marcuse's observation that, at the time, 'Canadians' images of current events were strongly defined by pictures and voices produced by American and British companies (sometimes with short Canadian features tacked on)'.[102]

In defining 'Canadian heritage', entrenched aspects of the British body politic and Canadian conservatism were upheld. One example of the IODE taking the initiative in broadcasting such pro-democratic content was in a patriotic radio series made in New Brunswick. In 1957, Mrs F. L. Miller, as part of New Brunswick IODE's Canadian Heritage Programme, organized a series of broadcasts around the topic of 'Canadian heritage'. It was the intention of the producers of this series to 'awaken the people of New Brunswick to a new consciousness of the freedoms and traditions which they are privileged to enjoy: freedoms and traditions which are becoming priceless in the twentieth century'.[103] Present in this broadcast was the intention to 'keep fast the ideals of British Democracy in New Brunswick'.[104] The broadcasts were centred around allegiances 'to the Crown of England and the justice, freedoms, and responsibilities it represents'.[105] The five-minute radio talks were given by 'respected' citizens, such as the lieutenant-governor of New Brunswick speaking, as 'the Queen's representative in New Brunswick', on 'The British Commonwealth and Canadian defence'; the premier speaking on 'The privilege of the vote in a democracy'; and the chief justice speaking on 'What British law has meant to New Brunswick'. An historical geographer discussed 'Our maritime heritage: a basis for a sound economy'.[106] In keeping with the

IODE's alignment with Britain, such a programme had much more in common with other parts of the Commonwealth than it did with the democracy of Canada's southern neighbour.

Civil defence

It was in the IODE's involvement in civil defence that there should have come the clearest re-alignment away from British influences and towards those of the USA. Because of its location in the home, separate from the public masculine spaces of citizenship, civil defence is largely absent in mainstream accounts or discussions of the Cold War. The success of civil defence, however, depended upon its ability to show the vital interdependence of home and national defence. As Guy Oakes argues, civil defence was constructed as the moral obligation of every household and 'construed the practices demanded by family preparedness as civic virtues indispensable to the American way of life'.[107] In contrast to British Heritage Programmes, which were representative of progressive conservatism, American civil defence was an individualistic activity, which tied national security to the character of family life and family values.

Elaine Tyler May has noted the usefulness of women's traditional role in American civil defence.[108] It was believed that continuing to cope in domestic settings after a nuclear war involved those household tasks, such as cooking, that were deemed women's work. Caring and nursing were other traditionally female activities to which women were expected to contribute both in the home and in the nuclear shelter. During the Cold War the threat of nuclear war was constantly conveyed to the American public, and its ability to survive such a war as depending upon American family values. Across the border in Canada, the IODE was a strong supporter of Canadian government civil defence programmes. In 1955 the National Chapter established civil defence liaison officers at the provincial, municipal and primary levels. The liaison officers attended special courses at the Canadian Civil Defence College at Arnprior, Ontario, on diverse topics which involved both women's and men's work. The tasks were general welfare, emergency clothing, emergency feeding, emergency lodging, registration and inquiry procedures, firefighting, radio monitoring, knots and casualty handling, personal services, evacuation, transport, chaplaincy, maintenance, recreation, medical services, supply, communication, care of pets, and personnel.[109] Gender identity was sometimes an important part of the IODE's contribution to civil defence. On the ground, the tasks that the IODE took an active part in were predominantly those considered to be women's work. In a letter to convenors,

IODE National Civil Defence Liaison Officer Mrs Osler, with substantial Second World War experience, said: 'There is one phase of civil defence training which no housewife or mother should overlook – basic home nursing. This Course is being taught by St John['s] Ambulance and the Canadian Red Cross.'[110]

Civil defence, according to a 1955 advertisement in *Echoes*, was 'a common sense way of dealing with any community disaster'. IODE members were urged to learn to do everything that they could to protect their own lives and the lives of their families. As citizens they should make sure that local civil defence organizations were strong and active.[111] In emphasizing the home, the IODE was arguably adopting American virtues of self-determination, personal responsibility and self-help. These were virtues believed to be anchored in the family –'the primary locus of their inculcation and practice' and the location of the 'moral structure' and the 'spiritual strength' of American home life.[112]

To explain the IODE's participation in an individualistic, American-influenced, civil defence as representing Canada's shift from a British colony to a nation situated in North America is not an adequate interpretation of the Order's involvement in civil defence. Canada's civil defence was distinctively 'Canadian', and the IODE's prominent position in civil defence was based upon its participation in the Second World War. This was a participation that placed work for the common good of community, nation and Empire as of prime importance, with everyone banding together to beat the foe. Such a discourse was very different from the Cold War emphasis on personal fear and individual preparedness. It was the IODE's work in the Second World War that stood it in good stead to help out during the Cold War. Mrs Osler and Mrs C. L. Brown represented the Order at an emergency clothing course in Arnprior in 1954. Out of the fourteen representatives in attendance, there was only one other woman.[113] The value of having the competent women of the IODE involved was recognized by Federal Co-ordinator Major-General Worthington, who noted: 'Since the Imperial Order Daughters of the Empire has been actively engaged in the collection and shipping of clothing over a period of years, it is natural to believe that the members of the Order will not only be vitally interested in participating in this phase of the Canadian Civil Defence programme but, also, will be able to contribute a valuable back-log of practical experience.'[114] While the work of the IODE was gendered, preparing to defend Canada came first. The IODE was held in such high regard not primarily because its members were wives and mothers, but because of their grounding in the British body politic, in progressive conservatism and defence of the nation.

Canadian civil defence was a unique brand. Unlike the USA's programme, however, Canadian civil defence was communitarian, pragmatically stressing 'community' above the individual home. This was evident from its emphasis on the importance of huge civil defence exercises, than on individuals securing the safety of their homes. Mrs Mitchie, wife of the Canadian governor-general and herself the Alberta provincial civil defence liaison officer for the IODE, associated the civil defence movement with the British body politic. Commenting on 'Operation Lifesaver', a mock evacuation of 40,000 people from Calgary in September 1955, she summed up the IODE's place in civil defence: 'Across Canada, many members of the Imperial Order Daughters of the Empire are participating in Civil Defence activities. The Order has always sought to further the national security. Here is a vital service in which many more of our members could make a valuable contribution.'[115]

National security through national community was the key to Canadian civil defence. The composition of national community operated along gendered terms. During 'Operation Lifesaver' IODE chapters in Calgary worked as units in a variety of tasks, from members who were nurses assisting at welfare stations to 'those who had taken special Civil Defence courses [and] were in their places at the registration tables or at the emergency feeding station'.[116] In this collaboration outside of the home, uniting as a nation to defend the nation was the major emphasis, and not at-home individual preparedness.

During the Cold War, the IODE's response to perceived threats to Canada caused a shift whereby colonial attachments weakened and there was a move to a focus on Canadian space. This shift was influenced by diverse ideologies from Britain and the practices of the USA. Gender was integral in both the identification and combating of the enemy. In a period remembered for its harsh treatment of difference, both personal and political, the IODE supported the status quo, its members promoting the conservatism of the era. For all that women's position in society was vastly different from what it had been at the turn of the century, the importance of maternal identity took on a continued, and specifically postwar dimension, as women's domain of home and children was believed to be under threat. While the IODE articulated British sentiments, at the same time it was the tactics of the USA that were adapted to fight Communism. It was out of the threats believed to be posed by Communists that the IODE articulated a clear vision of Canadian citizenship. That vision was still based upon British principles and Anglo-Celtic superiority, but was more encompassing in emphasizing the ability of immigrants to assimilate over their perceived racial origins. The Cold War forced a serious engagement with Canadian defence and nation building in the Canadian north. That arena is the subject of the next chapter.

Notes

1 *Echoes*, 192 (autumn 1948), 8.
2 For an example see Reg Whitaker and Gary Marcuse, *Cold War Canada: The Making of a National Insecurity State, 1945–1957* (Toronto: University of Toronto Press, 1994).
3 Editorial, *Echoes*, 231 (summer 1958), 3.
4 Mary A. Pease, 'Our threatened values', *Echoes*, 193 (Christmas 1948), 13.
5 *British Columbia Weekly* (New Westminster), 14 July 1948.
6 *Daily Colonist* (Victoria, British Columbia), 29 May 1949.
7 Editorial, *Echoes*, 228 (autumn 1957), 3.
8 Joanne Meyerowitz (ed.), *Not June Cleaver: Women and Gender in Postwar America, 1945–1960* (Philadelphia: Temple University Press, 1994).
9 *Echoes*, 191 (summer 1958), 23.
10 Mrs Cecil L. Brown, national convener of the Empire and world affairs committee, 'This perilous interval of peace', *Echoes* 214 (spring 1954), 24.
11 IODE Ontario provincial headquarters, Hamilton, 1949 Minutes Ontario Provincial Chapter IODE, 10. Provincial President Mary Brown.
12 Brown, 'This perilous interval of peace', *Echoes*, 214 (spring 1954), 24.
13 W. L. Morton, *The Canadian Identity*, 2nd edn (Madison: University of Wisconsin Press, 1972), 86.
14 John Conway, 'An adapted organic tradition', *Daedalus: Journal of the American Academy of Arts and Sciences*, 117: 4 (1988), 381–96.
15 *Ibid.*, 381–3.
16 'Communism and the Canadian woman', *Echoes*, 190 (spring 1948), 5–6.
17 *Echoes*, 203 (summer 1951), 15.
18 *Ibid.*
19 Mrs J. D. Detwiler, *Echoes*, 168 (autumn 1942), 44.
20 Editorial, *Echoes*, 202 (spring 1951), 3.
21 Amy Swerdlow, *Women Strike for Peace: Traditional Motherhood and Radical Politics in the 1960s* (Chicago and London: University of Chicago Press, 1993).
22 Franca Iacovetta, 'Parents, daughters, and Family Court intrusions into working-class life', in Franca Iacovetta and Wendy Mitchinson (eds), *On the Case: Explorations in Social History* (Toronto: University of Toronto Press, 1998), 312–37.
23 'Kidnapped by Communism', letter to the editor of the Vancouver *Daily Province*, quoted in *Echoes*, 193 (Christmas 1948), 12–13.
24 'Communism and the Canadian woman', 5.
25 See Denis Smith, *Diplomacy of Fear: Canada and the Cold War, 1941–1948* (Toronto: University of Toronto Press, 1988). Instead of being dictated to by the USA, Smith emphasizes Canada's 'choice' of action during the Cold War.
26 'Communism and the Canadian woman', 5–6.
27 *Ibid.*
28 Merrily Weisbord, *The Strangest Dream: Canadian Communists, the Spy Trials, and the Cold War*, 2nd edn (Montreal: Vehicule Press, 1994), 215.
29 Whitaker and Marcuse, *Cold War Canada*, argue (p. xi): 'Forces "bolstered" tended to be the forces of wealth and power; those that it undermined tended to be the elements of potential opposition to wealth and power.'
30 'Communism and the Canadian woman', 5–6. This conflation of political perspectives other than the IODE's was a static strategy throughout the Cold War. An *Echoes* editorial stated: 'We who believe in Democracy are honestly shocked at the regimentation of minds and affront to human dignity imposed upon citizens of dictator governed states, whether Communist, fascist or modern feudal in form. We

are convinced that we have compete freedom of judgment and expression and reasonably limited freedom of action', *Echoes*, 236 (autumn 1959), 3.

31 Whitaker and Marcuse, *Cold War Canada*, 27; see also Robert Bothwell and J. L. Granatstein (eds), *The Gouzenko Transcripts: The Evidence Presented to the Kellock–Taschereau Royal Commission of 1946* (Ottawa: Deneau Publishers and Company Ltd, 1982).

32 *Ibid.*, 37. Whitaker and Marcuse argue: 'International control of the atomic bomb and international access to the research that had produced the bomb was central.' See also Paul S. Boyer, *By the Bomb's Early Light: American Thought and Culture at the Dawn of the Atomic Age* (New York: Pantheon, 1985).

33 Merrily Weisbord, *The Strangest Dream*, 153. Weisbord writes that 'it would be decades before other broad-based lobbies for the international control of atomic power would dare to speak out'.

34 Boyer, *By the Bomb's Early Light*, 106.

35 Smith, *Diplomacy of Fear*, 236.

36 Whitaker and Marcuse, *Cold War Canada*, 110, 184.

37 Elaine Tyler May, *Homeward Bound: American Families in the Cold War Era* (New York: Basic Books, 1988), 94.

38 See Gary Kinsman, '"Character weakness" and "fruit machines": towards an analysis of the anti-homosexual security campaign in the Canadian Civil Service', *Labour/Le Travail*, 35: spring (1995), 133–62.

39 Whitaker and Marcuse, *Cold War Canada*, 263–64.

40 *Ibid.*, 366.

41 'IODE would halt visit of Red Dean', *Vancouver News Herald*, 27 October 1948.

42 'IODE asks Ottawa to bar Red Dean', *Varsity*, 27 October 1948.

43 Editorial, 'Veto is justified', *St Catharine's Standard*, 28 October 1948.

44 'Cleric hits IODE move to ban "Red Dean" tour', *Vancouver News Herald*, 29 October 1948. The *British Columbian* (New Westminster), 30 October 1948, drew further attention to the hypocricies of the IODE's reasons for seeking to ban the dean: 'Moreover, the implication – that the ordinary Canadian is not to be trusted to make his own selection of ideologies – is an indirect denial of the validity of the democratic theory.' Student newspapers were even more blunt. The University of British Columbia student newspaper the *Daily Ubyssey* (Vancouver), 3 November 1948, reported that the IODE, through its campaign, was inadvertently serving as a good publicist for the dean. Meanwhile, the 9 November 1948 editions of *Varsity* and the *McGill Daily*, the University of Toronto and McGill University student newspapers, accused the IODE of infringing upon the very tenets of democracy that it claimed to promote: the freedoms of speech and association. In their duplicate editorial, 'Is free speech a menace?', the papers stated that 'the IODE, which prides itself on its British Connection, might be surprised to learn that a soapbox in London's Hyde Park offers more freedom of expression than is found in IODE circles'.

45 NAC MG28 I 17, 7, 11, 115, February 1955. The IODE's information comes from the Alert Service, which claims to have got it from the *Canadian Tribune*, a Communist paper which it was monitoring. It announced that the petition was headed 'Appeal against the preparation for atomic war'.

46 *Echoes*, 218 (spring 1955), 7.

47 *Sudbury Daily Star*, 3 June 1958.

48 NAC MG28 I 17, 7, 29 May 1946.

49 Franca Iacovetta with Paula Draper and Robert Ventresca (eds), *A Nation of Immigrants: Women, Workers and Communities in Canadian History, 1840s–1960s* (Toronto: University of Toronto Press, 1998), 449.

50 NAC MG28 I 17, 183, 9 October 1946.

51 Anthony Richmond, *Post-War Immigrants in Canada* (Toronto: University of Toronto Press, 1967), 3. Freda Hawkins thinks that Mackenzie King's statement was unstartling, low key, and designed to 'preserve heritage'. Freda Hawkins, *Critical Years in Immigration: Canada and Australia Compared* (Montreal and Kingston: McGill–Queen's University Press, 1989), 36.

52 NAC MG28 I 17, 7, 8, 10 September 1947, National Executive Minutes. There were offices in the United Kingdom, and throughout Europe, South Africa and South America. In Germany there was co-operation with international refugee organizations for persons from displaced persons' camps. There was no provision for 'Oriental' immigration, except for wives and children of Canadian citizens of Chinese origin.

53 'IODE terms immigration "moral obligation" of Canada', *Vancouver News-Herald* (British Columbia), 29 May 1946. The article stated: 'A new policy of immigration, based on moral obligation to suffering countries and increased prosperity to Canada, has been suggested to the Dominion Government, Miss D. V. Taylor, of Ottawa, told the 46th annual meeting, National Chapter IODE, today.'

54 Robert F. Harney, 'So great a heritage as ours', in *If One Were to Write a History: Selected Writings* (Toronto: Multicultural History Society of Ontario, 1991), 333.

55 Richmond, *Post-War Immigration in Canada*, 15.

56 *Ibid.*, 7. In 1946 Order-in-Council 3112 provided for the admission from the United Kingdom and Italy of ex-servicemen from the Polish armed services. These were single men who agreed to remain in agricultural employment for a minimum period of two years. In all, 4,527 came to Canada under the scheme.

57 NAC MG28 I 17, 7, 6 November 1946.

58 NAC MG28 I 17, 7, 8 October 1947, National Executive Minutes. The young women were to be sent to Charlottetown, Saint John, Moncton, Montreal, Ste Agathe, Kitchener, Belleville, Ottawa, Oakville, Toronto, Winnipeg, Calgary and St Boniface.

59 *Ibid.*

60 *Daily Sentinel Review* (Woodstock, Ontario), 12 December 1956.

61 Glenbow Archives (hereafter GBOW), M 7127, File 59 IODE. According to one story Margaret was born in Scotland in 1045, the daughter of Gisela, wife of Saint Stephen of Hungary; she became known as the patron saint of Hungary and Scotland. A miscellaneous cutting from the scrapbook of Mrs C. S. Buchan (Frances) Calgary, Alberta, October 1955, says that 'the story behind the name chosen for the second new Imperial Order Daughters of the Empire chapter is that of Margaret, a young Hungarian born girl who was given assistance by Malcolm the Third of Scotland'. Private Collection of Audrey Webster, Calgary, Alberta.

62 GBOW, IODE Alberta Provincial Chapter Minutes, 17 May 1967. A picture of the Queen was framed and hung in the Calvin Hungarian Presbyterian Church.

63 'Communism and the Canadian woman', 5–6.

64 'IODE's aid to needy helps fight Communism', *Vancouver Herald*, 30 May 1956, and 'IODE material aid to needy overseas will fight Communism, president states', *Gazette* (Montreal), 29 May 1956.

65 NAC MG28 I 17, 13, 1, 5, 95, National Annual Meeting 1959. The national immigration and citizenship committee's report by Mrs Douglas Jennings.

66 NAC MG28 I 17, 4 February 1948, National Executive Minutes.

67 Saskatchewan Archives Board (hereafter SAB), R598 iv 15. *Canadian Scene* Annual Report 1958.

68 *Ibid.*

69 *Canadian Scene*, pamphlet (Toronto, 1994).

70 PANB, 6 April 1959, 4, Saint John Municipal Chapter.

71 'Wide-range of assistance given immigrants by IODE', *Daily News* (Prince Rupert, British Columbia), 29 May 1956.

72 Provincial Archives of Alberta (hereafter PAA), Acc. no. 83.456, Box no. 2, IODE Provincial Chapter Summary Reports, 15 January 1948–15 January 1955.

73 NAC MG28 I 17, 7, 7 February 1951.

74 Mrs G. L. Hamilton, national convener of immigration and canadianization, 'IODE helps newcomers to become Canadians', *Echoes*, 213 (Christmas 1953), 11.

75 NAC MG28 I 17, 13, 1, 5, 1959 National Meeting Minutes.

76 Franca Iacovetta, 'Making "new Canadians": social workers, women, and the reshaping of immigrant families', in Franca Iacovetta and Mariana Valverde (eds),

Gender Conflicts: New Essays in Women's History (Toronto: University of Toronto Press, 1992), 261–303, at 272.

77 *Ibid.*, 284.
78 GBOW, M7127, Box 5, #52, 5 December 1955.
79 'Speedy language training urged for immigrants', *Leader Post* (Regina, Saskatchewan), 29 May 1951.
80 *Ibid.*, 97.
81 Joan Church, History of the Province of Saskatchewan IODE, 1914–1994, Private Collection of Joan Church, Regina.
82 NAC MG28 I 17, 13, 1, 5, 97, 1959 National Meeting Minutes.
83 PANB Saint John Municipal Chapter, 1966–67.
84 PANB Provincial report of immigration and citizenship 1964–65.
85 PANB Passamaquoddy Chapter IODE of St Andrews, New Brunswick, 1965–66.
86 See Richmond, *Post-War Immigration in Canada*, 4.
87 *Echoes*, 192 (autumn 1948), 8.
88 *Echoes*, 236 (autumn 1959), 6–7.
89 NAC MG28 I 17, 14, 21 September 1961, Minutes of the democratic action committee, 1957–63. In 1961 $500 was sent by the IODE to the Alert Service to fund 10,000 alerts, memoranda, and pamphlets.
90 NAC MG28 I 17, 13, 1, 7, 97, National world affairs committee report.
91 NAC MG28 I 17, 14, 1963, Minutes of the democratic action committee, 1957–63.
92 'She's a redhead who's out to beat the Reds', *Telegram* (Toronto), 30 January 1959, 27.
93 PANB IODE Misc. files, sample copies of the alerts.
94 NAC MG28 I 17, 14, 78, 1963 National Meeting Minutes.
95 Guy Oakes, *The Imaginary War: Civil Defense and American Cold War Culture* (New York: Oxford University Press, 1994), 82.
96 *Echoes*, 192 (autumn 1948), 8.
97 *Ibid.*
98 'IODE out to combat Communism in Canada', *Edmonton Journal*, 26 May 1955.
99 NAC MG28 I 17, 14, Minutes of the democratic action committee 1957–63.
100 NAC MG28 I 17 14, Minutes of the democratic action committee 1957, suggestions from Saskatchewan.
101 *Echoes*, 236 (autumn 1959), 6–7.
102 Whitaker and Marcuse, *Cold War Canada*, 19.
103 PANB MC 200, MS 7/18, Mrs F. L. Miller, speech from the final broadcast.
104 *Ibid.*
105 *Ibid.*
106 *Ibid.*, geographer R. Whidden Ganong and Lieutenant-General E. W. Sansom.
107 Oakes, *The Imaginary War*, 8.
108 Tyler May, *Homeward Bound*, 103.
109 'IODE members across Canada prepare for civil defence', *Echoes*, 218 (spring 1955), 10.
110 NAC MG28 I 17, 8, 6 April 1955.
111 'Civil defence, what is civil defence?' *Echoes*, 218 (spring 1955), 23.
112 Oakes, *The Imaginary War*, 105.
113 *Ibid.*
114 NAC MG28 I 17, 8, 89, 3 March 1954, National Executive Minutes.
115 Mrs Thomas C. Mitchie, Alberta provincial defence liaison officer, 'Operation Lifesaver', *Echoes*, 220 (autumn 1955), 43.
116 *Ibid.*

CHAPTER EIGHT

Modernizing the north: women, internal colonization and indigenous peoples

The IODE's most recent projects reflect an Anglo-Canadian identity which is much changed from what it had been in the early years of the twentieth century. The old racial categories have broken down, and new Canada-centered constructions of citizenship have emerged. Instead of concentrating on assimilating immigrants, the IODE has shifted focus, a shift that began during the Cold War, to a group of citizens who, although living within Canadian territory, were previously considered 'foreign'. This shift represented the change in Canada's identity from that of a dominion in the Empire, with an identity centred on Britain, to that of a nation situated in Canadian geographic space. The decreasing confidence in colonial attitudes was reflected in the drifting away of the IODE from involvement with the Canadian government towards the spaces of charity and the home. This chapter draws out the irony manifest in the attempt to assimilate indigenous peoples into the national project, and make them the same as other Canadians, while clinging to the spatial and social difference of the north. As this chapter shows, through the IODE's work in the Canadian north, this colonization took place *within* a national boundary.

New horizons at home

The Canadian north was the last region to which the IODE turned its attentions. The geographic isolation of the north, and its perceived low economic value, meant that for the first half of the century the IODE saw the north to be outside its vision of Canada. This is ironic, because as a nation Canada had already developed a mythical identity through its northern location. From the late nineteenth century, 'the true north strong and free' provided justification for the rhetoric of a robust and healthy nation.[1] Yet no place was found in such rhetoric for the indigenous inhabitants, who were viewed as culturally backward and living in territories that were economically worthless.[2] The north evoked by southern Canadians was a vast and harsh land, a masculine zone of heroes and explorers, of freedom of movement, of escape and confrontation with nature in the raw – a distant place having little in common with the rest of Canada.[3]

There have been two major phases of IODE work in the north. As far back as 1927, the IODE was involved in raising funds for the Quebec-based Labrador Voluntary Education League's provision of educational supplies and summer schools in the north.[4] This work took place in the context of the undertakings of Grenfell in Labrador.[5] It was not until the late 1950s, however, that the Order turned attention in a concerted way to the Northwest Territories and the Yukon. This was part of a shift that saw welfare extended to peoples in the north, with aid previously focused upon regions outside of Canada – such as Korea, India and Africa – moving back into Canadian territory. Where aid to India had operated during the first half of the century, in the post-Second World War years medical supplies and technology went to Korea and Africa, and considerable aid to postwar Europe.

Extending aid to the Canadian north was part of the territorial completion of Canadian nationalism during the 1940s and 1950s. This was the time of Diefenbaker's 'northern vision', whereby the Canadian Government reached out to encompass the north in a social-democratic welfare state. Newfoundland's and Labrador's entry into confederation, and the spread of social programmes into the north, were believed to be a part of Canada's manifest destiny. The move to aiding Canada was part of a nationwide recognition of socio-economic disparities previously downplayed in the education and health of Canadian citizens. At this time all indigenous Canadians were grouped as one people by the IODE, as was expressed in a 1960 recommendation to the Government to assist Canadian citizens of indigenous origin: 'The IODE feels that in a country which gives large scale aid to underdeveloped countries in many parts of the World, it is essential that a research programme be instituted immediately to ensure that our own citizens of Indian origin achieve equality of opportunity with the utmost speed.'[6]

Directly related to the push to assimilate and modernize indigenous peoples was Canada's new identity as a leading nation in international affairs. This identity was to be fostered by domestic good example and harmony. In the course of setting an example in human rights to other countries, on 19 January 1962 new immigration regulations were introduced that laid primary stress on education, training and skills as the criteria of admissibility to Canada, regardless of the country of origin of the applicant. Freda Hawkins has written that the new law was intended to remove racial discrimination as 'the major feature of

Canada's immigration policy', and retained only one privilege for European immigrants over most non-Europeans in allowing them to sponsor a wider range of relatives.[7] This change officially ended the preference for British immigrants. Minister for Immigration Ellen Fairclough stated that the new regulations represented 'a conscientious and sincere effort on the part of the Government of Canada to enshrine the principles of equity and justice which will guide responsible officials in the discharge of their difficult and complex duties'.[8]

As Canada manoeuvred into a new position of strength on the world stage, its racist immigration policies were found to be an embarrassment. Ellen Fairclough was in fact a long-time IODE member who had held the national office for the immigration and citizenship division and had been prominent in the Ontario Provincial Chapter. It appears that, to Fairclough, Canada's world position was more important than such ingrained prejudice. She stated: 'it is my hope that the new immigration regulations will commend themselves to all members of parliament, regardless of party, to all Canadians and to prospective immigrants around the world'.[9] Freda Hawkins has suggested that the pressure for the changes came from senior officials in Canada, including the deputy minister for immigration, who saw that Canada could not operate effectively within the United Nations or in a multi-racial Commonwealth 'with the millstone of a racially discriminatory immigration policy around her neck'.[10]

In keeping with tradition, the IODE responded to the new regulations by supporting government policy. In 1964, having had time to mull over the new regulations, the IODE stated: 'Canada respects the universal declaration of human rights of the United Nations which outlaws discrimination by reason of national origin. Therefore, it seems out of place for the Order at this time to advocate what might seem like a discriminatory immigration policy.'[11] So as to preserve the democratic traditions and institutions of Canada 'the Order might endorse a non-discriminatory immigration policy and at the same time press for a more intensive programme of education for democratic citizenship among all Canadians, and particularly among immigrants'.[12] The IODE was forced to reflect on its long-standing preference for British immigrants, notably its 1922 resolution: 'Now, 40 years later, insisting on a "preponderance of British citizens amongst those admitted to the country" means that we are in favour of admitting people from the West Indies, India, Pakistan and the Commonwealth Countries in preference to people from the Netherlands, Denmark, Germany etc.'[13] In the 1920s, when only a minority of the subjects of the British Empire were 'white', 'coloured' people were blocked from immigrating to Canada in large numbers, so that the preponderance of white migrants to Canada did not give rise to questions about racial preferment. In 1964, however, the situation was much changed. Putting the interests of the British Commonwealth second to those of Canada, the IODE was disturbed by the prospect of non-white British subjects migrating to Canada. As it still believed that those of 'white' and 'European' ethnicity were superior to 'coloured' Commonwealth citizens, Commonwealth attachments were weakened. Although the IODE officially supported government policy, unofficially there was much continuity with its earlier prejudices. The IODE was aware of the Canadian government's missions and posts throughout Western Europe, while there were 'almost no missions in the coloured countries'.[14]

In this context, immigration became of less importance to the IODE than it had been, and national identity became a more secure and important part of the IODE's representation of Canadian identity. By focusing on Canadian citizens themselves, and on the spaces of Canada from a North American geographical standpoint, the IODE focused more intensively on indigenous peoples, made a call for national unity, and gave more attention to French Canada, going so far as to note that 'at the present time in Canada there is a need for promoting national unity. Our policy of promoting British immigration over any other group could be construed as a slight to the French Canadians and people of other than British origin.'[15]

This attention to French Canada was a response to the increasingly vocal call for the recognition of French Canadian distinctivness. Despite gestures by the IODE towards recognition of French Canada, change was slow. The IODE's neglect of the French language went unchecked until it began to risk embarrassment. In 1956, a draft letter from the Sherbrooke Municipal Chapter advised that the IODE would no longer be permitted to present naturalization greeting cards to new citizens in the courthouse unless they were printed in French as well as English.[16] The IODE's national convenor for immigration and canadianization agreed with this stance and expressed surprise that the problem had not arisen before. She thought that if bilingual cards were printed, they should be available to all interested chapters. The convener stated that 'government literature is printed in both languages and I feel that the Order should do the same in this respect'.[17] By 1975, however, some booklets were still being published in English only. The postmaster-general's special assistant announced that the Post Office could not help the IODE with its work; a polite way of telling them that their booklet was no longer suitable, because chapters had been placing the IODE's English-only booklet 'How to become a Canadian citizen' in post offices.

In intervening in the north, the IODE was associated with the Canadian government's effort to increase its activities, and so its presence, there. Intertwined with ambitions for the social welfare of the indigenous peoples was a clear economic agenda. From the beginning of the IODE's intervention in the north, mention was made of the economic and resource potential of the Arctic.[18] The IODE president stated in her opening speech at the 1959 National Meeting in Regina: 'The great mineral wealth of the Arctic is just beginning to be tapped. The Canadian Government is in the process of building roads to link strategic points and it is inevitable that communities will follow the industries as they are established.'[19]

After the Second World War, the government and private companies looked with increased interest to the resource potential of the north, combining economic potential with welfare and defence objectives in the region. Tapping into the economic potential of the north was a useful way for Canada to increase its presence there, both to confirm sovereignty over the land and to make money. In an imperial context, if Canada did not step up its development of the Arctic, the country risked forfeiting its sovereignty claims to the Americans or, worse still, the Russians. Recalling the early IODE work in the north, one member commented in interview: 'I don't know if this has come to light in any of your studies, probably not. The Canadian government were worried about the Russians coming in. We were afraid that if we didn't work in the north we might lose that part of Canada. So the government wanted us up there.'[20]

As argued in the previous chapter, the Cold War forced a new consideration of North American-situated defence concerns. In particular, the USA looked to the Canadian north, increasing its own presence there, building airbases and radar stations. In 1954 the Canadian Government decided to collaborate with the Americans to build the Distant Early Warning (DEW) Line, a system of radar-detecting stations, along the vast northern border at the 70th and 55th parallels, which would warn against long-range bomber attack.[21] Figure 8.1 shows the line. The DEW Line went beyond defence in outreach, with economic and welfare objectives also involved. Mineral exploration and infrastructure were located near the lines, and it made sense to concentrate the requested welfare services in the same places.[22] Such schemes had important implications for the people of the North. In 1955, an article in *The Canadian Geographer* contained the observation: 'the human geography of the Canadian Arctic is being rapidly recast'.[23] In the short run, the changes meant employment opportunities for indigenous peoples and, from another point of view, a new utility for people who had been seen as redundant. There were high hopes for the modernization and assimilation of native peoples.

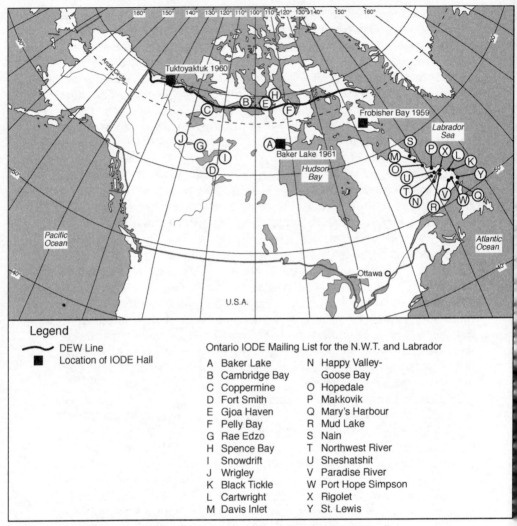

Figure 8.1   The IODE in the Canadian north (showing the DEW Line)

   The IODE set itself the objective of helping northern peoples 'catch up' and become a part of Canada through entering the paid labour force. To 'enable them to fit into a competitive industrial life', the IODE president told the 1959 National Meeting in Regina, 'the Eskimos must, therefore, be provided with educational and vocational training', as it was noted that 'they have marked ability for anything mechanical and are readily absorbed into industry'.[24] Resource extraction and the economic development of the north were seen as a way

[154]

out of starvation and appalling conditions, and there was a new feeling of goodwill towards a population perceived to be desperate. In 1959, for example, an article by an IODE member in *Echoes*, titled 'The Eskimo. His future is a challenge', claimed that 'the frontiers of civilization are pushing farther and farther northward, confronting the Eskimo with a new way of life, and he is going to require help in the process of adjustment'.[25]

Such intervention involved southern Canadians acting as guardians to indigenous peoples. They were treated as children, who needed to be brought up until they were old enough to look after themselves.[26] The objective was to help indigenous people to escape from their 'primitive' conditions, made all the more harsh by their cold environment, to obliterate differences and make the north a part of Canada. There was little perception, however, of indigenous peoples as 'Canadians'. On the contrary, this 'development' was undertaken with much the same attitude as the IODE had demonstrated in its work in India and Africa. Likewise, as Tester and Kulchyski have argued, the government saw indigenous peoples as freakish 'artifacts', to be counted, marvelled at and relocated.[27] None the less, such attitudes were a necessary part of the Canadian government's extension of social programmes into the north, appealing to a sense of improvement through intervention, as the social-democratic welfare state extended throughout Canada's diverse regions.

The first stage of the IODE's work was undertaken in direct consultation with government in line with the close cooperation typical of the IODE's long-standing relationship with the State. The work was surprisingly 'public sphere' in scope; that is, the IODE interacted in constructed public spaces with influential policy makers and was highly regarded by its colleagues. After members had attended a seminar on the 'Canadian Eskimo' in 1958, for instance, the IODE contacted the Federal Government to ask how it might help: 'We were told that while the Government was responsible for educational and welfare services, there were many other ways in which we could be of tremendous assistance.'[28] The Government suggested that the IODE build a community hall for the 'Eskimos' at Frobisher Bay, a fast-growing community of about 1,000 people. The plan was that the Government would provide a site, the 'Eskimos' would donate their labour and the IODE would pay the cost of materials of approximately $20,000. In this pilot project the IODE considered itself to be the first women's organization to commence work in the Arctic.[29] This claim was inaccurate, since women missionaries and church groups had long had a presence there, but as a Canadian patriotic order the IODE's presence, with citizenship at the heart of its operations, differed from that of a religious or benevolent organization.[30] Like the donation of battle-ships, bombers and scholarships, the hall was a considerable under-taking and demonstrated the IODE's enduring strategic Empire- and nation- building concern.

At the IODE National Meeting in Regina in 1959 the Canadian Eskimo Fund was established, the community hall at Frobisher Bay being its first project. In her opening address to members, the president set out the need for economic and cultural change:

> Conditions in the Arctic are changing in that the Caribou, which seven years ago were estimated to number 675,000, have decreased to approx-imately 200,000. A second great hardship is the decline in the price of furs. This situation, together with the fact that the frontiers of civiliza-tion are pushing farther and farther northward, is confronting the Eskimo with a new way of life, and he is going to require help from his fellow Canadians in adjusting himself to it.[31]

The message was that colonization was desirable and resistance was futile. It was inevitable that the north become a part of Canada and that northern people move beyond the harshness and deemed inade-quacy of traditional ways.

So it was with a great sense of optimism that the building of the community hall at Frobisher Bay went ahead. In this project, the IODE was very much a part of the Government's relocation scheme for Inuit. The hall was located at Apex Hill, a new settlement on the DEW Line, five miles from the main centre of Frobisher Bay. Apex Hill was desig-nated by the Government an 'Eskimo rehabilitation centre', a transi-tional housing centre for Eskimo families who were entering waged employment.[32]

The 1958–63 Canadian Eskimo Fund committee enjoyed an imme-diate accumulation of funds. The hall at Frobisher Bay was such a suc-cess that it was promptly followed by a hall at Tuktoyaktuk in 1960 and by another hall at Baker Lake in 1961.[33] Figure 8.1 shows the loca-tion of these halls. These buildings, also situated along the DEW Line, were similar in design and function to the Frobisher Bay hall. For the Tuktoyaktuk hall, the Government was to pay half the total cost according to the ratio of resident Inuit and non-Inuit.[34] This worked out at 45 per cent.

The three community halls were visible schemes symbolic of Cana-dian community and togetherness. In building them, the IODE attempted to influence the culture of the Inuit, encouraging a sense of community that would promote the Inuit's sense of belonging to Canada. In 1962, Mrs Robinson, as national president of the IODE, vis-ited the Arctic for two weeks and opened the Tuktoyaktuk hall. On her return, she told the *Toronto Star*: 'The hall has been given outright to the people up there. They can use it for their dances, for the showing of films, for anything they like.'[35] The 'anything they like', however, would preferably be the activities of Canadians of the south. Stereotypes concerning Inuit identity underpinned the hope for their adoption of 'southern' culture, such as western-style barn dances. It was noted in the records of the IODE Eskimo Fund in 1959 that 'the Eskimos, being a light-hearted people, have a flair for entertainment'.[36] In the north, the IODE asserted the symbols of its imagined Canada, deploying such markers in the landscape as the Union Jack and staff that were provided to the newly established Northwest Territories Court of Record in 1956, and in 1967 a Canadian flag to the Northwest Territories Court.[37]

Overall, there was an optimism about this first stage of work in the north. It occurred in a context of confident social welfare intervention and resource development, with the objectives of entrenching national sovereignty, serving the need to defend Canadian democracy against the perceived Communist threat and instituting the use of 'Eskimo' and 'Indian' as uncontested names. By 1969 little had changed in the perceived need for modernization and assimilation. In her president's report in 1969, Mrs Leggett made it clear that the north belonged to all Canadians and that IODE aid was seen as contributing to the extraction of wealth: 'The North is a challenge to all Canadians. It is a rich land with great natural wealth. Canadians should realize this and ensure that these resources are developed for the benefit of all Canadians.'[38] To become 'useful and participating members of Canadian society', indigenous peoples, she said, would ideally be trained so that they might achieve 'equality of opportunity' by providing the labour force of the north.[39]

The perception of resource development and welfare as the keys to assimilating indigenous peoples into the living standards of the Canadian south persisted into the 1970s. In 1972, a report on 'Operation Help Me' noted that the Inuit led a harsh life, with large groups starving to death in the 1950s as a consequence of being in a state of transition from their old ways of living to the use of new technology such as snowmobiles.[40] The report went on to state: 'Eskimos are obviously caught between two ages, one with technology and one old and traditional. They cannot return to their old ways but they could receive assistance from modern technology', especially in radio communications.[41]

By the beginning of the 1970s, the initial IODE grand schemes had given way to more modest and localized health and education projects, where, making up for government underfunding, the IODE supplied the latest technology and other highly valued hospital equipment, especially X-ray machines and hearing aids. The provision of such equipment reinforced the identity of Canada as modern and progressive, even in the far reaches of the Canadian north. In supplying the most up-to-date equipment, the IODE forged ahead with its endeavour of modernizing the north and introducing new technology, while at the same time situating itself in the realm of feminine domesticity, providing aid to women and children. More and more, the IODE came to rely upon informal women's networks, which often operated through high social connections and direct collaboration with the wives of public servants. In 1973, for example, Mrs Michener, wife of the governor-general, after a discussion with Commissioner Stuart M. Hodgson of the Northwest Territories, suggested to the IODE that it provide hearing aids.[42] Michener was also responsible for introducing infant incubators to the north.

The focus on Labrador

By 1977, many of the schemes initiated by the IODE had been taken over by the government, and IODE support was no longer as necessary in the north, particularly the Northwest Territories. So in 1979 the IODE turned to the second major phase of its work in the north: with the indigenous peoples of Labrador. There is no doubt that the work of the IODE in Labrador has been considerable, and it remains underpublicised. Especially in Ontario, Quebec and the Atlantic provinces, but all across Canada, IODE chapters have contributed to the many projects. It is estimated that more than $2 million was raised and spent in Labrador between 1979 and 1993.[43] Figure 8.1 maps the 1992 locations of aid to Labrador and the Northwest Territories from the IODE's Ontario provincial headquarters.

In this second phase of its work, the IODE's focus has been at the level of creating good future citizens in the form of native children. With its reliance on class-based informal networks maintained and reinforced, reminiscent of turn-of-the-twentieth-century philanthropists, IODE members worked mostly in the areas of education and health care. These emphases grew ever stronger as the IODE found itself still operating with awkward national and imperial ideals and, as a consequence, continued to retreat from more overt patriotic attempts into the 'feminine' spheres of care and nurture, of children in particular rather than of citizens in general. Deeper satisfaction was expressed about projects that gave 'boosts' to a variety of needs than was afforded by the highly visible hall building of the past. This change was summed up in the 1994 national president's comments regarding a new initiative with substance abusers: 'Now our "good works" are being channelled in a different direction. We are paving the way for a peer counselling program to help combat substance abuse in Labrador. If we can save the life of one child, if we can give one child renewed hope, our efforts will be rewarded.'[44] Gone was the language of tapping resource potential and fostering economic development. Instead talk was of 'good work,' individual hope, and charity. Such language was not unique at the time to the IODE. Other previously patriotic organizations, such as the Girl Guides and the YWCA, found themselves abandoning a rhetoric of imperialism in favour of one of inclusive community.

This change in scope is reflected in the re-presentation of the IODE's official status. Where in its beginning years the IODE had declared staunchly that it was a patriotic order and not a charitable or benevolent organization, it reversed its rhetoric. Today, the IODE is officially a charity, possessing a government-assigned charity number, and is somewhat fearful of being perceived as 'political' lest its status as a charity be taken away. Members today seem much more comfortable talking knitting and providing food for children than they do about the economic development of the north.

Whereas in the Northwest Territories education and welfare were areas of government intervention, in Labrador they increasingly became the responsibility of the IODE. Distant residential schools were no longer acceptable to either the Inuit or the Government, increasing the demand in local schools for IODE help. The IODE now has almost no direct contact with government; instead, it contacts individual teachers and nurses, asking them what their schools and hospitals need. Education is still seen by the IODE as an essential tool which the people of Labrador can use to improve their 'quality of life', the looser phrase now used in place of the emphasis on quickly becoming a part of Canada. Education is the key to becoming employable, and becoming employable is perceived as the way to a better life. In 1982 the IODE established a bursary to provide students from Labrador with funds for education in Canadian universities. It has also equipped an industrial arts room at Happy Valley–Goose Bay, a project that has served 'to help students stay in school and become employable'.[45] In 1981, the IODE paid the air transportation costs of $6,000 for approximately seventy students living in isolated villages to travel to a creative arts festival in Goose Bay.[46] Music has also been encouraged, and instruments have been provided to encourage the formation of bands. As it has always fostered the education of girls, the IODE's work in the north has involved girls together with boys, although, obviously, within a context of gender-specific roles. While a focus on reading and writing was extended to both, the colours of hats probably did not challenge colours constructed as masculine and feminine.

In its work the IODE acts as a metaphorical godmother, sending its domestic goods to help colonize the north and make it a part of Canada. Chapters across Canada 'adopt' underfunded schools in Labrador and supply them with equipment. As one Quebec member said:

> They don't have books to read, they need books. So what we do, in our chapter, is we send them books and magazines or we give them a new subscription to them, whatever they like. And for Christmas we send them favours, candies, and little chocolate Santa Clauses so that they can receive these things and have a little bit of Christmas, too, *just like we have*, because most of them are Inuit and they know nothing about having wonderful little parties. And we send them party hats.[47]

Because learning is not possible when children are cold and tired, the IODE prepares children for learning by providing food and clothing. The 'Snack-Pack Programme' in the schools of Labrador provides milk, juice, fruit and cheese. The same Quebec member describes how her chapter is occupied in providing clothing, and knitting slippers and tuque hats. Meanwhile, the Province of Ontario IODE operates a project called Footwear for Kids, where arrangements are made with different footwear manufacturers, and shipments of shoes are sent to different areas of Labrador. Socks also are provided.[48] The material donated by the IODE is not solely domestic. A member recalls arriving, unannounced, by helicopter at the tiny village of Red Bay, where she saw a group of school children using a map, and others in the community using skates and skis, all sent by the IODE.[49]

Female imperialism on the retreat

The second phase of the IODE's work in Labrador is no longer in tune with government policy, and is moreover in a period of crisis and retreat. Overall, the Canadian north has not been assimilated to become a part of Canada as the IODE sees it. In a postcolonial climate of greater acceptance of difference and state promotion of multiculturalism, the IODE's earlier vision for the Canadian north is outmoded.[50] There is no longer a threat of a Russian invasion, and economic ventures are more the responsibility of private companies. Organized opposition by indigenous peoples has forced government to recognize that full assimilation is not possible, or desirable, as suggested by the 1988 Canadian Multiculturalism Act's recognition of Nunavit and omission of Inuit (Eskimo) peoples.[51]

The work of making the north a part of the south makes sense only as long as the north is recognized as different from the south. The more that members of the IODE perceive the north as changing to become like the south, the less needy the north appears. People in the cities and other regions of Canada are now perceived to be in just as much need as are those in the north. Because of this irony, it is necessary to selectively sustain the north as different. The irony of encouraging difference while seeking assimilation is apparent in the arts, where the IODE has selectively fostered Inuit arts, crafts and legends. The national headquarters of the IODE in Toronto and the provincial headquarters in Hamilton, Ontario, are testimony to the regard that the IODE has for indigenous art. Here tokens of appreciation from the north abound. There are moosehair flowers, soap stone carvings and quilts made by school children.

The tours of the north made by IODE members reinforce the perception of the north as a place of difference. Prominent IODE members have made trips to inspect the work in the north, and return south to report on this distant part of Canada. The early trips to the Northwest Territories were full of pomp and ceremony, as presidents of the IODE were received by politicians and governors-general. In trips to Labrador, in 1979, 1981, 1985, 1987, 1989 and 1993, there was a much greater attempt at 'hands-on' interaction. In interviews, the women who went on some of these trips recalled their great enthusiasm and determination: 'It was a thrilling experience of a lifetime', said one woman who went to Labrador in 1993. 'It was beautiful, majestic, glorious scenery. I still dream about it. It's so different. You can't imagine.'[52] Another woman, on a 1989 tour, gave her impressions of Mud Lake's community: 'Mud Lake is a beautiful little community with well-kept homes, a pretty little church, and a two-room school with a small teacherage attached.'[53] The general tidiness, and indicators of Christian worship and education, led her to report that all was well.

The 'othering' of the north has much to do with its geography. Whereas in the first stage of IODE work in the north the landscape was seen as contributing to the plight and desperation of northern peoples, now, despite its harsh climate, the landscape is perceived as beautiful. Positive images contribute to the romanticizing of the place and the people who live there. In contrast to an urban landscape of dirt and concrete, there is something awesome and inspirational in the vastness and severity of the north. A woman on a 1980 coastal tour of Labrador reported that at times she felt she was in 'another world'.[54] Another woman observed: 'You really have to turn your head off, or turn it around, or do something. You can not judge normally. No, you can not. But it's fascinating to see. Oh, I find the people who've chosen to go there for their teaching career or a piece of their teaching career just marvellous. It's a different way of life there.'[55] There is a tendency to take a romantic, 'warm–fuzzy', view of the children. An IODE member who went to Labrador in the early 1980s said: 'But I like to think of the bright-eyed little kids of all kinds of funny mixed bloods and mixtures that I saw, wearing our boots or our mits, or having our breakfasts.'[56] Although the goal is to prevent 'Canadian' children from having to 'live like that in this land',[57] real 'rescue' is no longer the objective of a diverse Canadian identity.

Through the 1990s romantic notions of the people and the land of the north were increasingly replaced by a vision of despair. Ironically, whereas the initial concern was with issues of national security and economic growth, now aid to adults has been abandoned, with efforts instead concentrated on individual children and youth in general. Said one member: 'The children are beautiful. They have so little opportunity. Their traditional way of life and values have been destroyed. I'm dubious of a way out. They can't go back. It's a tragic situation. I hope they can be helped.'[58]

For some women of the IODE today, the north remains an almost mythical landscape of difference, despair and degradation. Thousands of women, especially in Ontario, continue to knit. They make garments for people they may never meet, but they feel a great sense of motivation to give to children they think of as 'the needy':

> We give them things to wear on their heads to keep them warm. Scarves, we're always knitting. Every night when I'm watching television – we never stop. Now, if I'm too tired, I don't knit. But if I'm wide awake, like I am now, I'll probably be knitting tonight. They [the garments]don't take long. Stuff to keep their hands warm. Something that they can pull down under their ears, because it's cold there in Labrador. Now we have to make the strong fentex-type slippers – something that doesn't wear out.[59]

Change is not happening to the extent that was desired, and the IODE is silent with respect to new self-governed territories and pending land claims.[60] 'You can't do much for these people' is what some members now believe,[61] and IODE help is seen by them as 'just another drop in the bucket', consisting of 'band aid solutions'. 'I hope they can change. It [the way of life] goes right back in their culture'.[62] 'They were living in tents, not houses until the 1950s. Now they're being brought into the twentieth century.'[63] A member in Saskatchewan expressed her sense of hopelessness in these words: 'But, you know, all of this talk about Davis Inlet. Substance abuse and all that. People don't realize the IODE was in there doing work long before this came out. So it's not because we haven't tried. And there's problems in some of those places that no volunteer organization is ever gonna solve. We can try, but really ...'.[64] The IODE's present lack of confidence in its work does not mean that the Order should be considered of little importance to the postwar history of the Canadian north. The IODE has skilfully utilized its identity as a voluntary group of affluent Anglo-Celtic women in going about its work. But the ideology behind the work is now old-fashioned and inappropriate to the demands of indigenous Canadians.

It is not just in the north that the IODE has faced crisis and retreat. Its citizenship work more generally has come under increasing challenge. Professionals are now employed as interpreters and government services provide English lessons. As the structure of citizenship courts changes, erosion of the IODE presence has varied from place to place according to the local actors. In New Brunswick the IODE no longer participates in the way that it used to: 'We always gave little welcome cards, Canadian flag pins or maple leafs. And they asked us not to do that anymore. In fact we find more and more that the government is taking over things like that.'[65] In general, the organization is no longer welcome or relevant at courts, except to provide food and refreshments.[66] The food that was so essential at the ports in the 1920s is now incidental at the courts. In Saskatchewan members still hold receptions and serve lunches,[67] and in 1994 British Columbia members served 170 cookies at one such reception,[68] but the days of handing out patriotic literature and gifts are drawing to a close.

The structure of the courts has changed over the last twenty years, adapting to demands for less ceremony, more vigorous cost-cutting, and the emphasis on multiculturalism. In 1993 the Government announced a plan to terminate the system of patronage under which citizenship court judges were appointed. A Saskatchewan member laments the day she heard about this change, and her spontaneous comment reflects the complexity and ambiguity of the IODE's work with immigrants, its backward and its forward look:

> I didn't hear all of this until this morning. This is where I said yesterday, let's get on that bandwagon. We had a citizenship court judge as our guest speaker at our banquet, and she had tears in her eyes when she heard. Now they're talking about doing away with the patronage and the amount of money that they're paying for these judges. But when they appointed these judges, we liked the system as it was before. We were very involved with teaching English in a lot of cases, helping [immigrants] with their questions, their rights and responsibilities, all of this. We were there for them, at every session, and often we would take them aside to make sure that they knew things. Well that's all at an end. The judges just sat down and talked to them. We never quite knew what the

judge was saying, and what was happening and what they knew to become Canadian citizens, and now it's going to be even less. They're going to be able to slip into this country as just anybody, and it's time for us to get on the bandwagon for this and say 'This isn't good enough.' But we'll be called radical. But why not be radical if we believe in something?[69]

The call to be radical in the face of a diminishing presence is not carried through to the IODE's official position. Gone are the days of the IODE proudly sharing its opinions on Canada and the Empire at citizenship courts, and its part in confidently combining capitalism, culture and imperialism with the objective of making the north a part of Canada is much diminished. As one contemporary member commented on the contact that members have through letters and photos from their 'adoptees' in the north: 'And it's wonderful, the contact. We had a marvellous teacher not too long ago, and she sent us a video all about the children. It was so much fun to see them out in the snow and everything, so this work is helping another area of the World – well of our own country.'[70] Such paradox and tension between national and imperial identities capture the IODE's complicated and shifting endeavours to make the north a part of Canada. In contemporary times, the IODE is confronted with a national climate in which the greater acceptance of difference challenges its ideas of citizenship; and, as its members age, the IODE is now attempting to colonize the north through individual patronage and domestic methods – a far cry from its earlier involvement in the sweeping momentum of governmental initiatives. The objective of making the north a part of Canada remains incomplete, contradictory and fragmented, a state of affairs indicative of the eclipsing of an imperial ideology by a diverse Canadian national identity. A vital part of this new diversity is that indigenous peoples have gained more agency, and the right to autonomy, rendering the IODE marginal.

Notes

1 Carl Berger, 'The true north strong and free', in Peter Russell (ed.), *Nationalism in Canada* (Toronto: University of Toronto Press, 1966), 3–26.
2 See R. Quinn Duffy, *The Road to Nunavut: The Progress of the Eastern Arctic Inuit Since the Second World War* (Montreal and Kingston: McGill–Queen's University Press, 1988).
3 Carl Berger, 'The true north strong and free'; Lisa Bloom, *Gender on Ice: American Ideologies of Polar Expeditions* (Minneapolis and London: University of Minnesota Press, 1993).
4 *Echoes* (1930), 11 and 15; *Echoes*, 150 (1938), 10.
5 Ronald Rompkey, *Grenfell of Labrador: A Biography* (Toronto: University of Toronto Press, 1991).
6 NAC MG28 I 17, no date, Canadian Eskimo Fund, 1959–63.

7 NAC MG28 I 17, loose document. Ellen Fairclough, 1962 Regulations and Statement, 1. Freda Hawkins, *Critical Years in Immigration: Canada and Australia
Compared* (Kingston and Montreal: McGill–Queen's University Press, 1989), 39.
8 *Ibid.*, 7.
9 *Ibid.*, 6.
10 Hawkins, *Critical Years in Immigration*, 39.
11 NAC MG28 I 17, 9, 1, 4 March 1964.
12 *Ibid.*
13 *Ibid.*
14 *Ibid.*
15 *Ibid.*
16 NAC MG28 I 17, 8, 5 September 1956.
17 *Ibid.*
18 NAC MG28 I 17, 26, 2, 1959.
19 *Ibid.*
20 Interview, 4 November 1994: Ottawa, Ontario.
21 Peter J. Usher, 'The north: metropolitan frontier, native homeland?', in L. D.
McCann (ed.), *A Geography of Canada. Heartland and Hinterland* (Scarborough,
Ontario: Prentice-Hall, 1982), 411–56, at 429. The DEW line was a combined
USA–Canada project. There would be radar-detecting stations crossing from Alaska
to the central Canadian Arctic to Baffin Island at the 70th parallel and a radar line
at the 55th parallel.
22 The McGill sub-Arctic research station opened in Schefferville in 1955. It was
funded by the Canadian Defence Research Board and the mining and construction
companies involved in the development of local iron-ore deposits. John T. Parry,
'Geomorphology in Canada', *The Canadian Geographer*, 11: 4 (1967), 280–311, at
292. Situated on the 55th parallel, it was the location or a new airstrip, and radar and
weather equipment. Two native bands were relocated to the area.
23 G. H. Michie and E. M. Neil, 'Cultural conflict in the Canadian Arctic', *The Canadian Geographer*, 5 (1955), 22–41, at 41.
24 NAC MG28 I 17, 26, 2, 1959.
25 'The Eskimo – his future is a challenge', *Echoes*, 236 (autumn 1959), 6.
26 Quinn Duffy, *The Road to Nunavut*, xxiii.
27 See Frank J. Tester and Peter Kulchyski, *Tamarniit (Mistakes): Innuit Relocation in
the Eastern Arctic, 1939–63* (Vancouver: University of British Columbia Press,
1994).
28 NAC MG28 I 17, 14, Minutes of the Eskimo affairs committee.
29 *Ibid.*
30 NAC MG28 I 17, no date, Canadian Eskimo Fund, 1959–1963. The Women's Auxil-
iary had been helping since the 1920s and there had also been women's missionary
work in the Arctic.
31 NAC MG28 I 17, 26, 2.
32 Quinn Duffy, *The Road to Nunavut*, 30.
33 *Echoes*, 240 (autumn 1960).
34 *Ibid.* This worked out at 45 per cent.
35 *Toronto Star*, 13 December 1962.
36 NAC MG28 I 17, 8, 5 November 1959, Eskimo Fund Frobisher Bay, 315.
37 May Kertland, *IODE. The Third Twenty-Five Years* (Toronto: G. Best Publishing),
1975.
38 NAC MG28 I 17, 13, 2, 14, 1969.
39 *Ibid.*
40 NAC MG28 I 17, 26, 1, Operation 'Help Me' typed July 1972.
41 *Ibid.*
42 *St Thomas Times* (Ontario), 19 June 1973.
43 National headquarters IODE, unpublished 1993 IODE report.
44 *Echoes*, 359 (1993–94), 4.
45 *Echoes*, 358 (1993), 1.

46 *Echoes*, 326 (1982), 16.
47 Interview, 22 November 1993: Montreal, Quebec.
48 Interview, 4 November 1994: Ottawa, Ontario.
49 Interview, 25 February 1994: Toronto, Ontario.
50 For a discussion of multiculturalism see Audrey Kobayashi, 'Multiculturalism: representing a Canadian institution', in James Duncan and David Ley (eds), *Place/Culture/Representation* (London and New York: Routledge, 1993), 205–31.
51 Section 2 of the 1988 Canadian Multiculturalism Act states: 'The Yukon and the Northwest Territories as well as Indian bands and band councils, are excluded from the application of the Act in compliance with the ongoing process of delegation of powers by the Government of Canada.' *The Canadian Multiculturalism Act* (Ottawa: Government Printer, 1988).
52 First interview, 24 February 1994: Toronto, Ontario.
53 Jean Throope, *Echoes*, 348 (1989–90), 6.
54 *Echoes*, 317 (1980), 6.
55 First interview, 24 February 1994: Toronto, Ontario.
56 Interview, 25 February 1994: Toronto, Ontario.
57 First interview, 24 February 1994: Toronto, Ontario.
58 *Ibid.*
59 Interview, November 1993: Montreal, Quebec. The interviewee is referring to a class of 9-year-olds 'adopted' by her chapter.
60 Ken Coates (ed.), *Aboriginal Land Claims in Canada: A Regional Perspective* (Toronto: Copp Clark Pitman, 1992).
61 Interview, 14 July 1993: St John's, Newfoundland.
62 Second interview, 24 February 1994: Toronto, Ontario.
63 First interview, 24 February 1994: Toronto, Ontario.
64 Interview, 20 April 1994: Meota, Saskatchewan.
65 Interview, 25 October 1993: Saint John, New Brunswick.
66 Interview, 25 February 1994: Toronto, Ontario.
67 Interview, 18 April 1994: Regina, Saskatchewan.
68 Interview, 29 April 1994: Vancouver, British Columbia.
69 Interview, 17 April 1994: Regina, Saskatchewan.
70 Interview, 4 November 1993: Ottawa, Ontario.

Conclusion

The IODE has played a key role in the making of Anglo-Canada in the image of Britain, and has been an important part of British imperial and Canadian national history. Due to gender-blind frameworks, however, historians have paid little attention to the IODE. Today, at a time when the countries are focusing on national, rather than imperial, histories, the IODE is mistakenly portrayed as British or 'international'. There is a sense in which it is seen as old-fashioned and as part of the past. Throughout the twentieth century, the IODE did manifestly age. As the grey hairs multiplied there has been a concerted effort to remain as innovative and 'up to date' as the IODE was when it started out with the marking of graves in 1900. As has happened with other women's organizations, the IODE has found many of its initial concerns to have been accomplished, or else professionalized, while others have been found to be no longer appropriate. Concern over an ageing demographic emerged in the mid-1960s, when the IODE asked 'Are we dinosaurs?'[1] The longevity of the IODE is impressive, and although membership never again reached the heights attained in the First World War and, after a boost during the Second World War, has steadily declined, the IODE has managed to leave a distinctive, if somewhat hidden and changing, imprint throughout the twentieth century.

Why the membership declined can be explained by a variety of factors. The peaks during wartime suggest that many women joined seeing in the IODE an avenue by which they could contribute to the war effort rather than out of a more general dedication to the philosophy of the IODE. The IODE was founded during the South Africa War, and thrived in membership during subsequent wars. Without those boosts, doubtless the otherwise gradual decline in membership would have been hastened, but it is difficult to imagine an alternative history for an organization whose identity was so bound up with the ultimate test of patriotism: war. Meanwhile, the intergenerational structure of the IODE has been able to keep the Order going, with new generations of women prompted to join because of the proffered continuity with the past and the promise of interaction with their peers, rather than being lured by new ideas.

Current members themselves view the declining membership in the context of women's changing place in society. The twentieth century saw huge changes in the lives of Western women, Canadian women included. In general, women have displayed decreasing interest in the work of women's organizations. As increasing numbers of women joined the paid workforce, there was simply not enough time for voluntary work. Interestingly, as welfare states have grown, many women in paid employment have found themselves occupied in 'women's work' that was previously the domain of the voluntary sector. 'Working women' were not available for meetings held in the afternoons, and their evenings were often spent doing housework and caring for children. Besides these reasons, current members sense that their ideas do not appeal to younger generations. There are suggestions that young women are now more self-absorbed, that they lack a sense of the importance of helping others, and are perhaps even lazy. Members see the secularizing of society and the advance of conspicuous consumption as related to the IODE's declining relevance – the latter factor seeming rather ironic given the IODE's image of white gloves and fur.

But what makes the IODE so interesting is its perseverance as an organization, and its ability to adapt and re-invent itself, building on ideas largely moulded at the beginning of the twentieth century. It might be assumed that as the British Empire declined, so too would the IODE. Here, the IODE's positioning as a national, as well as an imperial, organization is an important factor, one on which this book has focused. The IODE was able to latch on to a growing Canadian nationalism, at the same time as it reluctantly shed the imperial past and ideas that were seen as increasingly redundant in modern Canadian society. Such adaptation is applicable on a wider scale to the other former 'white dominions' or 'settler societies' of the British Empire, which have also developed national identities out of their imperial pasts, simultaneously fostering an attachment to the British Commonwealth. In its relationship to the Empire and the Canadian nation, the IODE has undergone changes that bear a resemblance to the histories of other imperial patriotic organizations, such as the Victoria League, the Girl Guides and Boy Scouts Movements, and the Royal Empire/Commonwealth Society.

Throughout the book I have used the history of the IODE to explain how the Order constructed a hegemonic Anglo-Canadian identity that was based upon mimicking Britain. Clearly, there was in that regard considerable regional variation within Canada, but I argue that a dominant, if changing, narrative did exist. Further, tracing the history of the IODE reveals a shifting focus from that of a Canada seeking a 'sense of power' within the British Empire to that of a nation situated in its own geographic space. How this process came about is the domain of my second argument: that the IODE's Anglo-Canadian identity was produced in a recursive relationship to the threats and resistance that, at specific moments, challenged its composition. There was a recurring sense that threats posed by *difference* forced the IODE to redefine the hegemonic. In the early years of the twentieth century it was the threat of immigrants from the less desirable positions on the racial hierarchy that led the IODE to value British immigrants. Similarly, it was because of the fear that immigrants would not assimilate that the IODE focused on canadianization and, in doing so, more clearly defined a Canadian identity based upon features of that Canadian space. War forced the IODE to defend and define itself against the enemy, serving the 'mother country' in an ever-strengthening capacity, while war memorialization, which continues today, perpetuated memory and simultaneously promoted imperial and national identity through the education of future generations. During the Cold War, Communism was the enemy, with the IODE focusing on the threat it posed to Canadian space and identity, and, in 'combating Communism', redefining the principles of Canadian democracy and citizenship away from those of Britain and towards those of North America.

For many Canadians, the British Commonwealth itself is no longer important. Canadian identity is now located in Canadian space, with conquest, progress, modernization and the assimilation of all difference no longer considered unquestioned objectives. 'White settler society' now appears to be a limited descriptor, one that fails to encompass the complexities of gender, race and class, and risks a reassertion of Anglo-Celtic dominance. The IODE's work in the Canadian north at once shows the most complete relocation of Anglo-Canadian identity from British imperial space to Canadian space, and captures the contemporary fragmentation of a previously totalizing Canadian identity. Despite this fragmentation of earlier universals, however, there remains a strong continuity with the past. IODE members still mention 'a bright future' for the Canadian north, but the discourse of modernization and canadianization is muted. One woman, when asked about how successful she considers the IODE's work in the north to have been, focused on providing children with food and education as the way to a bright future.[2] With the IODE's earlier belief in modernization and progress in question, its projects are becoming increasingly local, and there are doubts as to how much longer the Labrador project can last.

Twentieth-century changes in the lives of women included new voting rights, entry to the paid workforce in unprecedented numbers, opportunities in higher education and occupations previously reserved for men, and a generally increasing voice and influence. Ironically, as women's traditional place was challenged, and women were more than ever present in positions of power and influence, the IODE found itself most comfortable in the maternal spaces of charity work and benevolent and gendered care, without the overarching patriotic purpose it had asserted early in the twentieth century. As figures 9.1 and 9.2 show, no longer is the IODE visible marching through streets on Remembrance Day, presenting briefs to government, or having its latest opinions featured in newspapers. Instead activity continues in private and muted ways that are embarrassed about the past.

It is not possible for the IODE to simply forget the past. Rather its past is seen as a process of transformation, and that the IODE survives to the present is evidence of the importance of its adaptability. Literature on colonialism that generalizes about the colonizing process often implies a rupture in political rule or an event of cultural resistance as the defining moment in the identity of a nation. As the country's hegemonic identity has been controlled by Canada's Anglo-Celtic immigrants from the imperial centre, attempting to impose a white settler society, changes to the Canadian identity are not about making a clean break from the colonial to the post-colonial, erasing past rules and dominance. Rather, change is about the perpetuation of British values and their adaptation to Canadian space. As representative of this change, the IODE has continued to argue for the importance of the tenets and institutions of British colonialism, especially the monarchy, to Canada.

In 1968 the IODE presented a brief on the monarchy to the Special Joint Committee of the Senate and the House of Commons on the Constitution, urging renewed emphasis on the importance of the monarchy's place in Canada.[3] In the 1990s, amid increasingly general doubts in Canada and Britain, IODE members retained a strong sense of the importance of Canada's system continuing to be that of a federal constitutional monarchy, stating: 'I think that everybody needs something that is pretty well unobtainable. You need a focus';[4] and 'I think that the Queen is an enduring symbol, and that's something that you don't have to worry about going away. You need a head of state [who is] above and beyond ...'.[5] Another member expressed her belief that the monarchy offers a level of 'protection' missing from the govern-

Figure 9.1 Processing with the wreath to the Cenotaph, 1951 National Meeting in Ottawa

ment of the USA, and referred to Ronald Reagan as having been as 'crazy as a march hare. You know, I wouldn't let Ronald Reagan look after my own chequing account.'[6] The new Canadian flag and the repatriation of the Canadian Constitution were changes that many members of the IODE could accept only after some time had passed.

The biggest silence in the history of the IODE is in respect of the underlying importance of Canada's southern neighbour. The influence of the USA, as became very evident during the Cold War, was a large contributing factor to the IODE's focus on Canadian space. On the one hand, the IODE has considered the USA a republican enemy, threatening Canada with its politics and culture. Here endless work by IODE members in film and education, and in the general promotion of Anglo-Canadian culture, although not often documented as such, was undertaken to ward off American influences. In fact, however, if attachments to British institutions are stripped away, the IODE's brand of patriotism, with its emphasis on hard work and fundraising, has much in common with the patriotism of women's organizations'

Figure 9.2 IODE Thrift Store, April 1994, Calgary, Alberta

in the USA. Even during the Cold War, when Canada moved into its north for strategic reasons that involved a threat from the USA, the IODE remained caught up in the rhetoric of British democracy, while adopting American anti-Communist sentiments.

Another noteworthy silence is that over French Canada. Highly placed on the IODE's perceived hierarchy of races, French Canadians were sometimes referred to as a 'founding race'; but they were not considered a serious challenge to the dominant Anglo-Celtic Canadian identity of the IODE, and were left largely alone. The lack of mention of French Canada in IODE documents is startling. This book definitely represents 'one solitude' of Canada's history. Opposition to conscription during the two world wars, although considerable, was in the main geographically confined to Quebec, while IODE attention was centred on being a loyal member of the British Empire, and not on addressing domestic problems. It was not until the 1960s that the IODE paid attention to French Canada, as resistance to Anglo dominance mounted and there were demands for greater recognition of bilingualism and biculturalism.

[172]

CONCLUSION

The membership of the IODE is no longer a matter of class. Whereas the first IODE members could be regarded as a group of élite women in long white dresses, hats and gloves, often the wives of doctors, lawyers and business people, contemporary members are 'just ordinary people' who are 'much more relaxed'.[7] A contemporary member, who considers herself to be 'untypical', and with no family history of IODE membership, recalls the mid-1950s when her friends asked her to join: 'It seemed like a bit of an honour to be asked because it seemed like all the best people in town belonged to IODE.'[8] A Calgary members thinks that IODE has become more flexible, with fewer issues labelled 'Private and Confidential' – 'or, as they used to say, "on the different levels", especially at executive levels'; primary chapter members can now feel comfortable talking to national officers and are told to have fun while they are working.[9] Class change has varied provincially. The Prairie provinces of Alberta, Saskatchewan and Manitoba, and also Ontario, appear to be the more diverse, whereas provinces with smaller memberships, such as Prince Edward Island, have retained their homogeneity. A Charlottetown paper reported in the late 1950s that 'the IODE is not a class-conscious organization, though among its members are women whose social background is in the "upper brackets"'.[10]

As the hegemonic Anglo-Canadian identity fragmented, there was an opening up of membership to those of diverse religious beliefs. This is seen as a strength by a contemporary Roman Catholic member in Fredericton, who believes that the IODE gives a chance for women of other religious backgrounds to become involved: 'It doesn't matter what church you belong to, you can belong [to the IODE].'[11] Overall, however, the mainstream continues to be Christian, with a traditionalist interest in education:

> I went to my grandchildren's school for Christmas, and there was a lot of controversy about the school's being Christian when we have so many ethnics coming in. And I went to that programme and people who had the highest profile positions in those plays and concerts that they put on were the Indians, the Orientals, the whole bit. They loved it. You talk to the Jewish people. They say that when they went to school they loved the Christian Christmas: it was colourful, it was exciting. They had parts in plays, they did things. And why is it that, if such few people are criticizing it, we should be taking it away? Everybody's so afraid of our image. I really strongly believe that one of the strongest things that we should be supporting at all times ... [is] Canadians, being good, and good citizenship. Being good Canadians.[12]

In these contemporary attitudes towards race, religion and culture, despite an overall trend towards the acceptance of difference, little has

[173]

changed since the start of the IODE at the beginning of the twentieth century. While difference is sometimes accepted, there is the belief that assimilation is actually in the best interests of different religions and ethnicities. Indeed, this is presented as if it were a principle of the Christian Church.

In recent times, the founding patriotism that made the IODE unique as an organization of women primarily concerned with citizenship, and not necessarily with children, has been officially replaced by charitable endeavour and a distinct focus on children. Meanwhile, unofficially, patriotism has remained, with the focus no longer on Canada within the British Empire, but on the Canadian nation. Individual members continue their patriotic focus. A Regina member who rejects the perception that the IODE should be embarrassed for 'flag waving' proudly flies her flag on every Canadian occasion: 'I've had kids come to my door and say, "What have you got your flag out there for?" And I'll say, "Well this is such and such day, and I feel proud to be a Canadian, aren't you proud to be a Canadian?"'[13] A Calgary member was drawn to the IODE by its patriotism:

> I guess that one of the things was that it was patriotic. And I've always really been a proud Canadian ... I'm really concerned about my country ... I want to keep Canada a country that my family, my kids, and my grandkids can be safe in. And be proud of. So I guess that's why I work for Canada, because I think if you're working for the IODE you're working for your country.[14]

Patriotism may now be centred within Canada, but British colonial attitudes from the past remain the dominant influence, as can be seen in this New Brunswick member's assertion of her enduring patriotism:

> I've always been patriotic. I really have been. Probably unnecessarily. I can remember when we were first married and we were listening to a show on radio and they ended with God Save the King, and I stood up in bed just to be facetious. But that's how much I felt you should stand up for God Save the King. My husband laughed at me. He said, 'Really, you know, standing up in bed!'[15]

Over the years, fundraising has moved away from its early patriotic orientation to involve anything that makes money. There is continuity, though, and the retention of fundraisers of large scope and organization, such as operating coat checks and taking entries at exhibitions. In Vancouver municipal members have operated the coat check at Hastings Park for over thirty years.[16] On the opposite side of the country, in New Brunswick, a chapter took entries for the handicrafts building at the Atlantic National Exhibition. A participant noted that receiving $1,500 for their labour was a much easier way of raising money than baking or selling tags: 'It's an enjoyable way [of raising money], and we give prizes to school children for their entries and handicrafts.'[17] After the Second World War, fashion shows, a transmutation of previous pageants, became a popular and nationwide fundraising event for the IODE. For individual chapters, a large event such as a fashion show could raise enough money in a single evening to keep the chapter's budget going for a year.[18] While bridge parties were a common event in the past, enjoyed by many members, running, but not playing, bingo is now widespread. An Ontario member notes: 'In every chapter we have bingo and make fantastic money. Usually you work so hard to raise money, and now they're doing it the modern way of bingos.'[19] Similarly, a Saskatchewan member stated:

> Lots of it is bingo these days. I try with fundraising. A lot of times I've bought something and donated it for a raffle, and made up the tickets. But everybody hates buying tickets, and I'm not much for bake sales, a good tried and true. But I think that, a lot of times, you work for a few days doing the baking, and then you turn around and buy it back. We do catering, too, and we have the bridge club, fashion shows ... Some chapters make fruit cakes for Christmas and Christmas puddings. We used to have hockey pools for the Stanley Cup play-offs.[20]

While exercise and fitness were important parts of the IODE's constructions and justifications of racial preferences, competitive sports is another area of notable silence. Given the strong connections between the Empire's unity, drilling for war and competitive sports, it is ironic that the IODE was remiss in this powerful twentieth century agent of popular nationalism. But as a bastion of masculinity, more so than the spaces of politics and Parliament, commerce and academia, the sporting arena was not a domain of the IODE.

In *Cat's Eye*, the Canadian novelist Margaret Atwood describes interwar classroom activities at Queen Mary's school:

> Over the door to the cloakroom, so that you can feel you're being watched from behind, there's a large photograph of the King and Queen, the King with medals, the Queen in a white ballgown and diamond tiara ... Things are more British than they were last year. We learn to draw the Union Jack, using a ruler and memorizing the various crosses for St George of England, St Patrick of Ireland, St Andrew of Scotland, St David of Wales. Our own flag is red and has a Union Jack in one corner, although there's no saint for Canada. We learn to name all the pink parts of the map.[21]

In this description of Anglo-Canadian sensibilities fact meets fiction in that it was probably the IODE that placed the picture of the king and queen in Atwood's classroom, provided a school library, offered prizes for imperial essays and influenced the school curriculum. The IODE has been a vital part of Anglo-Canadian sensibilities, present in the hearts and minds of Canadians.

But rhetoric has never been enough for the IODE. It has worked hard to make an impact in education, health and welfare. At its foundation, the IODE was ahead of the governments concerned, displaying its initiative with the marking of graves in the South Africa War, and in providing bursaries for children of the war-dead after the First World War. Members of the IODE were listened to on school and health boards. During times of war and peace, but especially during the two world wars, and again with postwar civil defence work, and in the Canadian north, the IODE has been called upon by Canadian governments. Those governments took the IODE's recommendations seriously, and in its work the IODE was trusted to be organized and efficient. As times changed, and the IODE shifted from patriotism to charitable work, it lost none of the high regard in which Canadians have held it. Such respect is still particularly strong with regard to the IODE's contribution to the two world wars.

The IODE is an important part of imperial history. It made a substantial and arguably enduring effort during the twentieth century to produce and perpetuate Anglo-Canadian identity. Yet, because of a masculinist, imperial division of space, relegating women to a 'separate sphere', as a women's organization the IODE has not always been considered important; and despite the IODE's widespread influence it has not always been given the recognition that it deserves. As itself a supporter of a totalizing Canadian identity, being considered unimportant has not necessarily been a uniform disadvantage for the IODE. Rather, combining race and class positions, the IODE was able to access gendered feminine as well as masculine spaces. In this way, the IODE's history reveals a complex relationship to a patriarchy that is not as stable as it is often assumed to be. Although comprised of a group of women, the IODE is not to be treated as separate from patriarchy, masculine identity and public spaces, as it helped to produce those constructions as part of its overall standpoint as national and imperial citizens. Indeed, to push the argument further, the IODE was responsible for propping up patriarchy. In recent years deconstruction has been the fate of many categories previously considered absolute. As this history of the IODE indicates, now is perhaps the time for understandings of patriarchy to be complexified.

An examination of the IODE's history reveals that, in terms of their feminist politics, not all women's organizations are to be categorized in a straightforward manner. Women's historians since the 1970s have in the main looked to women's groups of the past as feminist forbears who can provide inspiration and examples for the present. Their focus was on overtly feminist groups, which had women as their central cause. On the contrary, the IODE was first and foremost patriotic, and often advanced a conservative politics. Yet, to label the IODE 'conservative' is not to do justice to the complex workings of feminist and patriarchal politics. In some of its patriotic work, even that which on the surface privileged a returned serviceman, such as the War Memorial Scholarships, the IODE was supportive of women. As with all areas of its educational work, the presence of members who believed women to be the equals of men and deserving of equality of opportunity, a considerable number of them teachers themselves, ensured that the IODE offered strong support for women's education at all levels. In the landmark cause of first-wave feminism, women's suffrage, the IODE was a central player, being perceived by the nation and the Empire as credible because of its patriotism. And it is worth repeating that among the IODE's membership were important firsts for Canadian women: two of the first women academics (Wilhelmina Gordon and Mary Bollert); Canada's first woman mayor (Charlotte Whitton); the first woman Canadian federal minister (Ellen Fairclough); the first woman provincial lieutenant-governor (Pauline McGibbon); and the first woman chancellor of a Canadian university (also Pauline McGibbon). For an organization that was premissed upon a willingness to speak out on citizenship, it makes sense that civic duty was taken seriously. The history of the IODE shows that feminist outcomes can stem from a variety of motives, and that the effects might be useful for Anglo-Celtic women, while detrimental to others.

As Anglo-Canadian identity was hegemonic, claiming total dominance and demanding the assimilation of all difference, it was threats and not silences that led the IODE to defend and define Canada. Until the 1960s, French Canada was perceived as non-threatening by the IODE, which accordingly paid it little attention. As French Canadian voices were heard, in the face of threats from those outside of Northern Europe and Britain, they were to some extent accommodated. Over the years, a series of challenges to Anglo-Celtic principles, from immigration, war and Communism, forced the IODE to define a national identity that was increasingly constructed within Canadian space and from Canadian subjectivities. Canadianization, war work, memorialization, education, health and welfare were some of the many ways of producing this identity. In recent times, the IODE has represented the fragmentation of such a totalizing identity. Although racial hierarchies are officially dismantled, prejudices continue, and there is still strong support for old universal attachments, such as the monarchy, and for a Canada within the Commonwealth. Rather than a clear break with the past, as the official donation of the IODE archive, and the name and badge changes, might at first indicate, there is an underlying continuity with the past and a re-presentation of a strongly mainstream tradition.

Maternal identity is the key and enduring, if changing, facet of the IODE's imperialism. While the race and class components of Anglo-Canadian identity are now destabilized, it is the gendered private spaces of charitable undertakings, construed as peripheral in the production of hegemonic space, that now offer the most stable domain for the IODE. Whereas, for the IODE, the maternal was constructed at the beginning of the twentieth century to support patriotism and citizenship, at the end of that century the maternal was constructed to support individual charitable endeavours. Due to such constructions, the IODE is able to carry on its re-presented ideas in spaces that shield its enduring patriotic motives. These are patriotic motives which have been transformed, and may have lost much of their confidence, but they demonstrate that times do not change as quickly as we might think. The history of the IODE and its part in the making of Anglo-Canada in the image of Britain demands that we constantly challenge those whom we choose as agents in explaining the past – and the present.

In focusing on the IODE this book makes a contribution to the new area of female imperialism. The IODE's unique position, as the oldest and largest female imperialist organization, is easy to argue for. The IODE was by far the most active organization of those comprised of twentieth-century female imperialists. It encompassed the most diverse membership, and carried out the widest variety of projects. That the IODE originated in Canada constitutes an intervention in British imperialism and in the developing nationalism of the white settler societies, because imperial histories have often seen imperialist attitudes as originating in Britain rather than in other parts of the Empire. That the IODE was largely confined to Canada reveals female imperialists' struggle for control of the Empire. That the IODE obeyed the Victoria League is evidence of the colonial deference to what was considered to be the superior imperial metropolis, one that it sought to emulate. The Victoria League may have barred the IODE from imperial expansion, but had the situation been different I doubt that the IODE would have flourished in New Zealand or Australia in the way it has in North America. Canada was central to the IODE's vision from the time of the 1901 Toronto take-over from the Montreal foundress Margaret Clark Murray, and the invention of an identity situated in North America has gained in strength ever since. Branches of the Victoria League in New Zealand, Australia and South Africa, while sharing a general resemblance to the IODE, especially in their educational and immigration work, were much smaller, retained a more rigid class structure and were happiest when hostessing at garden parties and attending imperial lectures in their privately cultivated spaces. This is to suggest that the myth of egalitarianism, which has been identified as important in images of masculinity in the white settler societies, does not necessarily apply either to femininity or to colonial élites more generally. And from Canada, along with its ability to encompass an ever-increasing cross-section of society and to roll up its sleeves and work, when it came to tea parties and getting dressed up the IODE has also trumped the other female imperialists with its formidable panache. The 1928 English Schoolgirl Tour showed the Order at its most organized; while its contribution to the war effort demonstrated the considerable size of its possible output. Canada's need to define itself against the USA was something that the other dominions had no immediate need to attempt, and helps us to understand the IODE's determination, as well as, paradoxically, some of its cultural influences. The IODE's history tells how British imperialism and settler nationalism worked in one twentieth-century white dominion. Always Canadian, its imperial foundations turned into national ambitions, while it's maternal identity experienced a loss of confidence and shifted from patriotism to charitable work. For the IODE, female imperialism and national identity were always intertwined, in an ever-evolving relationship that spanned a century.

Notes

1 Editorial, *Echoes*, 263 (summer 1966), 2.
2 Interview, 25 February 1994: Toronto, Ontario.
3 NAC MG28 I 17, 8, 1968, IODE crown and Canada committee.
4 Interview, 25 February 1994: Toronto, Ontario.
5 Interview, 20 April 1994: Meota, Saskatchewan.
6 Interview, 21 October 1993: Fredericton, New Brunswick.
7 Interview, 20 April 1994: Meota, Saskatchewan.
8 *Ibid.*
9 Interview, 24 April 1994: Calgary, Alberta.
10 *Charlottetown Patriot*, 6 June 1958.
11 Interview, 23 October 1993: Fredericton, New Brunswick.
12 Interview, 18 April 1994: Regina, Saskatchewan.
13 *Ibid.*
14 Interview, 24 April 1994: Calgary, Alberta.
15 Interview, 25 October 1993: Saint John, New Brunswick.
16 Interview, 27 April 1994: Vancouver, British Columbia.
17 Interview, 25 October 1993: Saint John, New Brunswick.
18 *Ibid.*
19 Interview, 9 October 1993: Campbellford, Ontario.
20 Interview, 20 April 1994: Meota, Saskatchewan.
21 Margaret Atwood, *Cat's Eye* (London, Sydney, Toronto and Auckland: Doubleday, 1988), 83–4.

Note on sources

Archival sources

Research for this book has involved the use of archival material, oral sources and photographic records. The National Archives of Canada (NAC) in Ottawa houses the largest IODE collection. MG28 I 17 Imperial Order Daughters of the Empire, volumes 1–75, is the meticulous collection that the IODE handed over in 1979. Its focus is on the affairs of the IODE at the national level, although the very structure of the Order meant that local areas were represented in the records. The collection includes: minutes of annual national meetings and annual reports 1900–79; national executive minutes 1901–74; reports to the national executive committee; minutes of national committees 1901–79; miscellaneous minutes 1900–45; constitution, structure and history 1900–79; general histories of the Order, giving accounts of its activities; miscellaneous correspondence; miscellaneous subject files 1901–77; chapter records 1900–74; scrapbooks and newspaper clippings.

There are numerous other collections at the NAC that contain information either from individual members of the IODE, such as Charlotte Whitton, or on Royal Commissions to which the IODE made submissions. Relevant British records are also in Ottawa, such as: MG28 I 336 Society of the Oversea Settlement of British Women; and selected records from the Fawcett Library (now the Women's Library), London. The Photography and Visual Images Division of National Archives has an IODE photograph collection.

There is a complete collection up to 1978 of the IODE's magazine *Echoes*, which is shared between the NAC's library and the National Library of Canada (NLC). *Echoes* has been published quarterly since 1901 under a series of long-serving editors, professional journalists who have brought together opinions from around the country, as well as putting forward their own views. The NLC, Ottawa, has an assortment of studies published by the IODE. Of particular use are: *Brief History of the IODE* (1981); Helen M. Yeo, *An Era of Change: Historical Narrative, 1901-1976* (1976, Royal Edward Chapter); *Welfare in Alberta: The Report of a Study Undertaken by the IODE Alberta Provincial Chapter* (1947); *Record of the Post-Graduate Scholarship Holders for the First Twenty Years of the First War Memorial Instituted by the National Chapter of Canada IODE* (1945); *Laurentian Chapter IODE: 1906–1976* (1976); *Canada Within the Empire* (1939, Toronto), and *IODE 1900–1925* (1925).

I have investigated the extent of IODE material held outside of Canada. There is not much. The Royal Commonwealth Society Library (RCSL) holds records of the Victoria League, and the following IODE records: L. M. Bruce, *IODE in Waterloo* (IODE, USA); *War Relief Records, Illinois Chapters; Golden Jubilee: 1900–1950*; G. de. C. Morrell, 'IODE in Bermuda', *West African Review*, 14:2, 64–70; and the colourful *Manitoba Souvenir* (1916). The Imperial War Museum, London (IWM) has a copy of Charlotte Whitton's 1944 *From Kith to Kin*.

Libraries, archives and private collections across Canada have various provincial IODE minute books, local chapter records and scrapbooks. The quality of the collections varies according to the members who took an interest in the history of the IODE and have donated records. I benefited from the private collection of Velma Laferty's (unpublished) 'History of IODE Alberta', Audrey Webster's scrapbook of Mrs C. S. Buchan (Frances), Calgary, Alberta; Bertha Miller's *Clark House* (1985, Fredericton, New Brunswick); Joan Church's Histories of IODE Saskatchewan, Regina; 1919–94, Eleanor Carrothers's collection, Quebec City; and the scrapbooks of Ruby Greer, Stanstead, Quebec. The value of personal scrapbooks is not to be underestimated. Many IODE chapters have assembled their individual histories through such representation.

The Glenbow Archives (GBOW), in Calgary, Alberta, has a useful collection, including individual chapter records, a summary of Alberta IODE Provincial reports, a summary of the findings and recommendations of the Alberta Welfare Study, carried out in August 1947, a 1959 book on the Provincial Chapter of Alberta, and Calgary Municipal Chapter's minutes and records. The Provincial Archives of Alberta (PAA), in Edmonton, has an assortment of the Lethbridge Municipal Chapter's records, the Provincial Chapter's summary reports for 1948–70 and reports of provincial meetings, and the Edmonton Municipal Chapter's records.

The British Columbia Archives and Records Service (BCARS), in Victoria, has Provincial Chapter minutes for British Columbia, Ethel

Stead's 1959 *History of the Imperial Order Daughters of the Empire in British Columbia*, parts 1 and 2, local chapter records, and assorted clippings. The City of Vancouver Archives (CVA) holds records of individual Vancouver chapters and the Municipal Chapter. The J. S. Matthews Newsclippings Microfilm 13–246–7, Orders: Imperial Order Daughters of the Empire, is useful. The Vancouver Public Library (VPL) has assorted newspaper clippings. At the University of British Columbia Special Collections (UBCSC) is a pamphlet file with Mabel Durham's article 'British Columbia's patriotic women', *The Canadian Magazine*, 49: 2 (June 1917).

The Provincial Archives of New Brunswick (PANB), Fredericton, holds the original minute book of the first IODE meeting in Fredericton on 15 January 1900. There are also Provincial Chapter records and scrapbooks. The Memorial University Library's Centre for Newfoundland Studies (MULNS), St John's, has an IODE competition about Canada's royal heritage with essays by Canadian school children, and the book *Light at Last: Triumph Over Tuberculosis in Newfoundland and Labrador 1900–1975* (St John's, Newfoundland: Jesperson Press, 1981), a publication containing evidence of an IODE chapter in Newfoundland during the First World War.

In Ontario, the Queen's University Archives (QUA), Kingston, has the Wilhelmina Gordon Collection. The Lorne Pierce Special Collection (LPSC), also held at Queen's University, has a number of rare IODE publications: *Record of the Post Graduate Scholarship Holders for the Years 1945–1990*, with a Foreword by Cecilia Furness, national officer and War Memorial secretary (1990); *Welfare in Alberta. The Report of a Study Undertaken by The Imperial Order Daughters of the Empire* (Alberta Provincial Chapter IODE, 1947); Charlotte Whitton's *From Kith to Kin* (IODE, 1944), and *The Imperial Order Daughters of the Empire: Chapters of the Order* (Ottawa: IODE, 1934). The Thomas Fisher Rare Book Library, at the University of Toronto, has IODE proofs of a collection called 'National pictures for Canadian schools' (1918), and *Imperial Order Daughters of the Empire Souvenir* (IODE 19th Annual Meeting, 1919).

The Provincial Chapter of Ontario (1070 Main Street West, Hamilton, Ontario) has the Ontario Provincial Chapter's annual reports and minutes,1920–92, scrapbooks, and recent documents such as mailing lists for the Canadian north. The National Chapter of Canada (40 Orchard View, Suite 254, Toronto) has the annual National Meetings' minutes for 1978–93, *Echoes* for 1979–94, and published sources such as *80th Anniversary, IODE Manitoba* (Provincial Chapter of Manitoba, 1992), and *IODE: A Brief History, 1900–1982.* (National Chapter, 1982).

The Public Archives and Records Office (PARO) in Charlottetown, Prince Edward Island, has records for the IODE Royal Edward Chapter 1901–87 and souvenir programmes. Helen Yeo's aforementioned book remains the most comprehensive source for the Island.

As for Quebec, I have found little source material, although the Colby-Curtis Museum, Stanstead, has assorted newspaper clippings.

The Saskatchewan Archives Board (SAB), Regina, has a large collection of individual chapter records, Regina and Saskatoon Municipal Chapter records, and Provincial IODE Saskatchewan records. There are also records of educational awards, scrapbooks, and correspondence

Interviews

I conducted forty-seven interviews across Canada with members of the IODE. The objectives of these interviews were to

- gather personal accounts of participation in the IODE;
- fill in regional details that were not available in the national records; and
- allow for oral history research that could verify and cross-refer to written sources.

The approach followed for the interviews was to use the contemporary structure of the IODE as a framework, setting out to interview one member in every 200 out of a 1992 total of 10,000. Hence the number of interviews per province corresponds as closely as possible to the proportion of national membership held by that particular province. The IODE, through its social network, itself acted as informants in identifying those who would be interviewed. This was arranged by using the IODE's structure to order the writing of letters first to the national headquarters, and with its permission writing to provincial presidents, asking for contacts. The details of the interviews are:

Alberta (12)
21 April, 1994: interview of a seven-member group, the Royal Canadian Legion, Calgary, Alberta.
24 April 1994: interview at an individual member's home, Calgary, Alberta.
26 April 1994: interview of a three-member group, the Canada Place Food Court, Edmonton, Alberta.
27 April 1994: interview of a single member, the YWCA Café, Edmonton, Alberta.

British Columbia (3)
29 April 1994: interview of a three-member group, member's home, Kerrisdale, Vancouver.

New Brunswick (4)
21 and 23 October 1993: interviews of single members in their homes, Fredericton.
25 October 1993: interviews with single members, at the Earl of Leinster Bed and Breakfast and the Union Club, Saint John.

Newfoundland (1)
14 July 1993: interview of a member in her home, St John's.

Ontario (10)
9 October 1993: interview of a member in her home, Campbellford.
4 November 1993: interview of a member, Christchurch Cathedral, Ottawa.
8 November 1993: interview of a four-member group, Briargate Retirement Home, Kingston.
23 February 1994: interview of a member, IODE Provincial Chapter of Ontario, Hamilton.
24 February 1994: two interviews, by telephone, of individual members, Toronto.
25 February 1994: interview of a member at my homestay, Toronto.

Prince Edward Island (5)
27 October 1993: interview of a five-member group in a member's home, Charlottetown.

Quebec (10)
22 November 1993: two interviews of individual members in their homes, Montreal.
12 and 13 February 1994: two interviews of individual members in their homes, Sillery.
28 August 1995: interview of a five-member group in a member's home, Stanstead.
31 August 1995: interview of a member in her home, Stanstead.

Saskatchewan (2)
18 April 1994: interview of a member in her home, Regina.
20 April 1994: interview of a member in her home, Meota.

Theses and dissertations

A single PhD thesis has been written about the IODE, which forms the research base for this book: Catherine Gillian Pickles, 'Representing twentieth-century Canadian colonial identity: the Imperial Order Daughters of the Empire (IODE)', Department of Geography, McGill University, 1996.

At the time of writing, five MA dissertations directly concerned with the IODE have been completed: Daniel Buteau, 'De L'Empire à la nation: L'Impérial Order Daughters of the Empire de 1938 à 1972', Université Laval, 1987; Marcel Dirk, 'Imperial Order Daughters of the Empire and the First World War', Institute of Canadian Studies, Carleton University, 1988; Lisa Gaudet, 'Nation's mothers, Empire's daughters: the Imperial Order Daughters of the Empire, 1920–1930', Department of History, Carleton University, 1993; Doreen Constance Hamilton, 'Origins of the IODE: a Canadian women's movement for God, king and country, 1900–1925', Department of History, University of New Brunswick, 1992; and Nadine Michele Small, 'Stand by the Union Jack: the Imperial Order Daughters of the Empire in the Prairie provinces during the Great War, 1914–18', Department of History, University of Saskatchewan, 1988.

BIBLIOGRAPHY

Alessio, Dominic David, 'Domesticating "the heart of the wild": female personifications of the Colonies, 1886–1940', *Women's History Review*, 6: 2 (1997), 239–69.

Anderson, Benedict, *Imagined Communities: Reflections on the Origin and Spread of Nationalism*, 2nd edn (London and New York: Verso, 1991 [1983]).

Anderson, Kay, *Vancouver's Chinatown: Racial Discourse in Canada, 1875–1980* (Montreal and Kingston: McGill–Queen's University Press, 1991).

Anderson, Kay, and Fay Gale (eds), *Inventing Places: Studies in Cultural Geography* (Melbourne: Longman, 1992).

Arnup, Katherine, Andrée Lévesque and Ruth Roach Pierson (eds), *Delivering Motherhood: Maternal Ideologies and Practices in the Nineteenth and Twentieth Centuries* (London and New York: Routledge, 1990).

Atwood, Margaret, *Cat's Eye* (London, Sydney, Toronto and Auckland: Doubleday, 1988).

Bacchi, Carol Lee, *Liberation Deferred? The Ideas of the English–Canadian Suffragists, 1877–1918* (Toronto: University of Toronto Press, 1983).

Bacchi, Carol Lee, 'Race regeneration and social purity: a study of the social attitudes of Canada's English-speaking suffragists', *Histoire sociale/Social History*, 11: 22 (1978), 460–74.

Barber, Marilyn, *Immigrant Domestic Servants in Canada*, Canada's Ethnic Groups, Booklet No. 16 (Ottawa: Canadian Historical Association and the Government of Canada's Multicultural Programme, 1991).

Barber, Marilyn, 'Sunny Ontario for British girls, 1900–30', in Jean Burnet (ed.), *Looking into My Sister's Eyes: An Exploration in Women's History* (Toronto: Multicultural History Society of Ontario, 1986), 55–73.

Barber, Marilyn, 'The women Ontario welcomed: immigrant domestics for Ontario homes, 1870–1930', in Alison Prentice and Susan Mann Trofimenkoff (eds), *The Neglected Majority: Essays in Canadian Women's History* (Toronto: McClelland & Stewart, 1985), vol 2: 102–21.

Barber, Marilyn, 'The gentlewomen of Queen Mary's Coronation Hostel', in Barbara K. Latham and Roberta J. Pazdro (eds), *Not Just Pin Money* (Victoria: Camosun College, 1984), 141–58.

Bauer, P. T., *Economic Analysis and Policy in Underdeveloped Countries* (Duke University Commonwealth Studies Centre, Durham, NC: Duke University Press, 1957).

Bell, Morag, 'A woman's place in "a white man's country": rights, duties and citizenship for the "new" South Africa, c. 1902', *Ecumene*, 2: 2 (1995), 129–48.

Bell, Morag, '"The pestilence that walketh in darkness": imperial health, gender and images of South Africa c. 1880–1910', *Transactions of the Insti* tute of British Geographers, n. s. 18 (1993), 327–41.

Bell, Morag, Robin Butlin and Michael Heffernan (eds), *Geography and Imperialism 1820–1940* (Manchester: Manchester University Press, 1995).

Berger, Carl, *The Sense of Power: Studies in the Ideas of Canadian Imperialism, 1867–1914* (Toronto: University of Toronto Press, 1970).

Berger, Carl, 'The true north strong and free', in Peter Russell (ed.), *Nationalism in Canada* (Toronto: University of Toronto Press, 1966), 3–26.

Bhabha, Homi K., *The Location of Culture* (London and New York: Routledge, 1994).

Bhabha, Homi K., 'Conference presentation', in Philomena Mariani (ed.), *Critical Fictions: The Politics of Imaginative Writing* (Seattle, WA: Bay Press, 1991).

Bhabha, Homi K. (ed.), *Nation and Narration* (London and New York: Routledge, 1990).

Blakeley, Brian L., 'The Society for the Oversea Settlement of British Women and the problems of Empire settlement, 1917–1936', *Albion*, 20: 3 (1988), 421–44.

Bloom, Lisa, *Gender on Ice: American Ideologies of Polar Expeditions* (Minneapolis and London: University of Minnesota Press, 1993).

Blunt, Alison and Gillian Rose (eds), *Writing Women and Space: Colonial and Postcolonial Geographies* (New York and London: Guilford Press, 1994).

Bothwell, Robert and J. L. Granatstein (eds), *The Gouzenko Transcripts: The Evidence Presented to the Kellock–Taschereau Royal Commission of 1946* (Ottawa: Deneau Publishers, 1982).

Boyer, Paul S., *By the Bomb's Early Light: American Thought and Culture at the Dawn of the Atomic Age* (New York: Pantheon, 1985).

Buckner, Phillip, 'Whatever happened to the British Empire?', *Journal of the Canadian Historical Association*, 4 (1994), 2–32.

Bush, Julia, *Edwardian Ladies and Imperial Power* (Leicester: University of Leicester Press, 2000).

Bush, Julia, 'Edwardian ladies and the "race" dimensions of British imperialism', *Women's Studies International Forum*, 21: 3 (1998), 277–89.

Bush, Julia, '"The right sort of woman": female emigrators and the emigration to the British Empire, 1890–1910', *Women's History Review*, 3: 3 (1994), 385–409.

Butler, Judith, 'Contingent foundations: feminism and the question of "postmodernism', in Judith Butler and Joan W. Scott (eds), *Feminists Theorize the Political* (London and New York: Routledge, 1992).

Burton, Antoinette, (ed.), *Gender, Sexuality and Colonial Modernities* (London and New York: Routledge, 1999).

Burton, Antoinette, *At the Heart of Empire: Indians and the Colonial Encounter in Late-Victorian Britain* (Berkeley, Los Angeles and London: University of California Press, 1998).

Burton, Antoinette, *Burdens of History: British Feminists, Indian Women, and Imperial Culture, 1865–1915* (Chapel Hill and London: University of North Carolina Press, 1994).

Burton, Antoinette, 'Colonial encounters in late-Victorian England: Pandita

Ramabai at Cheltenham and Wantage 1883–6', *Feminist Review*, 49: spring (1995), 29–49.

Callaway, Helen, *Gender, Culture and Empire: European Women in Colonial Nigeria* (Basingstoke: Macmillan, 1987).

Carrothers, W. A., *Emigration from the British Isles: With Special Reference to the Development of the Oversea Dominions* (London: P. S. King & Son, 1929).

Chaudhuri, Nupur and Margaret Strobel (eds), *Western Women and Imperialism: Complicity and Resistance* (Bloomington: Indiana University Press, 1992).

Church Harrison, R. J., *Modern Colonization* (London, New York, Melbourne, Sydney and Cape Town: Hutchinson's University Library, 1951).

Clancy-Smith and Frances Gouda (eds) *Domesticating the Empire: Race, Gender and Family Life in French and Dutch Colonialism* (Charlottesville and London: University of Virginia Press, 1998).

Cleverdon, Catherine Lyle, *The Woman Suffrage Movement in Canada* (Toronto: University of Toronto Press, 1950).

Clifford, James and G. E. Marcus, *Writing Cultures* (Berkeley: University of California Press, 1986).

Clio Collective, *Quebec Women: A History* (Toronto: Women's Press, 1987).

Coates, Ken, *Best Left as Indians: Native–White Relations in the Yukon Territories 1840–1973* (Montreal: McGill–Queen's University Press, 1991).

Coates, Ken (ed.), *Aboriginal Land Claims in Canada: A Regional Perspective* (Toronto: Copp Clark Pitman, 1982).

Constantine, Stephen (ed.), *Emigrants and Empire: British Settlement in the Dominions between the Wars* (Manchester: Manchester University Press, 1990).

Conway, John, 'An adapted organic tradition', *Daedalus: Journal of the American Academy of Arts and Sciences*, 117: 4 (1988), 381–96.

Cooper, H. L., A. Munich and S. Merrill Squier (eds), *Arms and the Woman: War, Gender, and Literary Representation* (Chapell Hill: University of North Carolina Press, 1989).

Davies, Robertson, *The Salterton Trilogy* (Toronto: Penguin, 1980).

Davin, Anna, 'Imperialism and motherhood', *History Workshop*, 5: spring (1978), 9–64.

Dawson, Michael, *The Mountie from Dime Novel to Disney* (Toronto: Between The Lines, 1998).

Dewar, David *Queen's Profiles* (Montreal: Office of Endowment and Public Relations, Queen's University, 1951).

Dirks, Nicholas B., 'Introduction: colonialism and culture', in Nicholas B. Dirks (ed.), *Colonialism and Culture* (Ann Arbor: University of Michigan Press, 1992), 1–25.

Dubinsky, Karen, *The Second Greatest Disappointment: Honeymooning and Tourism at Niagara Falls* (Toronto: Between The Lines, 1999).

Dubinsky, Karen, *Improper Advances: Rape and Heterosexual Conflict in Ontario. 1880-1929* (Chicago and London: University of Chicago Press, 1993).

Dubinsky, Karen, 'Vacations in the "contact zone": race, gender, and the traveler at Niagara Falls', in Ruth Roach Pierson and Nupur Chaudhuri (eds), with Beth McAuley, *Nation, Empire, Colony: Historicizing Gender and Race* (Indiana: Indiana University Press, 1998), 251–69.

Driver, Felix, *Geography Militant: Cultures of Exploration in the Age of Empire* (Oxford: Blackwell, 1999).

Duncan, James and Denis Cosgrove (eds), 'Colonialism and postcolonialism in the former British Empire', *Ecumene*, 2: 2 (1995), 127–8.

Elshtain, Jean Bethke, *Women and War* (New York: Basic Books, 1987).

Elshtain, Jean Bethke, *Public Man, Private Woman: Women in Social and Political Thought* (Princeton, NJ: Princeton University Press, 1981).

Fedorowich, Kent, *Unfit for Heroes: Reconstruction and Soldier Settlement in the Empire between the Wars* (Manchester: Manchester University Press, 1995).

Fentress, James and Chris Wickham *Social Memory* (Oxford and Cambridge, MA: Blackwell, 1992).

Forgacs, David (ed.) *An Antonio Gramsci Reader: Selected Writings 1916–1935* (New York: Schoken, 1988).

Foucault, Michel, *Power/Knowledge: Selected Interviews and Other Writings, 1972–1977* (New York: Pantheon, 1980).

Foucault, Michel, *The History of Sexuality* (New York: Pantheon Books, 1978), vol. 1.

Foucault, Michel, *The Order of Things: An Archaeology of the Human Sciences* (London: Tavistock, 1970).

Francis, Daniel, *National Dreams: Myth, Memory, and Canadian History* (Vancouver: Arsenal Pulp Press, 1997).

Frankenberg, Ruth, *White Women, Race Matters: The Social Construction of Whiteness* (Minneapolis: University of Minnesota Press, 1995).

Fussell, Paul, *The Great War and Modern Memory* (Oxford and New York: Oxford University Press, 1975).

Gill, Alan, *Orphans of the Empire* (Sydney, New York and Toronto: Vintage, 1998).

Gillett, Margaret, *We Walked Very Wearily: A History of Women at McGill* (Montreal: Eden Press Women's Publications, 1981).

Gillett, Margaret, 'Growing pains: Mrs Murray, Lady Minto, Mrs Nordheimer and the early years of the IODE', Address to the James McGill Society, Montreal, 24 January 2000.

Godlewska, Anne and Neil Smith (eds), *Geography and Empire* (Oxford and Cambridge, MA: Blackwell, 1994).

Gothard, Janice, '"The healthy wholesome British domestic girl": single female migration and the Empire Settlement Act, 1922–1930', in S. Constantine (ed.), *Emigrants and Empire: British Settlement in the Dominions between the Wars* (Manchester: Manchester University Press, 1990), 72–95.

Government of Canada, *A History of the Vote in Canada* (Ottawa: Minister of Public Works and Government Services Canada, 1997).

Government of Canada, *The Canadian Multiculturalism Act* (Ottawa: Government Printer, 1988).

Greenhill, Pauline, *Ethnicity in the Mainstream: Three Studies of English Canadian Culture in Ontario* (Montreal, Kingston and London: McGill–Queen's University Press, 1993).

Gregory, Derek, *Geographical Imaginations* (Oxford and Cambridge, MA: Blackwell, 1994).

Haggis, Jane, *Women and Colonialism: Untold Stories and Conceptual Absences. A Critical Survey* (Manchester: University of Manchester, Sociology Department Special Series, 1988).

Hall, Catherine, *White, Male, and Middle-Class: Explorations in Feminism and History* (New York: Routledge, 1992).

Hall, Catherine, '"From Greenland's icy mountains ... to Afric's golden sand": ethnicity, race and nation in mid-nineteenth-century England', *Gender and History*, 5: 2 (1993), 212–30.

Hammerton, James, *Emigrant Gentlewomen: Genteel Poverty and Female Emigration, 1830–1914* (London: Croom Helm, 1979).

Haraway, Donna, 'Ecce homo, ain't (ar'n't) I a woman, and inappropriate/d others: the human in a post-humanist landscape', in Judith Butler and Joan W. Scott (eds), *Feminists Theorize the Political* (London and New York: Routledge, 1992), 86–100.

Haraway, Donna, *Simians, Cyborgs, and Women: The Reinvention of Nature* (New York: Routledge, 1991).

Harding, Sandra, 'Rethinking standpoint epistemology: what is strong objectivity'? in Linda Alcoff and Elizabeth Potter (eds), *Feminist Epistemologies* (London and New York: Routledge, 1993), 49–82.

Harding, Sandra, *Whose Science? Whose Knowledge? Thinking from Women's Lives* (Ithaca, NY: Cornell University Press, 1991).

Harney, Robert F., *If One Were to Write a History: Selected Writings* (Toronto: Multicultural History Society of Ontario, 1991).

Harris, R. C. 'The simplification of Europe overseas', *Annals of the Association of American Geographers*, 67: 4 (1977), 469–83.

Hawkins, Freda, *Critical Years in Immigration: Canada and Australia Compared* (Kingston and Montreal: McGill–Queen's University Press, 1989).

Heffernan, Michael, 'For ever England: the Western Front and the politics of remembrance in Britain', *Ecumene*, 2: 3 (1995), 293–323.

Hobsbawn, Eric and Terence Ranger (eds), *The Invention of Tradition* (Cambridge: Cambridge University Press, 1983).

Hooks, Bell, *Yearning: Race, Gender and Cultural Politics* (Boston, MA: South End Press, 1990).

Hopkins, J. Castell, *The Canadian Annual Review of Public Affairs* (Toronto: Annual Review Publishing Co.), 1901–1930.

Huntington, Ellsworth, *The Character of the Races, as Influenced by Physical Environment, Natural Selection and Historical Development* (New York: Scribner, 1924).

Iacovetta, Franca with Paul Draper and Robert Ventresca, *A Nation of Immigrants: Women, Workers and Communities in Canadian History, 1840s–1960s* (Toronto: University of Toronto Press, 1998).

Iacovetta, Franca, 'Making "new Canadians": social workers, women, and the reshaping of immigrant families', in Franca Iacovetta and Mariana Valverde (eds), *Gender Conflicts: New Essays in Women's History* (Toronto: University of Toronto Press, 1992), 261–303.

Jackson, Peter and Jan Penrose (eds) *Constructions of Race, Place and Nation* (London: University College Press and Minneapolis: University of Minnesota Press, 1994).

Johnson, Nuala 'Cast in stone: monuments, geography, and nationalism', *Environment and Planning D: Society and Space*, 13 (1995), 51–6.

Jolly, Margaret, 'Colonizing women: the maternal body and Empire', in Sneja Gunew and Anna Yeatman (eds), *Feminism and the Politics of Difference* (St Leonards, New South Wales: Allen & Unwin, 1993),103–27.

Kay, Jeanne, 'Landscapes of women and men: rethinking the regional historical geography of the United States and Canada', *Journal of Historical Geography*, 17: 4 (1991), 435–52.

Kay, Jeanne, 'Commentary on articles by Meinig, Jordan, and Hornsby: the future of historical geography in the United States and Canada', *Annals of the Association of American Geographers*, 80: 4 (1990), 618–23.

Kealey, Linda (ed.) *A Not Unreasonable Claim* (Toronto: Women's Press, 1979).

Kelly, Dorothy and Susan M. Reverby (eds), *Gendered Domains: Rethinking Public and Private in Women's History* (Ithaca, NY: Cornell University Press, 1992).

Kennedy, Dane 'Empire migration in post-war reconstruction: the role of the Oversea Settlement Committee, 1919–1922', *Albion*, 20: 3 (1988), 403–19.

Jacobs, Jane M., *Edge of Empire: Postcolonialism and the City* (London and New York: Routledge, 1996).

Kerber, Linda J., 'Separate spheres, female worlds, woman's place: the rhetoric of women's history', *Journal of American History*, 75: 1 (1988), 9–39.

Kerber, Linda J., Untitled section in Linda J. Kerber, Nancy F. Cott, Robert Gross, Lynn Hunt, Carol Smith-Rosenberg, and Christine M. Stansell, 'Beyond roles, beyond spheres: thinking about gender in the early republic', *William and Mary Quarterly*, 46: 3 (1989), July, 565–85.

Kerby, Andrew, 'What Did You Do in the War Daddy?', in A. Godlewska and N. Smith (eds), *Geography and Empire* (Oxford and Cambridge, MA: Blackwell, 1994), 300–15.

Kertland, May, *IODE: the Third Twenty-Five Years* (Toronto: Best Publishing, 1975).

Kimble, George H. T. and Dorothy Good (eds) *Geography of the Northlands*, Special Publication 32 (New York: American Geographical Society, 1955).

Kinsman, Gary, '"Character weakness" and "fruit machines": towards an analysis of the anti-homosexual security campaign in the Canadian Civil Service', *Labour/Le Travail*, 35: spring (1995), 133–62.

Knapman, Claudia, *White Women in Fiji, 1835–1930: The Ruin of Empire?* (Sydney: Allen & Unwin, 1986).

Knowles, Valerie, *Strangers at Our Gates: Canadian Immigration and Immigration Policy, 1540–1990* (Toronto: Dundurn Press, 1992).

Kobayashi, Audrey (ed.), *Women, Work and Place* (Montreal and Kingston, Ontario: McGill–Queen's University Press, 1994).

Kobayashi, Audrey 'Coloring the field: gender, "race", and the politics of field-work', *Professional Geographer*, 46: 1 (1994), 73–80.

Kobayashi, Audrey, 'Multiculturalism: representing a Canadian institution', in James Duncan and David Ley (eds), *Place/Culture/Representation* (London and New York: Routledge, 1993), 205–31.

Kobayashi, Audrey and Linda Peake, 'Unnatural discourse: "race" and gender in geography', *Gender, Place and Culture*, 1: 2 (1994), 225–43.

Kobayashi, Audrey and Suzanne MacKenzie (eds) *Remaking Human Geography* (Boston: Unwin, 1989).

Laclau, Ernesto and Chantal Mouffe, *Hegemony and Socialist Strategy: Towards a Radical Democratic Politics* (London: Verso, 1985).

Lefebvre, Henri, *The Production of Space*, trans Donald Nicholson-Smith (Oxford and Cambridge, MA: Blackwell, 1991).

Lenin, Vladimir, *Imperialism, the Highest Stage of Capitalism: A Popular Outline* (New York: International Publishers, 1939 [1921]).

Lévesque, Andrée, *Making and Breaking the Rules. Women in Québec, 1919–1939* (Toronto: McClelland & Stewart, 1994).

Light, Alison, *Forever England: Femininity, Literature and Conservatism between the Wars* (London: Routledge, 1991).

Livingstone, David N., *The Geographical Tradition: Episodes in the History of a Contested Enterprise* (Oxford and Cambridge, MA: Blackwell, 1993).

Lloyd, Genevieve, 'Selfhood, war and masculinity', in Carol Pateman and Elizabeth Gross (eds), *Feminist Challenges: Social and Political Theory* (Boston, MA: Northeastern University Press, 1986), 63–76.

Lower, J. Arthur, *Canada:An Outline History*, 2nd edn (Toronto: McGraw-Hill Ryerson, 1991 [1973]).

MacDonald, S. P. Holden and S. Ardener (eds), *Images of Women in Peace and War: Cross-Cultural and Historical Perspectives* (London: Macmillan, 1987).

MacKenzie, John M. (ed.), *Imperialism and Popular Culture* (Manchester: Manchester University Press, 1986).

MacKenzie, John M. *Propaganda and Empire: The Manipulation of British Public Opinion, 1880–1960* (Manchester: Manchester University Press, 1984).

MacLaren, Angus, *Our Own Master Race: Eugenics in Canada 1885–1945* (Toronto: McClelland & Stewart, 1990).

Madrell, Avril M.C., 'Empire, emigration and school geography: changing discourses of imperial citizenship, 1880–1925', *Journal of Historical Geography*, 22: 4 (1996), 373–87.

Mangan, J. A. (ed.) *The Imperial Curriculum: Racial Images and Education in the British Colonial Experience* (London and New York: Routledge, 1993).

Mangan, J. A. (ed.) *Making Imperial Mentalities: Socialisation and British Imperialism* (Manchester: Manchester University Press, 1990).

Mangan, J. A. (ed.), *Pleasure, Profit, Proselytism: British Culture and Sport at Home and Abroad, 1700-1914* (London and Totowa, NJ: Frank Cass, 1988).

Mangan, J. A., *The Games Ethic and Imperialism Aspects of the Diffusion of an Ideal* (Middlesex: Viking, 1985).

McClintock, Anne, *Imperial Leather: Race, Gender and Sexuality in the Colonial Contest* (London and New York: Routledge, 1995).

McCormack, Ross, 'Networks among British immigrants and accommodation to Canadian society: Winnipeg, 1900–1914', *Histoire sociale/ Social History*, 17: 4 (1984), 357–74.

McCormack, Ross, 'Cloth Caps and Jobs: The Ethnicity of English Immigrants in Canada, 1900–1914', in Jorgen Dahlie and Tina Fernando (eds), *Ethnicity, Power and Politics in Canada* (Toronto: Methuen, 1981), 38-57.

McIntyre, W. David, *The Significance of the Commonwealth, 1965–90* (Basingstoke and London: Macmillan, 1991).

McIntyre, W. David, *The Commonwealth of Nations: Origins and Impact, 1869–1971* (Minneapolis: University of Minnesota Press, 1977).

McPherson, Kathryn, Cecilia Morgan and Nancy M. Forestell (eds), *Gendered Pasts: Historical Essays in Femininity and Masculinity in Canada* (Don Mills: Oxford University Press Canada, 1999).

Meyerowitz, Joanne (ed.), *Not June Cleaver: Women and Gender in Postwar America, 1945–1960* (Philadelphia, PA: Temple University Press, 1994).

Michie, G. H. and E. M. Neil, 'Cultural conflict in the Canadian Arctic', *The Canadian Geographer*, 5 (1955), 22–41.

Midgley, Clare (ed.), *Gender and Imperialism* (Manchester: Manchester University Press, 1998).

Miles, Miranda and Jonathan Crush, 'Personal narratives as interactive texts: collecting and interpreting migrant life-histories', *Professional Geographer*, 45: 1 (1993), 95–129.

Miller, Carman, *Painting the Map Red: Canada and the South Africa War, 1899–1902* (Montreal: McGill–Queen's University Press, 1993).

Mills, Sara, 'Knowledge, gender, and Empire', in Alison Blunt and Gillian Rose (eds), *Writing Women and Space: Colonial and Postcolonial Geographies* (New York and London: Guilford Press, 1994), 29–50.

Mills, Sara, *Discourses of Difference: An Analysis of Women's Travel Writing and Colonialism* (London and New York: Routledge, 1993).

Mitchener, Wendy, 'The WCTU: "for God, home and native land": a study in nineteenth-century feminism', in Linda Kealey (ed.), *A Not Unreasonable Claim* (Toronto, Women's Press, 1979), 151–67.

Monk, Una, *New Horizons: A Hundred Years of Women's Migration* (London: HMSO, 1963).

Morgan, Cecilia, '"Of slender frame and delicate appearance": the placing of Laura Secord in the narratives of Canadian loyalist history', in Joy Parr and Mark Rosenfeld (eds), *Gender and History in Canada* (Mississauga: Copp Clark, 1996).

Morton, Desmond and Glenn Wright, *Winning the Second Battle: Canadian Veterans and the Return to Civilian Life 1915–1930* (Toronto: University of Toronto Press, 1987).

Morton, W. L., *The Canadian Identity* 2nd edn (Madison: University of Wisconsin Press, 1972).

Mouffe, Chantal, *The Return of the Political* (London: Verso, 1993).

Mouffe, Chantal (ed.), *Dimensions of Radical Democracy: Pluralism, Citizenship and Community* (London and New York: Verso, 1992).

Myers, Gareth, '"From Stinkibar to the island metropolis": the geography of British hegemony in Zanzibar', in Anne Godlewska and Neil Smith (eds), *Geography and Empire* (Oxford and Cambridge, MA: Blackwell, 1994).

Oakes, Guy, *The Imaginary War: Civil Defense and American Cold War Culture* (New York: Oxford University Press, 1994).

Olson, Sherry H. and A. L. Kobayashi, 'The emerging ethnocultural mosaic', in Larry S. Bourne and David F. Ley (eds), *The Changing Social Geography of Canadian Cities* (Montreal, Kingston, London and Buffalo: McGill–Queen's University Press, 1993), 138–52.

Osborne, Brian S, 'Canadian nation building: a monumental approach to landscapes of power', Paper presented at the 9th International Conference of Historical Geographers Pre-Conference Symposium. *Landscape and Identity*, 28–30 June 1995, Garden Hotel, Singapore.

Paisley, Fiona, *Loving Protection? Australian Feminism and Aboriginal Women's Rights, 1919–39* (Carlton South: Melbourne University Press, 2000).

Paisley, Fiona, 'Citizens of their world: Australian feminism and indigenous rights in the international context, 1920s and 1930s', *Feminist Review*, 58: spring (1998), 66–84.

Palmer, Howard, *Immigration and the Rise of Multiculturalism* (Vancouver, Calgary, Toronto and Montreal: Copp Clark, 1975).

Palmer, Howard, 'Reluctant hosts: Anglo-Canadian views of multiculturalism in the twentieth century', in Gerald Tulchinsky (ed.), *Immigration in Canada: Historical Perspectives* (Toronto: Copp Clark Longman, 1994), 297–333.

Palmer, Howard, *Ethnicity and Politics in Canada since Confederation*, Booklet No. 17 (Ottawa: Canadian Historical Association with the support of the Government of Canada's Multiculturalism Programme, 1991).

Parker, Andrew, Mary Russo, Doris Sommer and Patricia Yeager (eds), *Nationalisms and Sexualities* (New York: Routledge, 1992).

Parr, Joy, *Labouring Children: British Apprentices to Canada, 1869–1924* (London: Croom Helm, Montreal and Kingston: McGill–Queen's University Press, 1981).

Parr, Joy and Mark Rosenfeld (eds) *Gender and History in Canada* (Mississauga: Copp Clark, 1996).

Parry, John T., 'Geomorphology in Canada', *The Canadian Geographer*, 11: 4 (1967), 280–311.

Pateman, Carole, *The Disorder of Women: Democracy, Feminism and Political Theory* (Cambridge: Polity, 1989).

Perry, Adele, *On the Edge of Empire: Gender, Race, and the Making of British Columbia, 1849–1871* (Toronto: University of Toronto Press, 2000).

Perry, Adele, '"Oh I'm just sick of the faces of men": gender imbalance, race, sexuality, and sociability in nineteenth-century British Columbia', *BC Studies*, 105–6: spring/summer (1995), 27–43.

Phillips, Anne, *Democracy and Difference* (University Park: Pennsylvania State University Press, 1993).

Pickles, Katie, 'Colonial Counterparts: The First Academic Women in Anglo-Canada, New Zealand and Australia', *Women's History Review*, 10: 2 (2001), 273-297.

Pickles, Katie, 'Empire Settlement and Single British Women as New Zealand Domestic Servants During the 1920s', *The New Zealand Journal of History*, 35: 1 (2001), 22-44.

Pickles, Katie, 'Exhibiting Canada: Empire, migration and the 1928 English Schoolgirl Tour', *Gender, Place and Culture*, 7: 1 (2000), 81–96.

Pickles, Katie, 'Forgotten colonizers: the Imperial Order Daughters of the Empire (IODE) and the Canadian north', *The Canadian Geographer*, 42: 2 (1998), 193–204.

Pickles, Katie (ed.), *Hall of Fame: Life Stories of New Zealand Women* (Christchurch: Clerestory Press, 1998).

Pickles, Katie, 'Edith Cavell – heroine. No hatred or bitterness for anyone?', *History Now*, 3: 2 (1997), 1–8.

Pierson, Ruth Roach, *'They're Still Women After All': The Second World War and Canadian Womanhood* (Toronto: McClelland & Stewart, 1986).

Pierson, Ruth Roach and Nupur Chaudhuri (eds), with Beth McAuley, *Nation, Empire, Colony: Historicizing Gender and Race* (Bloomington: Indiana University Press, 1998).

Pierson, Ruth Roach, '"Did your mother wear army boots?" Feminist theory and women's relation to war, peace and revolution', in S. MacDonald, P. Holden and S. Ardener (eds), *Images of Women in Peace and War: Cross-Cultural and Historical Perspectives* (London: MacMillan, 1987).

Plant, G. F., *Oversea Settlement: Migration from the United Kingdom to the Dominions* (London: Oxford University Press, 1951).

Porter, John, *The Vertical Mosaic: An Analysis of Social Class and Power in Canada* (Toronto: University of Toronto Press, 1965).

Pratt, Mary Louise, *Imperial Eyes: Travel Writing and Transculturation* (London and New York: Routledge, 1992).

Prentice, A., P. Bourne, G. C. Brandt, B. Light, W. Mitchinson and N. Black (eds), *Canadian Women: A History*, 2nd edn (Toronto: Harcourt Brace Jovanovich, 1996 [1988]).

Prentice, Alison and Susan Mann Trofimenkoff (eds), *The Neglected Majority: Essays in Canadian Women's History*, vol. 2 (Toronto: McClelland & Stewart, 1985).

Quinn Duffy, R. *The Road to Nunavut: The Progress of the Eastern Arctic Inuit since the Second World War* (Montreal and Kingston: McGill–Queen's University Press, 1988).

Ram, Kalpana and Margaret Jolly, *Maternities and Modernities: Colonial and Postcolonial Experiences in Asia and the Pacific* (Cambridge: Cambridge University Press, 1998).

Reimer, K. J., *The Environmental Effects of the DEW Line on the Canadian Arctic* (Victoria, British Columbia: Royal Roads Military College Environmental Group, 1993).

Richards, Thomas, *The Imperial Archive: Knowledge and the Fantasy of Empire* (London and New York: Verso, 1993).

Richmond, Anthony H., *Post-War Immigrants in Canada* (Toronto: University of Toronto Press, 1967).

Riedi, Elizabeth L., 'Imperialist women in Edwardian Britain: the Victoria League 1899–1914', PhD thesis, St Andrew's University, 1998.

Riley, Denise, *'Am I that Name?': Feminism and the Category of 'Women' in History* (Basingstoke: Macmillan, 1988).

Roberts, Barbara, *Whence They Came: Deportation from Canada, 1900–1935* (Ottawa: University of Ottawa Press, 1988).

Roberts, Barbara, '"Shovelling out the mutinous": political deportation from Canada before 1936', *Labour/Le Travail*, 18: fall (1986), 77–110.

Roberts, Barbara, '"A work of Empire: Canadian reformers and British female immigration', in Linda Kealey (ed.), *A Not Unreasonable Claim* (Toronto: Women's Press, 1979), 185–202.

Roberts, Wayne, '"Rocking the cradle for the world": the new woman and maternal feminism, Toronto, 1877–1914', in Linda Kealey (ed.), *A Not Unreasonable Claim* (Toronto: Women's Press, 1979), 15–46.

Rompkey, Ronald, *Grenfell of Labrador: A Biography* (Toronto: University of Toronto Press, 1991).

Rooke, P. T. and R. L. Schnell, *No Bleeding Heart: Charlotte Whitton, a Feminist on the Right* (Vancouver: University of British Columbia Press, 1987).

Rose, Gillian, *Feminism and Geography: The Limits of Geographical Knowledge* (Minneapolis: University of Minnesota Press, 1993).

Rose, Gillian and Miles Ogborn, 'Debate: feminism and historical geography', *Journal of Historical Geography*. 14: 4 (1988), 405–9.

Ruddick, Sara, *Maternal Thinking: Toward a Politics of Peace* (Boston, MA: Beacon Press, 1989).

Rutherdale, Myra, *Women and the White Man's God: Gender and Race in the Canadian Mission Field* (Vancouver: University of British Columbia Press, forthcoming).

Rutherdale, Myra, 'Revisiting colonization through gender: Anglican missionary women in the Pacific northwest and the Arctic, 1860–1945', *BC Studies*, 104: winter (1994), 3–23.

Ryan, Mary, *Women in Public: Between Banners and Ballots, 1825–1880* (Baltimore, MD: Johns Hopkins University Press, 1990).

Ryan, Mary, *Cradle of the Middle Class: The Family in Oneida County, New York, 1790–1865* (Cambridge and New York: Cambridge University Press, 1981).

Said, Edward, *Culture and Imperialism* (London: Verso, 1993).

Said, Edward, *Orientalism*, 2nd edn (New York: Vintage Books, 1994 [1978]).

Samuel, Raphael, *Theatres of Memory*, vol. 1: *The Past and Present in Contemporary Culture* (London and New York: Verso, 1994).

Samuel, Raphael, and Paul Thompson (eds), *The Myths We Live By* (London and New York: Routledge, 1990).

Schultz, John A., '"Leaven for the lump": Canada and Empire settlement, 1918–1939', in Stephen Constantine (ed.), *Emigrants and Empire: British*

Settlement in the Dominions between the Wars (Manchester: Manchester University Press, 1990), 150–73.

Semmel, Bernard, *Imperialism and Social Reform: English Social-Imperialist Thought, 1895–1914* (Cambridge, MA: Harvard University Press, 1960).

Sharpe, Jenny, *Allegories of Empire: The Figure of Woman in the Colonial Text* (Minneapolis: University of Minnesota Press, 1993).

Sheehan, Nancy M., 'Philosophy, pedagogy and practice: the IODE and the schools in Canada 1900–1945', *History of Education Review*, 2: 2 (1990), 307–21.

Sheehan, Nancy M., 'Women's organisations and educational issues, 1900–1930', *Canadian Women's Studies/Les Cahiers de la femme*, 7: 3 (1986), 90–4.

Sheehan, Nancy M., 'The IODE, the schools, and World War I', *History of Education Review*, 13:1 (1984), 29–44.

Shipley, Robert, *To Mark Our Place: A History of Canadian War Memorials* (Toronto: NC Press, 1987).

Smith, Denis, *Diplomacy of Fear: Canada and the Cold War, 1941–1948* (Toronto: University of Toronto Press, 1988).

Smith, Dorothy, *The Everyday World as Problematic: A Feminist Sociology* (Toronto: University of Toronto Press, 1987).

Smith-Rosenberg, Carol, 'The female world of love and ritual: relations between women in nineteenth century America', *Signs*, 1: 1 (1975), 1–29.

Spelman, Elizabeth V., *Unessential Woman: Problems of Exclusion in Feminist Thought* (Boston, MA: Beacon Press, 1988).

Spivak, Gayatri Chakravorty, *Outside in the Teaching Machine* (New York: Routledge, 1993).

Spivak, Gayatri Chakravorty, 'Negotiating the structures of violence', in Sarah Harasym (ed.) *The Post-Colonial Critic. Interviews, Strategies, Dialogues* (London and New York: Routledge, 1990), 138–51.

Spivak, Gayatri Chakravorty, 'Subaltern studies: deconstructing historiography', in Gayatri Chakravorty Spivak, *In Other Worlds: Essays in Cultural Politics* (New York: Routledge, 1987), 197–221.

Stanley, Timothy J., 'White supremacy and the rhetoric of educational indoctrination: a Canadian case study', in J. A. Mangan (ed.), *Making Imperial Mentalities: Socialism and British Imperialism* (Manchester: Manchester University Press, 1990), 144–62.

Stansell, Christine, *City of Women: Sex and Class in New York, 1789–1860* (New York: Knopf, 1986).

Stasiulis, Daiva and Nira Yuval-Davis (eds) *Unsettling Settler Societies: Articulations of Gender, Race, Ethnicity and Class* (London: Sage, 1995).

Strange, Carolyn, *Toronto's Girl Problem: The Perils and Pleasures of the City 1880–1930* (Toronto: University of Toronto Press, 1995).

Strobel, Margaret, *European Women and the Second British Empire* (Bloomington: Indiana University Press, 1991).

Stoddart, David R., *On Geography and its History* (New York: Blackwell, 1986).

Strong-Boag, Veronica, *The New Day Recalled: Lives of Girls and Women in*

English Canada, 1919–1939 (London and Markham, Ontario: Penguin, 1988).

Strong-Boag, Veronica, *The Parliament of Women: The National Council of Women of Canada, 1893–1929* (Ottawa: National Museums of Canada, 1976).

Strong-Boag, Veronica and Carole Gerson, *Paddling Her Own Canoe: The Times and Texts of E. Pauline Johnson (Tekahionwake)* (Toronto: University of Toronto Press, 2000).

Strong-Boag. Veronica, Sherrill Grace, Abigail Eisenberg and Joan Anderson (eds), *Painting the Maple: Essays on Race, Gender, and the Construction of Canada* (Vancouver: University of British Columbia Press, 1998).

Swaisland, Cecillie, *Servants and Gentlewomen to the Golden Land: The Emigration of Single Women from Britain to Southern Africa, 1820–1939* (Pietermaritzburg: University of Natal Press, 1993).

Swerdlow, Amy, *Women Strike for Peace: Traditional Motherhood and Radical Politics in the 1960s* (Chicago and London: University of Chicago Press, 1993).

Tarburk, K. L. (ed.), *R. Luxemburg and N. Bukharin, Imperialism and the Accumulation of Capital* (London: Penguin, 1972).

Taylor, Griffith T., 'The evolution and distribution of race, culture, and language', *Geographical Review*, 11 (1921), 54–119.

Tester, Frank J. and Peter Kulchyski, *Tamarniit (Mistakes): Innuit Relocation in the Eastern Arctic, 1939–63* (Vancouver: University of British Columbia Press, 1994).

Thomas, Nicholas, *Colonialism's Culture: Anthropology, Travel, and Government* (Princeton, NJ: Princeton University Press, 1994).

Trinh, T. Minh-ha, *Women, Native, Other* (Bloomington: Indiana University Press, 1989).

Trofimenkoff, Susan Mann and Alison Prentice (eds) *The Neglected Majority: Essays in Canadian Women's History* (Toronto: McClelland & Stewart, 1977).

Troloppe, Joanna, *Britannia's Daughters: Women of the British Empire* (London, Melbourne, Auckland and Johannesburg: Cresset, 1983).

Tylee, Claire M., *The Great War and Women's Consciousness: Images of Militarism and Womanhood in Women's Writings, 1914–64* (Basingstoke: Macmillan, 1990).

Tyler May, Elaine, *Homeward Bound: American Families in the Cold War Era* (New York: Basic Books, 1998).

Usher, Peter J., 'The north: metropolitan frontier, native homeland?', in L. D. McCann (ed.), *A Geography of Canada: Heartland and Hinterland* (Scarborough, Ontario: Prentice-Hall, 1982), 411–56.

Valverde, Mariana, '"When the mother of the race is free": race, reproduction, and sexuality in first-wave feminism', in Franca Iacovetta and Mariana Valverde (eds), *Gender Conflicts: New Essays in Women's History* (Toronto: University of Toronto Press, 1992), 3–36.

Valverde, Mariana, *The Age of Light, Soap, and Water: Moral Reform in English Canada, 1885–1925* (Toronto: McClelland & Stewart, 1991).

Vance, Jonathan, *Death So Noble: Memory, Meaning, and the First World War* (Vancouver: University of British Columbia Press, 1997).

Wagner, Gillian, *Children of the Empire* (London: Weidenfeld & Nicolson, 1982).

Ware, Vron, *Beyond the Pale: White Women, Racism and History* (London and New York: Verso, 1992).

Ware, Vron, 'Moments of danger: race, gender, and memories of Empire', *Journal of History and Theory*, 31: 4 (1992), 116–32.

Warner, Marina, *Monuments and Maidens: The Allegory of the Female Form* (New York: Atheneum, 1985).

Wallach Scott, Joan, *Gender and the Politics of History* (New York: Columbia University Press, 1988).

Warren, Allen, '"Mothers for the Empire?" The Girl Guides' Association in Britain, 1909–1939', in J. A. Mangan (ed.) *Making Imperial Mentalities: Socialisation and British Imperialism* (Manchester: Manchester University Press, 1990), 96–109.

Weisbord, Merrily, *The Strangest Dream: Canadian Communists, the Spy Trials, and the Cold War*, 2nd edn (Montreal: Vehicle Press, 1994).

West Linder, Norma and Hope Morritt, *Pauline: A Warm Look at Ontario Lieutenant-Governor Pauline McGibbon* (Sarnia: River City Press, 1979).

Whitaker, Reg and Gary Marcuse, *Cold War Canada: The Making of a National Insecurity State, 1945–1957* (Toronto: University of Toronto Press, 1994).

Whittick, Arnold, *War Memorials* (London: Country Life, 1946).

Whitton, Charlotte, *Canadian Women in the War Effort* (Toronto: MacMillan, 1942).

Wicks, Ben, *Promise You'll Take Care of My Daughter: The Remarkable War Brides of World War II* (Don Mills, Ontario: Stoddart, 1992).

Williams, Raymond, 'Selections from Marxism and literature', in Nicholas B. Dirks, Geoff Eley and Sherry B. Ortner (eds), *Culture/Power/History: A Reader in Contemporary Social Theory*, Princeton, NJ: Princeton University Press, 1994), 585–608.

Winter, Jay, *Sites of Memory, Sites of Mourning: The Great War in European Cultural History* (Cambridge and New York: Cambridge University Press, 1995).

Woodsworth, James S., *Strangers at Our Gates, or Coming Canadians*, 2nd edn (Toronto: University of Toronto Press, 1972 [1909]).

Woollacott, Angela, 'Inventing Commonwealth and Pan-Pacific Feminism: Australian women's internationalist activism in the 1920s–30s', *Gender and History*, 10: 3 (1998), 425–48.

Wurtele, Susan E., 'Assimilation through domestic transformation: Saskatchewan's Masonic Scholarship Project, 1922–23', *The Canadian Geographer*, 38: 2 (1994), 122–33.

Yeatman, Anna, *Postmodern Revisionings of the Political* (New York and London: Routledge, 1994).

Young, Iris Marion, *Justice and the Politics of Difference* (Princeton, NJ: Princeton University Press, 1990).

Young, Iris Marion, 'The ideal of impartiality and the civic public', in Iris Marion Young, *Throwing Like a Girl and Other Essays in Feminist Philosophy and Social Theory* (Bloomington: Indiana University Press, 1990), 92–113.

Young, Robert, *Colonial Desire: Hybridity in Theory, Culture and Race* (London and New York: Routledge, 1995).

Young, Robert, *White Mythologies: Writing History and the West* (London and New York: Routledge, 1990).

INDEX